Arthur E. Jongsma, Jr., Series Editor

Helping therapists help their clients...

Treatment Planners cover all the necessary elements for developing formal treatment plans, including detailed problem definitions, long-term goals, short-term objectives, therapeutic interventions, and DSM™ diagnoses.

- ❑ **The Complete Adult Psychotherapy Treatment Planner,** Fifth Edition* ...... 978-1-118-06786-4 / $60.00
- ❑ **The Child Psychotherapy Treatment Planner,** Fifth Edition* .... 978-1-118-06785-7 / $60.00
- ❑ **The Adolescent Psychotherapy Treatment Planner,** Fifth Edition* .... 978-1-118-06784-0 / $60.00
- ❑ **The Addiction Treatment Planner,** Fifth Edition* .... 978-1-118-41475-0 / $60.00
- ❑ **The Couples Psychotherapy Treatment Planner,** with DSM-5 Updates, Second Edition .... 978-1-119-06312-4 / $60.00
- ❑ **The Group Therapy Treatment Planner,** Second Edition .... 978-0-471-66791-9 / $60.00
- ❑ **The Family Therapy Treatment Planner,** with DSM-5 Updates, Second Edition .... 978-1-119-06307-0 / $60.00
- ❑ **The Older Adult Psychotherapy Treatment Planner,** with DSM-5 Updates, Second Edition .... 978-1-119-06311-7 / $60.00
- ❑ **The Employee Assistance (EAP) Treatment Planner** .... 978-0-471-24709-8 / $60.00
- ❑ **The Gay and Lesbian Psychotherapy Treatment Planner** .... 978-0-471-35080-4 / $60.00
- ❑ **The Crisis Counseling and Traumatic Events Treatment Planner,** with DSM-5 Updates, Second Edition .... 978-1-119-06315-5 / $60.00
- ❑ **The Social Work and Human Services Treatment Planner** .... 978-0-471-37741-2 / $60.00
- ❑ **The Continuum of Care Treatment Planner** .... 978-0-471-19568-9 / $60.00
- ❑ **The Behavioral Medicine Treatment Planner** .... 978-0-471-31923-8 / $60.00
- ❑ **The Mental Retardation and Developmental Disability Treatment Planner** .... 978-0-471-38253-9 / $60.00
- ❑ **The Special Education Treatment Planner** .... 978-0-471-38872-2 / $60.00
- ❑ **The Severe and Persistent Mental Illness Treatment Planner,** with DSM-5 Updates, Second Edition .... 978-1-119-06309-6 / $60.00
- ❑ **The Personality Disorders Treatment Planner** .... 978-0-471-39403-7 / $60.00
- ❑ **The Rehabilitation Psychology Treatment Planner** .... 978-0-471-35178-8 / $60.00
- ❑ **The Pastoral Counseling Treatment Planner** .... 978-0-471-25416-4 / $60.00
- ❑ **The Juvenile Justice and Residential Care Treatment Planner** .... 978-0-471-43320-0 / $60.00
- ❑ **The School Counseling and School Social Work Treatment Planner,** with DSM-5 Updates, Second Edition .... 978-1-119-06309-4 / $60.00
- ❑ **The Psychopharmacology Treatment Planner** .... 978-0-471-43322-4 / $60.00
- ❑ **The Probation and Parole Treatment Planner** .... 978-0-471-20244-8 / $60.00
- ❑ **The Suicide and Homicide Risk Assessment & Prevention Treatment Planner** .... 978-0-471-46631-4 / $60.00
- ❑ **The Speech-Language Pathology Treatment Planner** .... 978-0-471-27504-6 / $60.00
- ❑ **The College Student Counseling Treatment Planner** .... 978-0-471-46708-3 / $60.00
- ❑ **The Parenting Skills Treatment Planner** .... 978-0-471-48183-6 / $60.00
- ❑ **The Early Childhood Education Intervention Treatment Planner** .... 978-0-471-65962-4 / $60.00
- ❑ **The Co-Occurring Disorders Treatment Planner** .... 978-0-471-73081-1 / $60.00
- ❑ **The Sexual Abuse Victim and Sexual Offender Treatment Planner** .... 978-0-471-21979-8 / $60.00
- ❑ **The Complete Women's Psychotherapy Treatment Planner** .... 978-0-470-03983-0 / $60.00
- ❑ **The Veterans and Active Duty Military Psychotherapy Treatment Planner,** with DSM-5 Updates, Second Edition .... 978-1-119-06308-7 / $60.00

*Updated to DSM-5™

The **Complete Treatment and Homework Planners** series of books combines our bestselling *Treatment Planners* and *Homework Planners* into one easy-to-use, all-in-one resource for mental health professionals treating clients suffering from the most commonly diagnosed disorders.

- ❑ **The Complete Depression Treatment and Homework Planner** .... 978-0-471-64515-3 / $60.00
- ❑ **The Complete Anxiety Treatment and Homework Planner** .... 978-0-471-64548-1 / $60.00

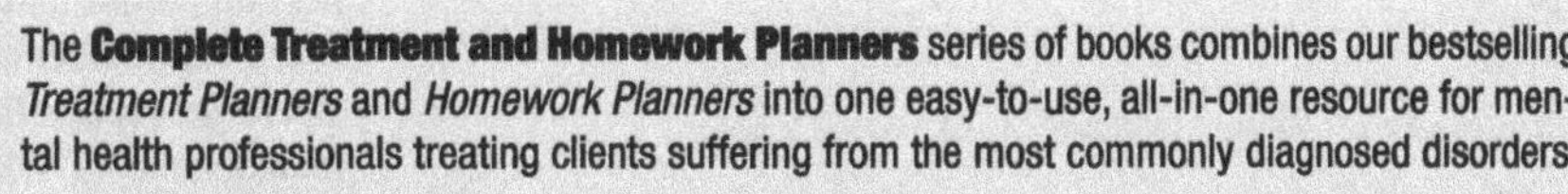

Over 1,000,000 Practice *Planners*® sold WILEY

The Veterans and Active Duty Military Psychotherapy Treatment Planner, with DSM-5 Updates, Second Edition

Practice*Planners*® Series

Treatment Planners

The Complete Adult Psychotherapy Treatment Planner, Fifth Edition
The Child Psychotherapy Treatment Planner, Fifth Edition
The Adolescent Psychotherapy Treatment Planner, Fifth Edition
The Addiction Treatment Planner, Fifth Edition
The Continuum of Care Treatment Planner
The Couples Psychotherapy Treatment Planner, with DSM-5 Updates, Second Edition
The Employee Assistance Treatment Planner
The Pastoral Counseling Treatment Planner
The Older Adult Psychotherapy Treatment Planner, with DSM-5 Updates, Second Edition
The Behavioral Medicine Treatment Planner
The Group Therapy Treatment Planner
The Gay and Lesbian Psychotherapy Treatment Planner
The Family Therapy Treatment Planner, with DSM-5 Updates, Second Edition
The Severe and Persistent Mental Illness Treatment Planner, with DSM-5 Updates, Second Edition
The Mental Retardation and Developmental Disability Treatment Planner
The Social Work and Human Services Treatment Planner
The Crisis Counseling and Traumatic Events Treatment Planner, with DSM-5 Updates, Second Edition
The Personality Disorders Treatment Planner
The Rehabilitation Psychology Treatment Planner
The Special Education Treatment Planner
The Juvenile Justice and Residential Care Treatment Planner
The School Counseling and School Social Work Treatment Planner, with DSM-5 Updates, Second Edition
The Sexual Abuse Victim and Sexual Offender Treatment Planner
The Probation and Parole Treatment Planner
The Psychopharmacology Treatment Planner
The Speech-Language Pathology Treatment Planner
The Suicide and Homicide Treatment Planner
The College Student Counseling Treatment Planner
The Parenting Skills Treatment Planner
The Early Childhood Intervention Treatment Planner
The Co-occurring Disorders Treatment Planner
The Complete Women's Psychotherapy Treatment Planner
The Veterans and Active Duty Military Psychotherapy Treatment Planner, with DSM-5 Updates

Progress Notes Planners

The Child Psychotherapy Progress Notes Planner, Fifth Edition
The Adolescent Psychotherapy Progress Notes Planner, Fifth Edition
The Adult Psychotherapy Progress Notes Planner, Fifth Edition
The Addiction Progress Notes Planner, Fifth Edition
The Severe and Persistent Mental Illness Progress Notes Planner, Second Edition
The Couples Psychotherapy Progress Notes Planner, Second Edition
The Family Therapy Progress Notes Planner, Second Edition
The Veterans and Active Duty Military Psychotherapy Progress Notes Planner

Homework Planners

Couples Therapy Homework Planner, Second Edition
Family Therapy Homework Planner, Second Edition
Grief Counseling Homework Planner
Group Therapy Homework Planner
Divorce Counseling Homework Planner
School Counseling and School Social Work Homework Planner, Second Edition
Child Therapy Activity and Homework Planner
Addiction Treatment Homework Planner, Fifth Edition
Adolescent Psychotherapy Homework Planner, Fifth Edition
Adult Psychotherapy Homework Planner, Fifth Edition
Child Psychotherapy Homework Planner, Fifth Edition
Parenting Skills Homework Planner
Veterans and Active Duty Military Psychotherapy Homework Planner

Client Education Handout Planners

Adult Client Education Handout Planner
Child and Adolescent Client Education Handout Planner
Couples and Family Client Education Handout Planner

Complete Planners

The Complete Depression Treatment and Homework Planner
The Complete Anxiety Treatment and Homework Planner

Practice*Planners*®

The Veterans and Active Duty Military Psychotherapy Treatment Planner, with DSM-5 Updates, Second Edition

Bret A. Moore

Arthur E. Jongsma, Jr.

WILEY

This book is printed on acid-free paper. ♾

Published by John Wiley & Sons, Inc., Hoboken, New Jersey.

Published simultaneously in Canada.

For general information on our other products and services please contact our Customer Care Department within the U.S. at (800) 762-2974, outside the United States at (317) 572-3993 or fax (317) 572-4002.

Wiley also publishes its books in a variety of electronic formats. Some content that appears in print may not be available in electronic books. For more information about Wiley products, visit our website at www.wiley.com.

Library of Congress Cataloging-in-Publication Data:

Moore, Bret A.
The veterans and active duty military psychotherapy treatment planner, with DSM-5 updates /Bret A. Moore, Arthur E. Jongsma, Jr.
p. cm. — (PracticePlanners' series)
"Published simultaneously in Canada"—T.p. verso.
Includes bibliographical references.
ISBN 978-1-119-06308-7 (paper : alk. paper)
ISBN 978-1-119-06437-4 (eMobi)
ISBN 978-1-119-06418-3 (ePub)
ISBN 978-1-119-06411-4 (ePDF)
1. Veterans—Mental health—United States--Handbooks, manuals, etc. 2. Soldiers—Mental health—United States—Handbooks, manuals, etc. 3. Psychotherapy—Planning—Handbooks, manuals, etc. 4. Psychology, Military—Handbooks, manuals, etc. I. Jongsma, Arthur E., 1943-II. Title.

UH629.3.M66 2009

616.89'1406—dc22

2009007396

Printed in the United States of America

SKY10048064_051723

To my brothers—Ed, Herm, and Ray—who honorably and meaningfully served our country in the military. Their unique and very personal experiences continue to impact them positively and negatively decades later. Thank you to a few very good men. I salute each of you!

—A.E.J.

To my beautiful wife, Lori, who has graciously endured my countless hours in front of the computer; my parents, David and Brynda Moore, who always provided encouragement and support in spite of my shortcomings; two former friends and mentors that left this world entirely too early, Dr. Richard Strait and Dr. Jack Scobey; and to the brave men and women in the military that protect our freedom and preserve our way of life.

—B.A.M.

CONTENTS

▽ Indicates that selected Objective/Interventions are consistent with those found in evidence-based treatments.

PRACTICE*PLANNERS*® SERIES PREFACE

Accountability is an important dimension of the practice of psychotherapy. Treatment programs, public agencies, clinics, and practitioners must justify and document their treatment plans to outside review entities in order to be reimbursed for services. The books in the Practice*Planners*® series are designed to help practitioners fulfill these documentation requirements efficiently and professionally.

The Practice*Planners*® series includes a wide array of treatment planning books including not only the original *Complete Adult Psychotherapy Treatment Planner*, *Child Psychotherapy Treatment Planner*, and *Adolescent Psychotherapy Treatment Planner*, all now in their fifth editions, but also *Treatment Planners* targeted to specialty areas of practice, including:

- Addictions
- Co-occurring disorders
- Behavioral medicine
- College students
- Couples therapy
- Crisis counseling
- Early childhood education
- Employee assistance
- Family therapy
- Gays and lesbians
- Group therapy
- Juvenile justice and residential care
- Mental retardation and developmental disability
- Neuropsychology
- Older adults
- Parenting skills
- Pastoral counseling
- Personality disorders
- Probation and parole
- Psychopharmacology
- Rehabilitation psychology
- School counseling and school social work
- Severe and persistent mental illness
- Sexual abuse victims and offenders

- Social work and human services
- Special education
- Speech-language pathology
- Suicide and homicide risk assessment
- Veterans and active military duty
- Women's issues

In addition, there are three branches of companion books that can be used in conjunction with the *Treatment Planners*, or on their own:

- ***Progress Notes Planners*** provide a menu of progress statements that elaborate on the client's symptom presentation and the provider's therapeutic intervention. Each *Progress Notes Planner* statement is directly integrated with the behavioral definitions and therapeutic interventions from its companion *Treatment Planner*.
- ***Homework Planners*** include homework assignments designed around each presenting problem (such as anxiety, depression, substance use, anger control problems, eating disorders, or panic disorder) that is the focus of a chapter in its corresponding *Treatment Planner*.
- ***Client Education Handout Planners*** provide brochures and handouts to help educate and inform clients on presenting problems and mental health issues, as well as life skills techniques. The handouts are included on CD-ROMs for easy printing from your computer and are ideal for use in waiting rooms, at presentations, as newsletters, or as information for clients struggling with mental illness issues. The topics covered by these handouts correspond to the presenting problems in the *Treatment Planners*.

The series also includes adjunctive books, such as *The Psychotherapy Documentation Primer* and *The Clinical Documentation Sourcebook*, containing forms and resources to aid the clinician in mental health practice management.

The goal of our series is to provide practitioners with the resources they need in order to provide high-quality care in the era of accountability. To put it simply: We seek to help you spend more time on patients, and less time on paperwork.

ARTHUR E. JONGSMA, JR.
Grand Rapids, Michigan

ACKNOWLEDGMENTS

It has been a genuine pleasure to work with Dr. Bret Moore on this project. When he first contacted me while he was on active duty as a psychologist serving in Iraq, I was so pleased as we had been searching for several months for a qualified expert in military treatment planning who had the time and inclination to write this book with me. He was a Godsend. Thank you, Bret, for your sensitive and very professional work.

No country maintains its freedom without a strong military and I want to acknowledge my debt of gratitude to those who have served and continue to serve in our military. I am hopeful that this book will make a small contribution toward giving back to the many who have served so honorably. I salute the men and women who, like my brothers, have sacrificed for the United States of America and for freedom around the world.

This *Planner* has adapted some content from previously written *Treatment Planners* for selected chapters. A footnote at the beginning of these chapters indicates their source. Chapter material was adapted from the following previous *Planners*: *The Complete Adult Psychotherapy Treatment Planner, The Addiction Treatment Planner,* and *The Couples Psychotherapy Treatment Planner*. We are indebted to the following coauthors of these books for granting permission to adapt their content for this *Military Treatment Planner*: L. Mark Peterson, Robert R. Perkinson, Timothy J. Bruce, K. Daniel O'Leary, and Richard E. Heyman. A hearty thank-you to these professionals for their good work and for allowing us to spread their treatment influence to the military population.

Once again, Sue Rhoda, my manuscript manager for the Practice*Planners*, has been wonderful in her contribution of organizational talent. She is so reliably competent and steady in good humor that working with her is a delight. Thank you, Sue.

I want to thank the editorial staff at John Wiley & Sons for their continued support and professionalism. No author has a better team at any publishing house in the world. Starting with Marquita Flemming, my editor, at least a dozen Wiley friends combine to put these books on the bookstore shelf. I am grateful to them.

Arthur E. Jongsma, Jr. PhD

Nearly ten years ago, I was beginning my career as a psychologist. Like many new clinicians, I struggled with developing and implementing treatment plans. Fortunately, I came across *The Complete Adult Psychotherapy Treatment Planner* written by Dr. Arthur E. Jongsma, Jr. and L. Mark Peterson. Ever since then, I have been able to work more effectively with my clients and provide a higher level of care. That's why I was so honored and pleased to be a part of this project and am immensely grateful that Art allowed me to coauthor this important book with him. Not only did this provide me with a much-needed distraction while I was deployed to Iraq, it provided me the opportunity to work with and learn from one of the most talented and influential behavioral health clinicians in the field today. Thank you, Art.

I want to thank Sue Rhoda for her expert guidance in formatting and editing the chapters. Although I have never met her in person, she seems to be a woman with a warm spirit and a very generous nature.

I am also grateful for the support and encouragement from the editorial staff at John Wiley & Sons, particularly Marquita Flemming. After meeting her in Boston at the 2008 annual convention of the American Psychological Association, I knew that this process would move quickly and efficiently and that the final product would be of the highest quality.

There is no group that I respect more than the men and women that serve so bravely in our Armed Forces. I had the pleasure to meet and work with thousands of these unique and special individuals during my 27 months in Iraq as a psychologist. Not a day goes by that I don't think about the incredibly brave and selfless acts I saw on a regular basis over there. It was an honor to serve alongside them. If this book improves the life of just one service member or veteran, then it was a success. Like Art, I bow to the men and women that serve us today, and those like my late grandfathers, Ferrell Abel and Charles Moore, that fought for our freedom in decades past.

Bret A. Moore, PsyD

INTRODUCTION

ABOUT PRACTICE*PLANNERS*® TREATMENT PLANNERS

Pressure from third-party payors, accrediting agencies, and other outside parties has increased the need for clinicians to quickly produce effective, high-quality treatment plans. *Treatment Planners* provide all the elements necessary to quickly and easily develop formal treatment plans that satisfy the needs of most third-party payors and state and federal review agencies.

Each *Treatment Planner*:

- Saves you hours of time-consuming paperwork.
- Offers the freedom to develop customized treatment plans.
- Includes over 1,000 clear statements describing the behavioral manifestations of each relational problem, and includes long-term goals, short-term objectives, and clinically tested treatment options.
- Has an easy-to-use reference format that helps locate treatment plan components by behavioral problem or *DSM-5* diagnosis.

As with the rest of the books in the Practice*Planners*® series, our aim is to clarify, simplify, and accelerate the treatment planning process, so you spend less time on paperwork, and more time with your clients.

ABOUT *THE VETERAN'S AND ACTIVE DUTY MILITARY PSYCHOTHERAPY TREATMENT PLANNER*

The need for effective and tailored treatment for veterans and service members is at a critical point in today's society. At the time of this writing, Operation Iraqi Freedom is in its seventh year and Operation Enduring Freedom is in its ninth. Over a million men and women have returned from long and stressful combat deployments and many of our Soldiers, Sailors, Airmen, and Marines are currently serving their second, third, and even fourth tour in Iraq and/or Afghanistan. Consequently, the estimated number of military members suffering from psychiatric and social problems is in the hundreds of thousands. In addition to the current conflicts that are creating a need for effective care for our service members and veterans, our Veterans Affairs hospitals are serving countless veterans from prior wars and conflicts such as Vietnam, Korea, Bosnia, and the Persian Gulf War.

Military and non-military clinicians are being confronted with difficult clinical presentations such as posttraumatic and acute stress disorders, generalized anxiety disorder, depression, and substance abuse, and are treating veterans and service members suffering from suicidal and homicidal ideation, relationship problems, social anxiety, and panic symptoms on a daily basis. Furthermore, clinicians are helping service members psychologically prepare for deployments as well as facilitate adjustment after returning home. Considering the debt that is owed these men and women and the necessity of brief and targeted psychological interventions to return service members back to the fight as soon as possible, there is probably no other group for which the importance of evidence-based, effective, and practical treatment planning is greater.

Another important issue for clinicians working with veterans and service members, which is not unlike those working with other groups, is that most agencies that serve veterans and service members are required or elect to obtain accreditation from outside auditors, such as the Joint Commission on the Accreditation of Health Organizations (JCAHO), Council on Accreditation (COA), or the Commission on Accreditation of Rehabilitation Facilities (CARF). Payors, internal auditors, and various governmental bodies often demand documentation of positive outcomes for the veterans and service members whom we serve. With these many changes in the field, the need for better organization, treatment techniques, and documentation becomes self-evident.

To fill this need, we have developed *The Veteran's and Active Duty Military Psychotherapy Treatment Planner.* This *Planner* suggests thousands of prewritten behavioral definitions, objectives, goals, and interventions for a variety of problem areas experienced by the men and women who serve or have served in the military. It is our belief that this book will be useful to any clinician working with this population. It was not written for any particular clinical discipline and will be of relevance to the psychologist, social worker, psychiatrist, counselor, psychiatric nurse, and case manager. Goals and interventions are written for a variety of types and levels of intensity of problems faced by veterans and service members. It is our hope that this *Planner* will allow clinicians to quickly and accurately develop and implement helpful treatment plans for those they treat.

It should be noted that throughout the planner a distinction between veteran and service member is made. The term veteran refers to an individual that has left military service and service member refers to current Active Duty, National Guard, and Reserve military members.

INCORPORATING EVIDENCE-BASED TREATMENT INTO THE *TREATMENT PLANNER*

Evidence-based treatment (that is, treatment that is scientifically shown in research trials to be efficacious) is rapidly becoming of critical importance to the mental health community as insurance companies are beginning to offer preferential pay to organizations using it. In fact, the APA Division 12 (Society of Clinical Psychology) lists of empirically supported treatments have been referenced by a number of local, state, and federal funding agencies, which are beginning to restrict reimbursement to these treatments, as are some managed care and insurance companies. Furthermore, military medical centers and Veterans Affairs hospitals have made utilizing evidence-based treatment the norm, which is not only related to cost and efficiency, but to providing the highest level of care possible.

In this first edition of *The Veteran's and Active Duty Military Psychotherapy Treatment Planner* we have made an effort to empirically inform some chapters by highlighting Short-term Objectives (STOs) and Therapeutic Interventions (TIs) that are consistent with psychological treatments or therapeutic programs that have demonstrated some level of efficacy through empirical study. Watch for this icon as an indication that an Objective/Intervention is consistent with those found in evidence-based treatments: ▽EBT

References to their empirical support have been included in the reference section as Appendix B. For information related to the identification of evidence-based practices (EBPs), including the benefits and limitations of the effort, we suggest Bruce and Sanderson (2005); Chambless et al. (1996, 1998); Chambless and Ollendick (2001); Drake, Merrens, and Lynde (2005); Hofmann and Tompson (2002); Nathan and Gorman (2002); and Stout and Hayes (2005).

In this *Planner*, we have included STOs and TIs consistent with EBPs that are more psychotherapeutic in nature, and that have been found efficacious for problems common to veterans and service members. Examples include treatment for posttraumatic stress disorder, insomnia, and nightmares. We have also included STOs and TIs reflective of psychotherapeutic approaches that have shown efficacy for disorders typically found in this group (e.g., cognitive behavior therapy for depression, exposure based therapy for posttraumatic stress symptoms). Beyond references to the empirical studies supporting these interventions, we have provided references to therapist- and client-oriented books and treatment manuals that describe the use of identified EBPs or treatments consistent with their objectives and interventions. Of course, recognizing that there are STOs and TIs that practicing clinicians have found useful but that have not yet received empirical scrutiny, we have included those that reflect common best practice among experienced clinicians. The goal is to provide a range of treatment plan options, some studied empirically, others reflecting common clinical practice, so the user can construct what they believe to be the best plan for a particular client.

Criteria for Inclusion of Evidence-Based Therapies

The EBPs from which STOs and TIs were taken have different levels of empirical work supporting them. Some have been well established as efficacious for the changes they target (e.g., stress disorders). Others have less support, but nonetheless have demonstrated efficacy.

At minimum, efficacy needed to be demonstrated through a clinical trial or large clinical replication series with features reflecting good experimental design (e.g., random assignment, blind assignments, reliable and valid measurement, clear inclusion and exclusion criteria, state-of-the-art diagnostic methods, and adequate sample size or replications). Well established EBPs typically have more than one of these types of studies demonstrating their efficacy, as well as other desirable features such as demonstration of efficacy by independent research groups and specification of client characteristics for which the treatment was effective.

Because treatment literatures for various problems develop at different paces, treatment STOs and TIs that have been included may have the most empirical support for their problem area, but less than that found in more heavily studied areas. For example, Dialectical Behavior Therapy (DBT) has the highest level of empirical support of tested psychotherapies for borderline personality disorder (BPD), but that level of evidence is lower than that supporting, for example, exposure-based therapy for phobic fear and avoidance. The latter has simply been studied more extensively, so there are more trials, replications, and the like. Nonetheless, within the psychotherapy outcome literature for BPD, DBT clearly has the highest level of evidence supporting its efficacy and usefulness. Accordingly, STOs and TIs consistent with DBT have been included in this edition. Lastly, all interventions, empirically supported or not, must be adapted to the particular veteran or service member in light of his/her personal circumstances, strengths, and vulnerabilities. The STOs and TIs included in this *Planner* are written in a manner to suggest and allow this adaptability.

Summary of Required and Preferred SPMI EBT Inclusion Criteria

Required

- Demonstration of efficacy through at least one randomized controlled trial with good experimental design, or
- Demonstration of efficacy through a large, well-designed clinical replication series.

Preferred

- Efficacy has been shown by more than one study.

- Efficacy has been demonstrated by independent research groups.
- Client characteristics for which the treatment was effective were specified.
- A clear description of the treatment was available.

HOW TO USE THIS *TREATMENT PLANNER*

Use this *Treatment Planner* to write treatment plans according to the following progression of six steps:

1. **Problem Selection.** Although the veteran/service member may discuss a variety of issues during the assessment, the clinician must determine the most significant problems on which to focus the treatment process. Usually a primary problem will surface, and secondary problems may also be evident. Some other problems may have to be set aside as not urgent enough to require treatment at this time. An effective treatment plan can only deal with a few selected problems or treatment will lose its direction. Choose the problem within this *Planner* that most accurately represents your veteran's/service member's presenting issues or the one that needs immediate attention (e.g., returning a service member to duty).
2. **Problem Definition.** Each veteran/service member presents with unique nuances as to how a problem behaviorally reveals itself in his or her life. Therefore, each problem that is selected for treatment focus requires a specific definition about how it is evidenced in the particular individual. The symptom pattern should be associated with diagnostic criteria and codes such as those found in the *DSM-5* or the *International Classification of Diseases*. This *Planner* offers such behaviorally specific definition statements to choose from or to serve as a model for your own personally crafted statements.
3. **Goal Development.** The next step in developing your treatment plan is to set broad goals for the resolution of the target problem. These statements need not be crafted in measurable terms but can be global, long-term goals that indicate a desired positive outcome to the treatment procedures. This *Planner* provides several possible goal statements for each problem, but one statement is all that is required in a treatment plan.
4. **Objective Construction.** In contrast to long-term goals, objectives must be stated in behaviorally measurable language so that it is clear to review agencies, health maintenance organizations, managed care organizations, and relevant command authorities when the veteran/service member has achieved the established objectives. The objectives presented in this *Planner* are designed to meet this demand for accountability, while maximizing treatment effectiveness. Numerous alternatives are presented to allow construction of a variety of treatment plan possibilities for the same presenting problem.

5. **Intervention Creation.** Interventions are the actions of the clinician designed to help the veteran/service member complete the objectives. There should be at least one intervention for every objective. If the veteran/service member does not accomplish the objective after the initial intervention, new interventions should be added to the plan. Interventions should be selected on the basis of the individual's needs and the treatment provider's full therapeutic repertoire. This *Planner* contains interventions from a broad range of therapeutic approaches, and we encourage the provider to write other interventions reflecting his or her own training and experience.

   Some suggested interventions listed in the *Planner* refer to specific books that can be assigned to the veteran/service member for adjunctive bibliotherapy. Appendix A contains a full bibliographic reference list of these materials, including these two popular choices: *Read Two Books and Let's Talk Next Week: Using Bibliotherapy in Clinical Practice* (2000) by Mainman and DiMenna, and *Rent Two Films and Let's Talk in the Morning: Using Popular Movies in Psychotherapy* (2nd ed.; 2001) by Hesley and Hesley (both books are published by Wiley). For further information about self-help books, mental health professionals may wish to consult *The Authoritative Guide to Self-Help Resources in Mental Health, Revised Edition* (2003) by Norcross et al. (available from Guilford Press, New York).
6. **Diagnosis Determination.** The determination of an appropriate diagnosis is based on an evaluation of the veteran's/service member's complete clinical presentation. The clinician must compare the behavioral, cognitive, emotional, and interpersonal symptoms that the veteran/service member presents with the criteria for diagnosis of a mental illness condition as described in *DSM-5*. Despite arguments made against diagnosing individuals in this manner, diagnosis is a reality that exists in the world of mental health care and in the military. Not only is it a necessity for billing and reimbursement, but often times it is required for disposition of a case such as retaining or discharging a service member from military service or filing for disability compensation claim for a veteran. It is the clinician's thorough knowledge of *DSM-5* criteria and a complete understanding of the assessment data that contribute to the most reliable, valid diagnosis.

Congratulations! After completing these six steps, you should have a comprehensive and individualized treatment plan ready for immediate implementation and presentation to the veteran/service member. A sample treatment plan for posttraumatic stress disorder is provided at the end of this introduction.

A FINAL NOTE ON TAILORING THE TREATMENT PLAN TO THE VETERAN/SERVICE MEMBER

One important aspect of effective treatment planning is that each plan should be tailored to the individual veteran's/service member's problems and needs. Treatment plans should not be mass-produced, even if veterans/service members have similar problems. The individual's strengths and weaknesses, unique stressors, social network, family circumstances, and symptom patterns must be considered in developing a treatment strategy. Drawing upon our own years of clinical experience, we have put together a variety of treatment choices. These statements can be combined in thousands of permutations to develop detailed treatment plans. Relying on their own good judgment, clinicians can easily select the statements that are appropriate for the individuals whom they are treating. In addition, we encourage readers to add their own definitions, goals, objects, and interventions to the existing samples. As with all of the books in the *Treatment Planners* series, it is our hope that this book will help promote effective, creative treatment planning—a process that will ultimately benefit the veteran/service member, clinicians, military unit, and mental health and military communities.

REFERENCES

Bruce, T. J., & Sanderson, W. C. (2005). Evidence-based psychosocial practices: Past, present, and future. In C. Stout and R. Hayes (Eds.), *The Handbook of Evidence-Based Practice in Behavioral Healthcare: Applications and New Directions.* Hoboken, NJ: John Wiley & Sons.

Chambless, D. L, Baker, M. J., Baucom, D., Beutler, L. E., Calhoun, K. S., Crits-Christoph, P., … Woody, S. R. (1998). Update on empirically validated therapies: II. *The Clinical Psychologist,* 51(1), 3–16.

Chambless, D. L., & Ollendick, T. H. (2001). Empirically supported psychological interventions: Controversies and evidence. *Annual Review of Psychology,* 52, 685-716.

Chambless, D. L., Sanderson, W. C., Shoham, V., Johnson, S. B., Pope, K. S., Crits-Christoph, P., … McCurry, S. (1996). An update on empirically validated therapies. *The Clinical Psychologist,* 49(2), 5–18.

Drake, R. E., & Goldman, H. (2003). *Evidence-based Practices in Mental Health Care.* Washington, D.C.: American Psychiatric Association.

Drake, R. E., Merrens, M. R., & Lynde, D. W. (2005). *Evidence-Based Mental Health Practice: A Textbook.* New York: W.W. Norton & Company.

Hofmann, S. G., & Tompson, M. G. (2002). *Treating Chronic and Severe Mental Disorders: A Handbook of Empirically Supported Interventions.* New York: Guilford.

Nathan, P. E., & Gorman, J. M. (Eds.). (1998). *A Guide to Treatments That Work.* New York: Oxford University Press.

Nathan, P. E., & Gorman, J. M. (Eds.). (2002). *A Guide to Treatments That Work (Vol. II).* New York: Oxford University Press.

Stout, C., & Hayes, R. (1995). *The Handbook of Evidence-Based Practice in Behavioral Healthcare: Applications and New Directions.* New York: John Wiley & Sons.

SAMPLE TREATMENT PLAN

POSTTRAUMATIC STRESS DISORDER

BEHAVIORAL DEFINITIONS

1. Has been exposed to a traumatic event involving actual or perceived threat of death or serious injury.
2. Reports response of intense fear, helplessness, or horror to the traumatic event.
3. Experiences disturbing and persistent thoughts, images, and/or perceptions of the traumatic event.
4. Describes a reliving of the event, particularly through dissociative flashbacks.
5. Displays significant psychological and/or physiological distress resulting from internal and external clues that are reminiscent of the traumatic event.
6. Experiences disturbances in sleep.
7. Experiences intense anger and irritability.
8. Reports feelings of letting his/her fellow comrades, unit, and country down.
9. Acknowledges increased interpersonal conflict with friends, fellow comrades, and superiors.

LONG-TERM GOALS

1. Eliminate or reduce the negative impact trauma related symptoms have on social, occupational, and family functioning.
2. Return to the level of psychological functioning prior to exposure to the traumatic event.
3. Regain the "warrior" mentality.

SHORT-TERM OBJECTIVES

1. Describe in detail the history and nature of the PTSD symptoms.

THERAPEUTIC INTERVENTIONS

1. Within an atmosphere of warm acceptance, informed active listening, and unconditional positive regard, explore and assess the veteran/service member's type, intensity, and

frequency of PTSD symptoms and the impact on his/her social, occupational, and interpersonal functioning (or assign "How the Trauma Affects Me" in the *Adult Psychotherapy Homework Planner*, 2nd ed. by Jongsma).

2. Talk with the service member's first line supervisor (e.g., Squad Leader, Platoon Sergeant, First Sergeant) to assess the degree the PTSD symptoms have impacted the service member's job performance.

2. Describe the precipitating traumatic event in detail.

1. Assist the veteran/service member in describing the details of the traumatic event (most significant event if there are more than one); encourage the veteran/service member to be aware of as many details of the event as possible while focusing on how he/she felt before the event, at the time of the event, and after it was over (e.g., anxiety, dread, shame, guilt, disgust), the most vivid parts of the recollection, and any sounds or smells that he/she remembers; process the emotions associated with retelling of this story (frequent retelling is a form of exposure therapy).

3. Verbalize an understanding of the treatment rationale for PTSD.

1. Educate the veteran/service member about how effective treatments for PTSD utilize virtual reality, imaginal, and *in vivo* exposure techniques to desensitize an individual's fears, and cognitive restructuring to assist the individual in viewing the world in a much less dangerous manner.

2. Assign the veteran/service member to review information

on cognitive restructuring, exposure therapy, and relaxation training in *Reclaiming Your Life from a Traumatic Experience: A Prolonged Exposure Treatment Program Workbook* by Rothbaum, Foa, and Hembree.

4. Verbalize an understanding that cognitions contribute to the maintenance of fear and avoidance.

1. Explain to the veteran/service member the concept of how thoughts impact our feelings and behavior, particularly in maintaining fear and reinforcing avoidance of perceived threats; use an example that relates to his/her situation (e.g., a person's up-armored vehicle was hit with an improvised explosive device, and every time he/she sees an up-armored vehicle he/she remembers the past traumatic event, assumes he/she will get attacked again, and avoids all up-armored vehicles).

5. Identify, challenge, and replace negative and self-defeating fearful thoughts that contribute to avoidance.

1. Assist the veteran/service member in developing an awareness of his/her automatic thoughts that are consistent with maintaining the view that the world is a hostile and dangerous place and injury and death is inevitable.
2. Assign the veteran/service member to keep a daily log of automatic thoughts associated with themes of threat and danger (e.g., "Negative Thoughts Trigger Negative Feelings" in the *Adult Psychotherapy Homework Planner*, 2nd ed. by Jongsma); process the journal material to challenge distorted thinking patterns with reality-based thoughts.
3. Reinforce the veteran's/service member's positive cognitions

that foster a sense of safety and security and decrease fearful and avoidance behavior (see "Positive Self-Talk" in the *Adult Psychotherapy Homework Planner*, 2nd ed. by Jongsma).

6. Participate with Prolonged Exposure treatment.

1. Utilize imaginal or virtual reality exposure as a way to recount/relive the emotional experience for an extended period of time (e.g., 60–90 minutes; see *Prolonged Exposure Therapy for PTSD: Emotional Processing of Traumatic Experiences-Therapist Guide* by Foa, Hembree, and Rothbaum).
2. Utilize *in vivo* exposure as a way to gradually expose the person to objects, situations, and places that create significant anxiety for the veteran/service member (see *Prolonged Exposure Therapy for PTSD: Emotional Processing of Traumatic Experiences-Therapist Guide* by Foa, Hembree, and Rothbaum).

7. Learn and implement thought stopping to manage intrusive unwanted thoughts.

1. Teach the veteran/service member thought-stopping in which he/she internally voices the word "stop" and/or imagines something representing the concept of stopping (e.g., a stop sign or light) immediately upon noticing unwanted trauma or otherwise negative, unwanted thoughts (or assign "Making Use of the Thought-Stopping Technique" in the *Adult Psychotherapy Homework Planner*, 2nd ed. by Jongsma).

DIAGNOSIS

ICD-9-CM	*ICD-10-CM*	*DSM-5* Disorder, Condition, or Problem
309.81	F43.10	Posttraumatic Stress Disorder

ADJUSTMENT TO KILLING

BEHAVIORAL DEFINITIONS

1. Displays frequent and intense negative emotions related to killing another human (e.g., guilt, remorse, sadness, anger, shame).
2. Reports constant ruminations about killing another human.
3. Avoids activities that may lead to killing another human again (e.g., future combat missions).
4. Avoidance of activities that serve as reminders of killing (e.g., shooting a weapon during training).
5. Reports onset of spiritual and moral conflicts related to the killing.
6. Exhibits sleep disturbances.
7. Reports increased substance use to forget killing incident(s).
8. Reports onset of suicidal ideation related to the killing.

—. ____
____

—. ____
____

—. ____
____

LONG-TERM GOALS

1. Resolve cognitive and emotional conflicts surrounding killing another human.
2. Engage in activities that require use of a weapon.
3. Facilitate reconciliation of spiritual and moral conflicts with the killing.
4. Improve both quantity and quality of sleep.
5. Decrease substance use.
6. Eliminate suicidal ideation.

__. ______________________________
____

__. ______________________________
____

__. ______________________________
____

SHORT-TERM OBJECTIVES

1. Acknowledge the different emotions related to the killing. (1, 2)

2. Gain awareness of negative emotions. (3, 4)

3. Gain awareness of the connection between thoughts and emotions. (5, 6, 7, 8)

THERAPEUTIC INTERVENTIONS

1. Assess the different types of emotions (e.g., shame, guilt, anxiety, anger, fear, etc.) associated with killing another human and experienced by the veteran/service member by conducting a clinical interview.

2. Assess the severity of the veteran's/service member's emotions and the impact on current functioning using interview and psychological testing.

3. Teach the veteran/service member techniques on how to become more aware of negative emotions (e.g., scan body for physiological cues).

4. Assist the veteran/service member with correctly labeling his/her emotions.

5. Explain to the veteran/service member the concept of how thoughts impact emotions.

6. Teach the veteran/service member about the cognitive therapy concept of automatic thoughts.

7. Assist the veteran/service member with implementing an automatic thought record/journal on thoughts about the killing incident.

8. Teach the veteran/service member about cognitive errors (e.g., judging, catastrophizing, labeling, all-or-nothing thinking, self-blaming, etc.) and how he/she uses these errors when thinking about the event (or assign "Negative Thoughts Trigger Negative Feelings" in the *Adult Psychotherapy Homework Planner*, 2nd ed. by Jongsma).

4. Replace negative ruminations with more adaptive thoughts. (9, 10, 11)

9. Assist the veteran/service member in testing the reality of the negative thoughts through environmental experiments (e.g., talking with other veterans/service members about their thoughts and beliefs about killing).

10. Assist the veteran/service member in replacing his/her negative thoughts with more adaptive ones through the use of reality testing experiments, therapeutic confrontation, and Socratic questioning.

11. Reinforce the veteran's/service member's positive, reality-based cognitive messages that enhance self-confidence and increase adaptive action (or assign "Positive Self-Talk" in the *Adult Psychotherapy Homework Planner*, 2nd ed. by Jongsma).

5. Reduce anxiety and prepare emotionally for future combat/training missions. (12, 13, 14, 15)

12. Review worst, best, and most likely case scenarios regarding future missions for the veteran/service member.

13. Instill a sense of confidence and capability in the veteran/service member regarding future missions by reviewing his/her past training and successful performance.

14. Teach the veteran/service member various relaxation techniques (e.g., deep muscle relaxation, imagining pleasant scenes, deep breathing exercises, etc.) that he/she can apply to ameliorate his/her anxiety about killing.

15. Utilize the imaginal exposure of a systematic desensitization technique to reduce the veteran's/service member's clinically significant levels of anxiety associated with combat situations that may lead to another killing incident.

6. Report restful sleep. (16, 17)

16. Assess the veteran's/service member's sleep pattern and whether a sleep disruption has followed the killing incident.

17. Instruct the veteran/service member on behavioral practices conducive to good sleep (or assign "Sleep Pattern Record" in the *Adult Psychotherapy Homework Planner*, 2nd ed. by Jongsma) that includes not using caffeine four hours prior to bedtime, not ruminating, exercising in the mornings, getting out of bed if not able to fall asleep within 15 minutes, not eating spicy meals/snacks prior to sleep, removing cues to time that may promote "clock watching" (see the chapter on Insomnia in this *Planner*).

7. Keep an appointment with a prescribing practitioner to evaluate for appropriateness of medication to assist with sleep. (18, 19)

18. Refer the veteran/service member to a prescribing practitioner to assess whether he/she would benefit from medication to assist with sleep.

19. Monitor the veteran's/service member's medication compliance, effectiveness, and side effects; be alert to medication abuse.

8. Verbalize current spiritual and moral conflicts. (20, 21, 22)

20. Normalize and empathize with the veteran's/service member's spiritual and moral conflicts.

21. Refer the veteran/service member to a chaplain or other spiritual and moral leader in the military.

22. Instruct the veteran/service member to read the book *On Killing* by Lieutenant Colonel Dave Grossman; process his/her reaction to the material.

9. Acknowledge apprehension about going on combat/training missions. (23)

23. Normalize the veteran/service member's apprehension and anxiety about going on future combat/training missions.

10. Gain a greater sense of confidence and comfortableness with a weapon. (24, 25)

24. Acknowledge the veteran's/service member's discomfort with maintaining a weapon and explore his/her reasons behind the discomfort.

25. Encourage the veteran/service member to participate in shooting ranges or spend time breaking down and cleaning his/her weapon.

11. Understand how killing another human can impact the mind and create temporary changes in the body's physiology. (22, 26)

22. Instruct the veteran/service member to read the book *On Killing* by Lieutenant Colonel Dave Grossman; process his/her reaction to the material.

26. Teach the veteran/service member how conflicted thoughts can affect emotions and physiological functioning.

12. Verbalize that substance use has become a problem. (27, 28, 29)

27. Perform or refer the veteran/service member for an in-depth substance use evaluation.

28. Refer the veteran/service member for a medical evaluation if substance dependence is suspected.

29. Perform or refer the veteran/service member for substance use disorder treatment if necessary (see the chapters on Substance Abuse/Dependence and Opioid Abuse/Dependence in this *Planner*).

13. Relate the details of the killing and express the grief and guilt associated with the action. (30, 31, 32, 33)

30. Using empathy and compassion, support and encourage the veteran/service member to tell in detail the story of the killing.

31. Ask the veteran/service member to list all the regrets he/she has concerning the killing; process that list.

32. Use a Rational Emotive Therapy approach to confront the veteran's/service member's unreasonable statements of responsibility for the action and compare them to more reality-based statements.

33. Treat the veteran's/service member's experience as one of grieving, explain the stages of the process (see the chapter on Grief/Complicated Bereavement in this *Planner*).

14. State the strength, frequency, and triggers of the suicidal ideation. (34)

34. Assess the veteran's/service member's risk of suicide, taking into account his/her history of

attempts, access to lethal means, current psychosocial stressors, and future orientation.

15. Cooperate with procedures to increase personal safety. (35, 36)

35. Restrict the veteran's/service member's access to weapons at home and work.

36. Encourage the veteran/service member to spend more time with family and friends; monitor the tendency to isolate himself/herself.

—. ____________________

—. ____________________

—. ____________________

—. ____________________

—. ____________________

—. ____________________

DIAGNOSTIC SUGGESTIONS

ICD-9-CM	*ICD-10-CM*	*DSM-5* Disorder, Condition, or Problem
V62.2	Z56.9	Other Problem Related to Employment
V62.89	Z65.8	Religious or Spiritual Problem
309.0	F43.21	Adjustment Disorder, With Depressed Mood
308.3	F43.0	Acute Stress Disorder
309.81	F43.10	Posttraumatic Stress Disorder
296.xx	F32.x	Major Depressive Disorder, Single Episode
296.xx	F33.x	Major Depressive Disorder, Recurrent Episode
______	______	____________________
______	______	____________________

ADJUSTMENT TO THE MILITARY CULTURE

BEHAVIORAL DEFINITIONS

1. Complains of difficulty with following rules and orders.
2. Exhibits sadness, frustration, anxiety, and/or feelings of hopelessness due to the loss of autonomy and independence.
3. Reports a persistent pattern of being reprimanded for insubordination, misconduct, disrespect, and/or failure to follow orders and adhere to military customs and courtesies.
4. Fails to meet minimum physical fitness, academic, and professional standards.
5. Exhibits a decline in mental and/or physical functioning as a result of decreased sleep.
6. Decides to go "Absent Without Leave" as a means to escape the stress of military life.
7. Reports a desire to leave the military and become a civilian.
8. Reports strong feelings of homesickness and isolation.

—. ____

____

—. ____

____

—. ____

____

LONG-TERM GOALS

1. Enhance ability to adapt to the structure, expectations, and hierarchical organization of the military.
2. Reduce the frequency of formal and informal reprimands.

3. Develop adaptive means for dealing with the physical and mental stress of military service.
4. Improve physical fitness and pass the required physical fitness test administered by the representative branch of service.

__. ____

____

__. ____

____

__. ____

____

SHORT-TERM OBJECTIVES

1. Describe the circumstances of military life that are contributing to the current adjustment problems. (1, 2, 3)
2. Identify the different emotions related to the problems adjusting to military life. (4, 5)
3. Identify positive aspects of serving in the military. (6, 7, 8)

THERAPEUTIC INTERVENTIONS

1. Explore the service member's current military stressors that are causing frustration, feelings of hopelessness, depression, and anxiety.
2. Assign the service member to create a list of stressors contributing to his/her current situation and rank them from most to least troubling.
3. Assist the service member in identifying similar dissatisfaction situations in the past and clarify outcomes; process reasons behind both positive and negative outcomes.
4. Assign the service member to create a list of the various emotions caused by his/her challenges in adjusting to the military culture.
5. Explore any stigma that may make it difficult for the service member to identify and accept his/her emotions (e.g., emotions make you weak and ineffective).
6. Assign the service member to develop a list of what he/she

likes about serving in the military.

7. Facilitate a role-play situation in which the service member and therapist switch roles and the service member is required to convince the therapist that the military can be a positive environment.
8. Encourage the service member to act or role-play "as if" he/she were a model/squared away service member while at work.

4. Identify and implement changes that will reduce the negative emotions brought on by the adjustment. (9, 10)

9. Brainstorm with the service member healthy ways of coping with stress and improving mood (e.g., progressive muscle relaxation, replacing negative thoughts with positive ones); monitor response and progress.
10. Teach the service member anger management techniques (e.g., deep breathing, taking a time out) to control his/her level of frustration and reduce the likelihood of acting impulsively.

5. Implement problem-solving strategies that promote adaptive responses to stressful situations. (11, 12)

11. Teach the service member how to apply the 7-step Military Problem-Solving Process to his/her current situation (e.g., recognize and define the problem, gather facts and make assumptions, define end states or goals and establish criteria for success, develop possible solutions, analyze the pros and cons and compare possible solutions, select and implement a solution, analyze the solution for effectiveness).
12. Identify a current problem and practice applying the problem-solving process with the service member in session; develop an action plan for real world

implementation and then review and process the outcome.

6. Implement increased assertiveness when dealing with interpersonal conflicts. (13, 14)

13. Utilize role-playing techniques (e.g., empty chair, role reversal) to teach the service member various methods for being more assertive in personal and professional situations.

14. Instruct the service member to read books on assertiveness (e.g., *The Complete Idiot's Guide to Assertiveness* by Davidson; *How to Grow a Backbone: 10 Strategies for Gaining Power and Influence at Work* by Marshall); process the content and application to current life problems.

7. Develop alternative ways of satisfying the need for independence. (15, 16)

15. Encourage the service member to develop activities that he/she enjoys and can participate in alone if so desired (e.g., hiking, fishing, biking); or assign "Identify and Schedule Pleasant Activities" in the *Adult Psychotherapy Homework Planner*, 2nd ed. by Jongsma.

16. Assist the service member in setting clear and strict boundaries when he/she has time off from work (e.g., decline to fill in at work for a peer).

8. Identify and develop activities outside of the military that provide a sense of pleasure and self-worth. (17)

17. Encourage the service member to participate in non-military related outings/activities that promote a sense of connectedness to others and the community (e.g., attend church socials, volunteer at an animal shelter).

9. Establish social supports that understand the challenges of being in the military. (18, 19).

18. Assist the service member in developing a list of current and past service member acquaintances who understand challenges of military life and with whom he/she could develop friendships.

19. Encourage the service member to attend an activity at a local Veterans of Foreign Wars (VFW).

10. Utilize already existing supports within the military that assist with the challenges of adjusting to military life. (20, 21)

20. Encourage the service member to talk with his/her unit chaplain about his/her problems adjusting to the military culture.

21. Assist the service member in making contact with local base/post services that help service members adjust to military life (e.g., Single Soldiers Club).

11. Develop a trusting and open relationship with a superior within the chain of command. (22)

22. Encourage the service member to talk with his/her Squad Leader, Platoon Sergeant, 1st Sergeant or anyone he/she trusts about the current situation.

12. Effectively communicate with significant others regarding current difficulties. (23).

23. Include the service member's significant other or family members in conjoint sessions to deal with problems that are impacting all parties involved.

13. Increase overall physical fitness. (24, 25, 26).

24. Encourage the service member to meet with a certified instructor at his/her local base/post in order to develop a physical fitness training plan.

25. Provide encouragement and positive feedback when physical fitness gains are made.

26. Teach the service member imagery techniques (e.g., imagining success versus failure at fitness tasks) that can improve his/her performance on the required physical fitness test.

14. Verbalize acceptance of the role of authority and follow orders of superiors without resistance. (27, 28, 29)

27. Teach the service member the need for authority and chain of command to promote order and safety in the face of threat and chaos during attack.

28. Explore the service member's civilian patterns of resistance to

authority and emphasize the need for a new reaction within the military setting.

29. Assist the service member in listing the negative consequences that will occur (e.g., lack of promotion, possible confinement, disciplinary assignments) if a pattern of resistance to authority continues.

15. Implement coping skills for dealing with loneliness. (30, 31)

30. Explore the service member's feelings of isolation and possible homesickness (see the chapter on Homesickness/Loneliness in this *Planner*).

31. Role-play situations in which the service member can reach out to others to establish social contact (or assign "Restoring Socialization Comfort" in the *Adult Psychotherapy Homework Planner*, 2nd ed. by Jongsma).

—. ______________________

—. ______________________

—. ______________________

—. ______________________

—. ______________________

—. ______________________

DIAGNOSTIC SUGGESTIONS

ICD-9-CM	*ICD-10-CM*	*DSM-5* Disorder, Condition, or Problem
V62.89	Z60.0	Phase of Life Problem
V62.2	Z56.9	Other Problem Related to Employment
309.0	F43.21	Adjustment Disorder, With Depressed Mood
296.xx	F32.x	Major Depressive Disorder, Single Episode
296.xx	F33.x	Major Depressive Disorder, Recurrent Episode
301.7	F60.2	Antisocial Personality Disorder
301.83	F60.3	Borderline Personality Disorder
______	______	______________________
______	______	______________________

AMPUTATION, LOSS OF MOBILITY, DISFIGUREMENT

BEHAVIORAL DEFINITIONS

1. Experienced a complete or partial loss of limb(s) during a combat or training mission or from an accident.
2. Has significant physical limitations due to limb loss including reduced movement or range of motion.
3. Received significant bodily burns during a combat or training mission or from an accident.
4. Reports clinically significant psychological distress resulting from loss of mobility, disfigurement, and social and occupational functioning.
5. Verbalizes feelings of hopelessness regarding future occupational opportunities.
6. Reports decreased satisfaction with life.
7. Exhibits marital and family conflicts.
8. Reports suicidal ideation.

—. ____

____

—. ____

____

—. ____

____

LONG-TERM GOALS

1. Accept the nature of the injury and understand its psychological and physical consequences.
2. Learn to compensate for any physical, occupational, interpersonal, and/or social limitations that the injury may create.

3. Develop an appreciation for existing physical abilities and attributes.
4. Return to pre-injury levels of self-esteem and confidence.

__. ____

____

__. ____

____

__. ____

____

SHORT-TERM OBJECTIVES

1. Describe in detail the history and nature of the injury and the impact on functioning. (1, 2)

2. Verbalize feelings about the injury. (3, 4)

THERAPEUTIC INTERVENTIONS

1. Encourage the veteran/service member to discuss the injury as much as he/she feels comfortable; maintain an awareness that some veterans/service members may also have posttraumatic stress disorder and describing the incident may bring up intense feelings.
2. Assess the veteran's/service member's type, intensity, and frequency of ongoing, injury-related symptoms and the impact on social, occupational, and interpersonal functioning.
3. Assist the veteran/service member in identifying his/her feelings associated with the injury (e.g., sadness, anger, hopelessness, fear); process those feelings in session.
4. Assign the veteran/service member to keep a "feelings log" for the purpose of rating his feelings throughout the day and identifying times, situations, objects, or people that intensify the negative feelings (or assign the "Pain and Stress Journal" in the

Adult Psychotherapy Homework Planner, 2nd ed. by Jongsma).

3. Cooperate with a psychiatric evaluation to assess for the need for psychotropic medication. (5, 6)

5. Arrange for an evaluation for a prescription of psychotropic medication(s) if the veteran/service member requests it, if he/she is likely to be noncompliant with psychotherapy, or if occupational and social functioning are seriously impaired.

6. Monitor the veteran/service member for prescription compliance, side effects, and overall effectiveness of the medication; consult with the prescribing practitioner at regular intervals.

4. Cooperate fully with all medical appointments and recommendations. (7)

7. Educate the veteran/service member about the importance of attending all assigned medical appointments, as well as the importance of following all medical treatment recommendations (e.g., take medication as prescribed, change bandages daily).

5. Verbalize an understanding that losing a limb, the ability to walk, stand, or hold a child, and/or bodily disfigurement is a loss that must be grieved. (8, 9, 10)

8. Educate the veteran/service member on the concept of grieving and that it is not just related to the death of a loved one.

9. Educate the veteran/service member about the five stages of grief (i.e., denial, anger, bargaining, depression, acceptance) and how it is not necessarily an all-or-none or stepwise progression; assist the veteran/service member in identifying which stage he/she is in.

10. Assign the veteran/service member to read material on grief (e.g., *The Grief Recovery Handbook: The Action Program*

for Moving Beyond Death, Divorce and Other Losses by James and Friedman; *How Can It Be All Right When Everything Is All Wrong*? by Smedes; or *When Bad Things Happen to Good People* by Kushner); process the material read.

6. Verbalize an understanding that the grief process is unique for each individual. (11)

11. Educate the veteran/service member on how grief is dealt with differently by different people and how the process may be impacted by culture, and that some grieve for short periods of time while others grieve for longer periods of time.

7. Cooperate with occupational therapy services. (12, 13)

12. Refer the veteran/service member for occupational therapy services; monitor and reinforce the veteran's/service member's compliance.

13. Educate the veteran/service member on how occupational therapy will assist him/her in functioning at a higher level in his/her job and everyday life.

8. Cooperate with physical therapy services. (14, 15)

14. Refer the veteran/service member for physical therapy services; monitor and reinforce the veteran's/service member's compliance.

15. Educate the veteran/service member on how physical therapy will help increase mobility, strength, and physical stamina, which has an impact on life satisfaction.

9. Participate in conjoint or family therapy. (16)

16. Provide conjoint or family therapy to assist the veteran/service member in overcoming the hurt associated with the loss and to help strengthen the family support system.

10. Participate in a support group. (17)

17. Encourage the veteran/service member to investigate various support groups that focus on his/her disability/injury; provide the veteran/service member with the following web links: http://www.amputee-coalition.org/, http://www.americanamputee.org/library/supportgroups.aspx, http://www.burnsurvivor.com/.

11. Verbalize an understanding and acceptance that outer "beauty" is diversely defined and that physical scars do not detract from a person's inner beauty and strength. (18, 19).

18. Discuss with the veteran/service member how physical deformities can be difficult to accept, but that most people do adjust with time.

19. Assign the veteran/service member to read *Tiny Dancer: The Incredible True Story of a Young Burn Victim's Journey from Afghanistan* by Flacco; process the content.

12. Develop a greater appreciation for individual strengths and abilities. (20, 21)

20. Assist the veteran/service member in developing an identity of someone with numerous abilities versus someone with a disability or limitation.

21. Assign the veteran/service member to read *To the Left of Inspiration: Adventures in Living with Disabilities* by Schneider; process thoughts about the content.

13. Identify and replace cognitive self-talk that is engaged in to support discouragement. (22, 23, 24, 25)

22. Assist the client in developing an awareness of his/her automatic thoughts that reflect a discouraging schemata.

23. Assign the client to keep a daily journal of automatic thoughts associated with discouraging feelings (e.g., "Negative Thoughts Trigger Negative Feelings" in the *Adult Psychotherapy Homework Planner*, 2nd ed. by Jongsma, or "Daily Record of Dysfunctional

Thoughts" in *Cognitive Therapy of Depression* by Beck, Rush, Shaw, and Emery); process the journal material to challenge depressive thinking patterns and replace them with reality-based thoughts.

24. Assign "behavioral experiments" in which discouraging automatic thoughts are treated as hypotheses/predictions, reality-based alternative hypotheses/predictions are generated, and both are tested against the client's past, present, and/or future experiences.

25. Reinforce the client's positive, reality-based cognitive messages that enhance self-confidence and increase adaptive action (see "Positive Self-Talk" in the *Adult Psychotherapy Homework Planner*, 2nd ed. by Jongsma).

14. Participate in the National Veterans Wheelchair Games. (26)

26. Provide information about and encourage the veteran/service member to participate in the National Veterans Wheelchair Games (www.wheelchairgames.va.gov/).

15. Verbalize a decision about a desire to remain in the military with a disability. (27, 28, 29)

27. Explore the service member's thoughts and feelings regarding remaining in the military.

28. Instruct the service member to talk with his/her chain of command, primary care provider, and case manager regarding developing a plan for remaining in the military.

29. Instruct the service member to request a referral from his/her primary care provider to the Center for the Intrepid at Brooke Army Medical Center in San Antonio, Texas.

16. Meet with military medical personnel if medical separation from service is desired or required. (30)

30. Encourage the service member to attend and participate in all medical separation appointments.

17. Meet with Veterans Affairs representative regarding disability compensation if separated from service. (31, 32)

31. Identify the veteran's Veterans Affairs appropriate geographical region and facilitate contact with a Veterans Affairs representative from that region.

32. Provide the veteran with information regarding his/her Veterans Affairs benefits (www.vba.va.gov/VBA/).

18. Attend scheduled Veterans Affairs medical appointments. (33)

33. Stress the importance of the veteran attending all scheduled medical appointments at his/her local Veterans Affairs facility, including compensation evaluations and regular healthcare appointments.

—. ______________________

—. ______________________

—. ______________________

—. ______________________

—. ______________________

—. ______________________

DIAGNOSTIC SUGGESTIONS

ICD-9-CM	*ICD-10-CM*	*DSM-5* Disorder, Condition, or Problem
309.0	F43.21	Adjustment Disorder, With Depressed Mood
296.xx	F32.x	Major Depressive Disorder, Single Episode
296.xx	F33.x	Major Depressive Disorder, Recurrent Episode
293.83	F06.31	Depressive Disorder Due to Another Medical Condition, With Depressive Features
305.00	F10.10	Alcohol Use Disorder, Mild
303.90	F10.20	Alcohol Use Disorder, Moderate or Severe
305.50	F11.10	Opioid Use Disorder, Mild
304.00	F11.20	Opioid Use Disorder, Moderate or Severe
______	______	______________________
______	______	______________________

ANGER MANAGEMENT AND DOMESTIC VIOLENCE

BEHAVIORAL DEFINITIONS

1. Reports a history of explosive, aggressive outbursts out of proportion to any precipitating stressors, leading to assaultive acts or destruction of property.
2. Displays overreactive hostility to insignificant irritants.
3 Engages in physical and or emotional abuse against significant other.
4. Makes swift and harsh judgmental statements to or about others.
5. Displays body language suggesting anger, including tense muscles (e.g., clenched fist or jaw), glaring looks, or refusal to make eye contact.
6. Uses passive-aggressive patterns (e.g., social withdrawal, lack of complete or timely compliance in following directions or rules, complaining about authority figures behind their backs, uncooperative in meeting expected behavioral norms) due to anger.
7. Displays a consistent pattern of challenging or disrespectful attitudes toward authority figures.
8. Uses abusive language meant to intimidate others.
9. Engages in rationalization to deflect responsibility for the abuse.
10. Blames others for aggressive and abusive behavior.

__. ____

__. ____

__. ____

LONG-TERM GOALS

1. Decrease overall intensity and frequency of angry feelings, and increase ability to recognize and appropriately express angry feelings as they occur.
2. Develop an awareness of current angry behaviors, clarifying origins of, and alterations to, aggressive behavior.
3. Refrain from physically and emotionally abusive behavior against significant other.
4. Come to an awareness and acceptance of angry feelings while developing better control and more serenity.
5. Become capable of handling angry feelings in constructive ways that enhance daily functioning.
6. Demonstrate respect for others and their feelings.

__. ____

____

__. ____

____

__. ____

____

SHORT-TERM OBJECTIVES

1. Identify situations, thoughts, feelings that trigger anger, angry verbal and/or behavioral actions, and the targets of those actions. (1)
2. Cooperate with a medical evaluation to assess possible organic contributors to poor anger control. (2)
3. Cooperate with a psychiatric evaluation for possible treatment

THERAPEUTIC INTERVENTIONS

1. Thoroughly assess the various stimuli (e.g., situations, people, thoughts) that have triggered the veteran's/service member's anger and the thoughts, feelings, and actions that have characterized his/her anger responses.
2. Refer the veteran/service member to a physician for a complete physical exam to rule out organic contributors (e.g., brain damage, tumor, elevated testosterone levels) to poor anger control.
3. Assess the veteran/service member for the need for

with psychotropic medications to assist in anger control and take medications consistently, if prescribed. (3, 4)

psychotropic medication to assist in control of anger; refer him/her to a psychiatric provider for an evaluation and prescription of medication, if needed. ▼

4. Monitor the veteran/service member for prescription compliance, effectiveness, and side effects; provide feedback to the prescribing practitioner. ▼

▼ 4. Keep a daily journal of persons, situations, and other triggers of anger; record thoughts, feelings, and actions taken. (5, 6)

5. Ask the veteran/service member to keep a daily journal in which he/she documents persons, situations, and other triggers of anger, irritation, or disappointment (or assign "Anger Journal" in the *Adult Psychotherapy Homework Planner*, 2nd ed. by Jongsma); routinely process the journal toward helping the veteran/service member understand his/her contributions to generating his/her anger. ▼

6. Assist the veteran/service member in generating a list of anger triggers; process the list toward helping the veteran/service member understand the causes and extent of his/her anger. ▼

▼ 5. Verbalize an increased awareness of anger expression patterns, their possible origins, and their consequences. (7, 8, 9, 10).

7. Assist the veteran/service member in coming to the realization that he/she is angry by reviewing triggers and frequency of angry outbursts. ▼

8. Assist the veteran/service member in identifying ways that key life figures (e.g., father, mother, teachers) have expressed angry feelings and how these experiences have positively or negatively influenced the way he/she handles anger. ▼

9. Ask the veteran/service member to list ways anger has negatively impacted his/her daily life (e.g., injuring others or self, legal conflicts, loss of respect from self and others, destruction of property); process this list. ▽

10. Expand the veteran's/service member's awareness of the negative effects that anger has on his/her physical health (e.g., increased susceptibility to disease, injuries, headaches). ▽

▽ 6. Agree to learn alternative ways to think about and manage anger. (11, 12)

11. Assist the veteran/service member in reconceptualizing anger as involving different components (cognitive, physiological, affective, and behavioral) that go through predictable phases (e.g., demanding expectations not being met leading to increased arousal and anger leading to acting out) that can be managed. ▽

12. Assist the veteran/service member in identifying the positive consequences of managing anger (e.g., respect from others and self, cooperation from others, improved physical health); ask the veteran/service member to agree to learn new ways to conceptualize and manage anger. ▽

▽ 7. Learn and implement calming strategies as part of managing reactions to frustration. (13, 14)

13. Teach the veteran/service member calming techniques (e.g., muscle relaxation, paced breathing, calming imagery) as part of a tailored strategy for responding appropriately to angry feelings when they occur. ▽

14. Assign the veteran/service member to implement calming techniques in his/her daily life

when facing anger trigger situations; process the results, reinforcing success and redirecting for failure.

8. Identify, challenge, and replace anger-inducing self-talk with self-talk that facilitates a less angry reaction. (15, 16)

15. Explore the veteran's/service member's self-talk that mediates his/her angry feelings and actions (e.g., demanding expectations reflected in should, must, or have to statements); identify and challenge biases, assisting him/her in generating appraisals and self-talk that corrects for the biases and facilitates a more flexible and temperate response to frustration.

16. Assign the veteran/service member a homework exercise in which he/she identifies angry self-talk and generates alternatives that help moderate angry reactions; review implementation; reinforce success, providing corrective feedback toward improvement.

9. Learn and implement thought-stopping to manage intrusive, unwanted thoughts that trigger anger. (17)

17. Assign the veteran/service member to implement a "thought-stopping" technique on a daily basis between sessions (or assign "Making Use of the Thought-Stopping Technique" in the *Adult Psychotherapy Homework Planner*, 2nd ed. by Jongsma); review implementation; reinforce success, providing corrective feedback toward improvement.

10. Verbalize feelings of anger in a controlled, assertive way. (18, 19)

18. Use instruction, modeling, and/or role-playing to teach the veteran/ service member assertive communication; if indicated, refer him/her to an assertiveness training class/group for further instruction.

19. Conduct conjoint sessions to help the veteran/service member implement assertion, problem-solving, and/or conflict resolution skills in the presence of his/her significant others.

11. Learn and implement problem-solving and/or conflict resolution skills to manage interpersonal problems. (19, 20)

19. Conduct conjoint sessions to help the veteran/service member implement assertion, problem-solving, and/or conflict resolution skills in the presence of his/her significant others.

20. Teach the veteran/service member conflict resolution skills (e.g., empathy, active listening, "I messages," respectful communication, assertiveness without aggression, compromise); use modeling, role-playing, and behavior rehearsal to work through several current conflicts.

12. Practice using new anger management skills in session with the therapist and during homework exercises. (21, 22, 23)

21. Assist the veteran/service member in constructing a client-centered strategy for managing anger that combines any of the somatic, cognitive, communication, problem-solving, and/or conflict resolution skills relevant to his/her needs.

22. Select situations in which the veteran/service member will be increasingly challenged to apply his/her new strategies for managing anger.

23. Use any of several techniques, including relaxation, imagery, behavioral rehearsal, modeling role-playing, or *in vivo* exposure/behavioral experiments to help the veteran/service member consolidate the use of his/her new anger management skills.

13. Decrease the number, intensity, and duration of angry outbursts, while increasing the use of new skills for managing anger. (24)

24. Monitor the veteran's/service member's reports of angry outbursts toward the goal of decreasing their frequency, intensity, and duration through the veteran's/service member's use of new anger management skills (or assign "Alternatives to Destructive Anger" in the *Adult Psychotherapy Homework Planner*, 2nd ed. by Jongsma); review progress, reinforcing success and providing corrective feedback toward improvement.

14. Attend a structured domestic violence treatment program. (25)

25. Refer the veteran/service member to a structured domestic violence program that consists of least a six-month program and focuses on issues of power and control, gender roles, and beliefs that create and maintain violence.

15. Identify social supports that will help facilitate the implementation of anger management skills. (26)

26. Encourage the veteran/service member to discuss his/her anger management goals with trusted persons who are likely to support his/her change.

16. Implement relapse prevention strategies for managing possible future trauma-related symptoms. (27, 28, 29, 30, 31)

27. Discuss with the veteran/service member the distinction between a lapse and relapse, associating a lapse with an initial and reversible angry outburst and relapse with the choice to return routinely to the old pattern of anger.

28. Identify and rehearse with the veteran/service member the management of future situations or circumstances in which lapses back to anger could occur.

29. Instruct the veteran/service member to routinely use the new

anger management strategies learned in therapy (e.g., calming, adaptive self-talk, assertion, and/or conflict resolution) to respond to frustrations.

30. Develop a "coping card" or other reminder on which new anger management skills and other important information (e.g., calm yourself, be flexible in your expectations of others, voice your opinion calmly, respect others' point of view) are recorded for the veteran's/service member's later use.

31. Schedule periodic "maintenance" sessions to help the veteran/service member maintain therapeutic gains.

17. Read a book or treatment manual that supplements the therapy by improving understanding of anger and anger management. (32)

32. Assign the veteran/service member to read material that educates him/her about anger and its management (e.g., *Overcoming Situational and General Anger: Client Manual* by Deffenbacher and McKay, *Of Course You're Angry* by Rosselini and Worden, or *The Anger Control Workbook* by McKay).

18. Identify the advantages and disadvantages of holding on to anger and of forgiveness; discuss with therapist. (33, 34)

33. Discuss with the veteran/service member forgiveness of the perpetrators of pain as a process of letting go of his/her anger.

34. Assign the veteran/service member to read *Forgive and Forget* by Smedes.

19. Write a letter of forgiveness to the perpetrator of past or present pain and process this letter with the therapist. (35)

35. Ask the veteran/service member to write a forgiving letter to the target of anger as a step toward letting go of anger; process this letter in session.

___. ____________________ ___. ____________________

____________________ ____________________

___. ____________________ ___. ____________________

____________________ ____________________

___. ____________________ ___. ____________________

____________________ ____________________

DIAGNOSTIC SUGGESTIONS

ICD-9-CM	*ICD-10-CM*	*DSM-5* Disorder, Condition, or Problem
312.34	F63.81	Intermittent Explosive Disorder
296.xx	F31.xx	Bipolar I Disorder
296.89	F31.81	Bipolar II Disorder
312.8	F91.x	Conduct Disorder
310.1	F07.0	Personality Change Due to Another Medical Condition
V61.12	Z69.12	Encounter for Mental Health Services for Perpetrator of Spouse or Partner Violence, Physical
V62.83	Z69.82	Encounter for Mental Health Services for Perpetrator of Nonspousal Adult
301.7	F60.2	Antisocial Personality Disorder
301.83	F60.3	Borderline Personality Disorder
301.0	F60.0	Paranoid Personality Disorder
301.81	F60.81	Narcissistic Personality Disorder
________	________	____________________
________	________	____________________

ANTISOCIAL BEHAVIOR IN THE MILITARY

BEHAVIORAL DEFINITIONS

1. Reports an adolescent history of consistent rule-breaking, lying, stealing, physical aggression, disrespect for others and their property, and/or substance abuse resulting in frequent confrontation with authorities.
2. Exhibits a failure to conform to military norms with respect to following orders, respecting superiors, and adhering to military customs and traditions.
3. Displays a pattern of interacting in a confrontive, aggressive, and/or argumentative manner with superiors.
4. Exhibits little or no remorse for causing harm or showing disrespect to others.
5. Displays a consistent pattern of blaming others for what happens to him/her.
6. Displays a disregard for the truth as evidenced by lying to superiors and manipulating/conning fellow service members.
7. Engages in frequent physical and/or verbal altercations with superiors and/or fellow service members.
8. Has a history of reckless behaviors that reflect a lack of regard for self and others that may have safety implications, particularly in the deployed setting.
9. Engages in a pattern of sexual promiscuity, which negatively impacts unit cohesion.
10. Frequently receives disciplinary actions for disruptive and disrespectful behavior.
11. Reports threats by superiors of being dishonorably discharged from the military.

Most of the content of this chapter (with only slight revisions) originates from A. E. Jongsma, Jr., L. M. Peterson, and T. J. Bruce, *The Complete Adult Psychotherapy Treatment Planner*, 4th ed. (Hoboken, NJ: John Wiley & Sons, 2006).

12. Has had frequent visits to military behavioral health professionals to discuss possibly being separated from the military for a personality disorder.
13. Displays a failure to function as a productive unit team member.

—. ____

—. ____

—. ____

LONG-TERM GOALS

1. Accept responsibility for own behavior and keep behavior within the acceptable limits of military rules and regulations.
2. Develop and demonstrate a healthy sense of respect for military norms, superiors, and the need for engaging in traditional military customs and traditions.
3. Improve method of relating to superiors; be less demanding, defiant, and hostile toward others.
4. Develop an understanding and acceptance of the need for conforming to prevailing military social boundaries on behavior.
5. Eliminate behavior that results in disciplinary actions for misconduct.
6. Engage in behavior that leads to greater unit and team cohesion.

—. ____

—. ____

—. ____

SHORT-TERM OBJECTIVES

1. Admit to illegal and/or unethical behavior that has trampled on military customs, traditions, and/or laws and the rights and

THERAPEUTIC INTERVENTIONS

1. Explore the history of the service member's pattern of illegal and/or unethical behavior and confront his/her attempts at

feelings of other service members. (1, 2)

minimization, denial, or projection of blame.

2. Review the consequences for the service member and others of his/her antisocial behavior (e.g., comrades may undeservingly be punished for someone else's behavior, others are put at risk in hostile environments).

2. Verbalize an understanding of the benefits for self and others when he/she abides by military rules and regulations. (3, 4)

3. Teach the service member that the basis for all military relationships is trust that the other person will treat one with respect and honor and will always be there to "watch their back."

4. Teach the service member the need for following military rules and laws as the basis for trust and success that ensures such a hierarchical organization will succeed and that the "mission" will be accomplished.

3. Make a commitment to live within the rules, laws, and regulations of the military. (5, 6)

5. Solicit a commitment from the service member to conform to a lifestyle that respects and adheres to military rules, laws, and regulations (or assign "Crooked Thinking Leads to Crooked Behavior" in the *Adult Psychotherapy Homework Planner*, 2nd ed. by Jongsma).

6. Emphasize the reality of negative consequences for the service member if he/she continues to disobey military rules, laws, and regulations (e.g., dishonorable discharge, confinement, reduction in rank and/or pay, extra duty).

4. List relationships that have been damaged because of disrespect, disloyalty, aggression, and/or dishonesty. (7, 8)

7. Review relationships that have been lost or significantly damaged due to the service member's antisocial attitudes and practices such as disloyalty, dishonesty, or aggression (or

assign "How I Have Hurt Others" in the *Adult Psychotherapy Homework Planner*, 2nd ed. by Jongsma).

8. Confront the service member's lack of sensitivity to the needs and feelings of others.

5. Acknowledge a pattern of self-centeredness in virtually all relationships. (8, 9, 10)

8. Confront the service member's lack of sensitivity to the needs and feelings of others.

9. Point out the self-focused, "me-first," look-out-for-number-one attitude that is reflected in the service member's antisocial behavior.

10. Discuss how the "me-first" approach to life is inconsistent with military values and traditions; process any feelings in session.

6. Make a commitment to be honest and reliable with his/her superiors and comrades. (11, 12, 13)

11. Teach the service member the value for self of honesty and reliability in all relationships, since he/she benefits from approval by his superiors and comrades as well as increased trust and respect.

12. Teach the service member the positive effect that honesty and reliability have for others, since they are not disappointed or develop distrust due to lies and broken promises.

13. Ask the service member to make a commitment to be honest and reliable.

7. Verbalize an understanding of the benefits to self and others of being empathetic and sensitive to the needs of fellow comrades. (3, 14, 15)

3. Teach the service member that the basis for all military relationships is trust that the other person will treat one with respect and honor and will always be there to "watch their back."

14. Attempt to sensitize the service member to his/her lack of

empathy for others by revisiting the consequences of his/her behavior on others. Use role reversal techniques.

15. Confront the service member when he/she is rude, disrespectful, or not being sensitive to other service members' boundaries.

8. List three actions that will be performed that will be acts of kindness and thoughtfulness toward other service members. (16)

16. Assist the service member in listing three actions that he/she will perform as acts of service or kindness for other service members (e.g., volunteer to work an extra shift, volunteer for a duty such as trash detail that is typically an undesirable task).

9. Indicate the steps that will be taken to make amends or restitution for damage caused by past behaviors. (17, 18, 19)

17. Assist the service member in identifying those who have been hurt/disrespected by his/her antisocial behavior.

18. Teach the service member the value of apologizing for damage caused as a means of accepting responsibility for behavior and of developing sensitivity to the feelings of others (or assign "Letter of Apology" in the *Adult Psychotherapy Homework Planner*, 2nd ed. by Jongsma).

19. Encourage the service member's commitment to specific steps that will be taken to apologize and make restitution to those who have been impacted by his/her antisocial behavior.

10. Verbally demonstrate an understanding of the rules, responsibilities, and duties related to employment. (20)

20. Review the rules and expectations that must govern the service member's behavior in the military work setting.

11. Attend work reliably, and treat superiors and coworkers with respect. (21, 22)

21. Monitor the service member's attendance at work and reinforce reliability as well as respect for authority.

22. Ask the service member to make a list of behaviors and attitudes that must be modified in order to decrease his/her conflict with authorities; process the list.

12. Increase statements of accepting responsibility for own behavior. (23, 24, 25)

23. Confront the service member when he/she makes blaming statements or fails to take responsibility for his/her own actions, thoughts, or feelings.

24. Explore the service member's reasons for blaming others for his/her own actions (e.g., history of physically abusive punishment, parental modeling, fear of rejection, low self-esteem).

25. Give verbal positive feedback to the service member when he/she takes responsibility for his/her own behavior.

13. Verbalize an understanding of how childhood experiences of pain have led to an imitative pattern of self-focused protection and aggression toward others. (26, 27)

26. Explore the service member's history of abuse, neglect, or abandonment in childhood; explain how the cycle of abuse or neglect is repeating itself in the service member's behavior.

27. Point out that the service member's pattern of emotional detachment in relationships and self-focused behavior is related to a dysfunctional attempt to protect self from pain.

14. Verbalize a desire to forgive perpetrators of childhood abuse. (28)

28. Teach the service member the value of forgiving the perpetrators of hurt versus holding on to hurt and rage and using the hurt as an excuse to continue antisocial practices.

15. Practice trusting a significant other with disclosure of personal feelings. (29, 30, 31)

29. Explore the service member's fears associated with placing trust in others.

30. Identify some personal thoughts and feelings that the service member could share with a significant other as a means of beginning to demonstrate trust in someone.

31. Process the experience of the service member making himself/herself vulnerable by self-disclosing to someone.

16. Acknowledge intent and/or motivation to remain in the military. (32, 33)

32. Explore with the service member if it is his/her intent to remain in the military.

33. Explore the impact of a dishonorable discharge on the service member's future (e.g., federal employment, student loans).

__. ____________________________

__. ____________________________

__. ____________________________

__. ____________________________

__. ____________________________

__. ____________________________

DIAGNOSTIC SUGGESTIONS

ICD-9-CM	*ICD-10-CM*	*DSM-5* Disorder, Condition, or Problem
V71.01	Z72.811	Adult Antisocial Behavior
309.3	F43.24	Adjustment Disorder, With Disturbance of Conduct
312.34	F63.81	Intermittent Explosive Disorder
312.30	F91.9	Unspecified Disruptive, Impulse-Control, and Conduct Disorder
303.90	F10.20	Alcohol Use Disorder, Moderate or Severe
301.7	F60.2	Antisocial Personality Disorder
301.81	F60.81	Narcissistic Personality Disorder
________	________	____________________
________	________	____________________

ANXIETY

BEHAVIORAL DEFINITIONS

1. Reports excessive and/or unrealistic worry that is difficult to control occurring more days than not for at least six months about a number of events or activities, which may or may not be military related.
2. Experiences motor tension (e.g., restlessness, muscle soreness, shakiness, muscle tension, or bruxism).
3. Complains of autonomic hyperactivity (e.g., palpitations, shortness of breath, dry mouth, nausea, insomnia, sweating, or diarrhea).
4. Displays hypervigilance (e.g., feeling constantly on edge, experiencing concentration difficulties, irritability, and exaggerated startle response).

—. ____

____

—. ____

____

—. ____

____

LONG-TERM GOALS

1. Reduce overall frequency, intensity, and duration of the anxiety so that daily functioning is not impaired.
2. Stabilize anxiety level while increasing ability to function on a daily basis.

---

3. Resolve the core conflict that is the source of anxiety.
4. Enhance ability to effectively cope with the full variety of life's responsibilities.

__. ____

____

__. ____

____

__. ____

____

SHORT-TERM OBJECTIVES

1. Describe current and past experiences with the worry and anxiety symptoms complete with their impact on functioning and attempts to resolve it. (1)
2. Complete psychological tests designed to assess worry and anxiety symptoms. (2)
3. ▽ Cooperate with an evaluation by a prescribing practitioner for psychotropic medication. (3, 4, 5)

THERAPEUTIC INTERVENTIONS

1. Assess the focus, excessiveness, and uncontrollability of the veteran's/service member's worry and the type, frequency, intensity, and duration of his/her anxiety symptoms.
2. Administer a patient-report measure to help assess the nature and degree of the veteran's/service member's worry and anxiety symptoms (e.g., *The Penn State Worry Questionnaire* by Meyer, Miller, Metzger, and Borkovec) and the impact those symptoms have on functioning (e.g., *OQ-45.2* by Burlingame, Lambert, and Reisinger).
3. Refer the veteran/service member to a prescribing practitioner for a psychotropic medication consultation. ▽
4. Monitor the veteran's/service member's psychotropic medication compliance, side effects, and effectiveness; confer regularly with the prescribing practitioner. ▽

5. If appropriate, contact the service member's chain of command if side effects from medication will put him/her or others at risk (e.g., drowsiness, changes in reaction time).

4. Verbalize an understanding of the cognitive, physiological, and behavioral components of anxiety and its treatment. (6, 7, 8)

6. Discuss how generalized anxiety typically involves excessive worry about unrealistic threats, various bodily expressions of tension, overarousal, and hypervigilance, and avoidance of what is threatening that interact to maintain the problem (see *Mastery of Your Anxiety and Worry—Therapist Guide* by Craske, Barlow, and Zinbarg).

7. Discuss how treatment targets worry, anxiety symptoms, and avoidance to help the veteran/service member manage worry effectively and reduce overarousal and unnecessary avoidance.

8. Assign the veteran/service member to read psychoeducational sections of books or treatment manuals on worry and generalized anxiety (e.g., *Mastery of Your Anxiety and Worry—Workbook* by Craske, and Barlow).

5. Learn and implement calming skills to reduce overall anxiety and manage anxiety symptoms. (9, 10, 11, 12)

9. Teach the veteran/service member relaxation skills (e.g., progressive muscle, imagery, diaphragmatic breathing) and how to discriminate better between relaxation and tension; teach the veteran/service member how to apply these skills to his/her daily life (e.g., *Progressive Relaxation Training* by Bernstein and Borkovec; *Treating GAD* by Rygh and Sanderson).

10. Assign the veteran/service member homework each session in which he/she practices relaxation exercises daily for at least 15 minutes; review and reinforce success while providing corrective feedback toward improvement.

11. Assign the veteran/service member to read about progressive muscle relaxation and other calming strategies in relevant books or treatment manuals (e.g., *Progressive Relaxation Training* by Bernstein and Borkovec; *Mastery of Your Anxiety and Worry—Workbook* by Craske, and Barlow).

12. Use biofeedback techniques to facilitate the veteran's/service member's success at learning relaxation skills.

6. Verbalize an understanding of the role that cognitive biases play in excessive irrational worry and persistent anxiety symptoms. (13, 14, 15)

13. Discuss examples demonstrating that unrealistic worry typically overestimates the probability of threats and underestimates or overlooks the veteran's/service member's ability to manage realistic demands (or assign "Past Successful Anxiety Coping" in *Adult Psychotherapy Homework Planner,* 2nd ed. by Jongsma).

14. Assist the veteran/service member in analyzing his/her fear by examining the probability of the negative expectation occurring, the real consequences of it occurring, his/her ability to control the outcome, the worst possible outcome, and his/her ability to accept it (see "Analyze the Probability of a Feared Event" in *Adult Psychotherapy*

Homework Planner, 2nd ed. by Jongsma, and *Anxiety Disorders and Phobias* by Beck and Emery). ▽

15. Help the veteran/service member gain insight into the notion that worry is a form of avoidance of a feared problem and that it creates chronic tension. ▽

▽ 7. Identify, challenge, and replace biased, fearful self-talk with positive, realistic, and empowering self-talk. (16, 17, 18)

16. Explore the veteran's/service member's schema and self-talk that mediate his/her fear response, then challenge the biases; assist him/her in replacing the distorted messages with reality-based alternatives and positive self-talk that will increase his/her self-confidence in coping with irrational fears. ▽

17. Assign the veteran/service member a homework exercise in which he/she identifies fearful self-talk and creates reality-based alternatives; review and reinforce success, providing corrective feedback toward improvement. ▽

18. Teach the client to implement a thought-stopping technique (thinking of a stop sign and then a pleasant scene) or aversion technique (snapping rubber band on the wrist) for worries that have been addressed but persist (or assign "Making Use of the Thought-Stopping Technique" in the *Adult Psychotherapy Homework Planner,* 2nd ed. by Jongsma); monitor and encourage the veteran's/service member's use of the technique in daily life between sessions. ▽

8. Undergo gradual repeated imaginal exposure to the feared negative consequences predicted by worries and develop alternative reality-based predictions. (19, 20, 21, 22)

19. Direct and assist the veteran/service member in constructing a hierarchy of two to three spheres of worry for use in exposure (e.g., worry about harm while on combat missions, future duty assignments, relationships).

20. Select initial exposures that have a high likelihood of being a successful experience for the veteran/service member; develop a plan for managing the negative effect engendered by exposure; mentally rehearse the procedure.

21. Ask the veteran/service member to vividly imagine worst-case consequences of worries, holding them in mind until anxiety associated with them weakens (up to 30 minutes); generate reality-based alternatives to that worst case and process them (see *Mastery of Your Anxiety and Worry—Therapist Guide* by Craske, Barlow, and Zinbarg).

22. Assign the veteran/service member a homework exercise in which he/she does worry exposures and records responses (see *Mastery of Your Anxiety and Worry—Workbook* by Craske, and Barlow; or *Generalized Anxiety Disorder* by Brown, O'Leary, and Barlow); review, reinforce success, and provide corrective feedback toward improvement.

9. Learn and implement problem-solving strategies for realistically addressing worries. (23, 24)

23. Teach the veteran/service member problem-solving strategies with a focus on the Military Problem Solving Process involving recognizing and defining the problem,

gathering facts and making assumptions, defining end states and establishing criteria, developing possible solutions, analyzing pros and cons and comparing possible solutions, selecting and implementing solutions, and analyzing solutions for effectiveness.

24. Assign the veteran/service member a homework exercise in which he/she problem-solves a current problem (see *Mastery of Your Anxiety and Worry—Workbook* by Craske, and Barlow; or *Generalized Anxiety Disorder* by Brown, O'Leary, and Barlow); review, reinforce success, and provide corrective feedback toward improvement.

10. Learn and implement relapse prevention strategies for managing possible future anxiety symptoms. (25, 26, 27, 28)

25. Discuss with the veteran/service member the distinction between a lapse and relapse, associating a lapse with an initial and reversible return of worry, anxiety symptoms, or urges to avoid and relapse with the decision to continue the fearful and avoidant patterns.

26. Identify and rehearse with the veteran/service member the management of future situations or circumstances in which lapses could occur (e.g., after conflict with a superior, exposure to a traumatic event).

27. Instruct the veteran/service member to routinely use relaxation, cognitive restructuring, exposure, and problem-solving exposures as needed to address emergent worries, building them into his/her life as much as possible.

28. Develop a "coping card" on which coping strategies and other important information (e.g., "Breathe deeply and relax," "Challenge unrealistic worries," "Use problem-solving") are written for the veteran's/service member's later use.

11. Utilize a paradoxical intervention technique to reduce the anxiety response. (29)

29. Develop a paradoxical intervention (see *Ordeal Therapy* by Haley) in which the veteran/ service member is encouraged to have the problem (e.g., anxiety) and then schedule that anxiety to occur at specific intervals each day (at a time of day/night when the client would be clearly wanting to do something else) in a specific way and for a defined length of time.

12. Complete a Cost Benefit Analysis of maintaining the anxiety. (30)

30. Ask the veteran/service member to evaluate the costs and benefits of worries (e.g., complete the Cost Benefit Analysis exercise in *Ten Days to Self-Esteem* by Burns) in which he/she lists the advantages and disadvantages of the negative thought, fear, or anxiety; process the completed assignment.

13. Identify the major life conflicts from the past and present that form the basis for present anxiety. (31, 32, 33)

31. Assist the veteran/service member in becoming aware of key unresolved life conflicts and in starting to work toward their resolution.

32. Reinforce the veteran's/service member's insights into the role of his/her past emotional pain and present anxiety.

33. Ask the veteran/service member to develop and process a list of key past and present life conflicts that continue to cause worry;

separate conflicts into military and civilian lists if so desired.

14. Maintain involvement in work, family, and social activities. (34)

34. Support the veteran/service member in following through with military duty responsibilities, family, and social activities rather than escaping or avoiding them to focus on panic.

15. Return for a follow-up session to track progress, reinforce gains, and problem-solve barriers. (35)

35. Schedule a "booster session" for the veteran/service member for one to three months after therapy ends.

16. Develop an alternate plan of care/follow-up if deployment is pending. (36)

36. Identify behavioral health supports that will be available at the location where the service member will be deployed.

__. ____________________

__. ____________________

__. ____________________

__. ____________________

__. ____________________

__. ____________________

DIAGNOSTIC SUGGESTIONS

ICD-9-CM	ICD-10-CM	DSM-5 Disorder, Condition, or Problem
300.02	F41.1	Generalized Anxiety Disorder
300.09	F41.8	Other Specified Anxiety Disorder
300.00	F41.9	Unspecified Anxiety Disorder
309.24	F43.22	Adjustment Disorder, With Anxiety
______	______	____________________
______	______	____________________

ATTENTION AND CONCENTRATION DEFICITS

BEHAVIORAL DEFINITIONS

1. Reports a childhood history of attention/concentration problems that may or may not have been diagnosed as Attention Deficit Disorder.
2. Exhibits a persistent pattern of attention/concentration problems during adulthood.
3. Reports difficulties paying attention in a variety of settings on most issues even though the issues may be of importance (e.g., training meetings, pre-mission briefings, college classes).
4. Complains of being easily distracted.
5. Exhibits a pervasive pattern of disorganization in his/her life.
6. Reports starting many projects and an inability to finish most, if any, of them.
7. Reports frequent complaints by superiors about lapses in attention/concentration during meetings, training, and combat missions.
8. Reports an inability to read for extended periods of time and is typically unable to recall what was read.
9. Complains of often misplacing/losing personal items (e.g., keys, wallet, identification).
10. Reports often asking others to repeat what was said during conversations.

—. ____
____

—. ____
____

—. ____
____

LONG-TERM GOALS

1. Increase levels of attention/concentration in all settings.
2. Minimize impact of attention/concentration deficits in daily life through the use of effective coping skills.
3. Increase perceived level of effectiveness in work, academic, and social arenas.
4. Improve overall satisfaction with periods of personal time and extracurricular activities.

—. ____

____

—. ____

____

—. ____

____

SHORT-TERM OBJECTIVES

1. Describe the history of the attention/concentration deficits. (1, 2)
2. Complete psychological testing and provide collateral information regarding the attention/concentration complaints. (3)

THERAPEUTIC INTERVENTIONS

1. Assess the history of the veteran's/service member's attention deficits and the course of progression including onset, frequency, and duration, and how they have impacted occupational, social, and academic functioning.
2. Evaluate the impact that the veteran's/service member's symptoms have had on his/her daily functioning; note worsening of symptoms and potential aggravating factors.
3. Administer psychological testing to the veteran/service member to rule out Attention Deficit Disorder (ADD); provide feedback to veteran/service member and any other relevant parties.

3. Participate in a medical examination to determine if the deficits are related to physical illness/insult or substance use. (4)

4. Refer the veteran/service member for a medical evaluation to assess for deficits related to recent injuries/insults (e.g., traumatic brain injury, exposure to toxins, drugs, and alcohol).

4. Cooperate with an evaluation by a prescribing practitioner to assess for the appropriateness of psychotropic medication. (5)

5. Refer the veteran/service member for a psychiatric evaluation for psychotropic medications to alleviate attention/concentration deficits (e.g., amphetamines, Bupropion).

5. Comply with recommendations resulting from the medical and psychiatric examinations. (6, 7, 8)

6. Process the results of the psychiatric, medical, and psychological evaluations with the veteran/service member and address any questions he/she may have.

7. Coordinate a conjoint session with significant others for the primary purposes of assisting with medication compliance and increasing social support.

8. Monitor the veteran/service member for medication compliance, effectiveness, and complications from side effects.

6. Identify and rank order specific work-related problems that result from attention/concentration deficits and cause the most difficulty. (9)

9. Assist the veteran/service member in creating a hierarchical list of his/her work-related problems, ranking them from most to least troublesome.

7. Implement problem-solving strategies that will mitigate work problems caused by attention/concentration deficits. (10, 11, 12)

10. Teach the veteran/service member problem-solving strategies focusing on the Military Problem Solving Process (e.g., recognize and define the problem, gather facts and make assumptions, define end states or goals and establish criteria for success, develop possible solutions, analyze and

compare possible solutions, select and implement solutions, and analyze solutions for effectiveness); apply the process to work-related problems starting with a problem with a rating in the middle of the hierarchical problem list.

11. Teach the veteran/service member organization and planning skills including the routine use of a calendar and daily task list.

12. Develop with the veteran/service member a procedure for classifying and managing mail and other papers as well as scheduled appointments.

8. Implement behavioral strategies for improving quality of conversations. (13, 14, 15, 16, 17)

13. Assign and monitor behavioral techniques for the veteran/service member for improving conversations with others (e.g., keep conversations brief, bring up topics that are of interest to the veteran/service member, take notes after the conversation and use the notes to initiate the discussion of a follow-up conversation); encourage the veteran/service member to acknowledge and reward himself/herself for successful interactions.

14. Use instruction, modeling, and role-playing to build the veteran's/service member's general social and/or communication skills (see *Social Effectiveness Training* by Turner, Beidel, and Cooley).

15. Assign the veteran/service member to read about general social and/or communication skills in books or treatment

manuals on building social skills (e.g., *Your Perfect Right* by Alberti and Emmons; *Conversationally Speaking* by Garner).

16. Review social situations in which the veteran/service member was intrusive or talked excessively without thoughtfulness; redirect for more social success using modeling, role-playing, and instruction.

17. Teach the veteran/service member problem-solving techniques that require thought before taking action to apply to interpersonal conflict situations (or assign "Applying Problem-Solving to Interpersonal Conflict" in the *Adult Psychotherapy Homework Planner,* 2nd ed. by Jongsma or "Negotiating Skills for Success" in the *Addiction Treatment Homework Planner*, 4th ed. by Finley and Lenz).

9. Learn and implement skills to reduce the disruptive influence of distractibility. (18, 19, 20)

18. Assess the veteran's/service member's typical attention span by having him/her do various tasks to the point that he/she indicates distraction; use this as an approximate measure of the veteran's/service member's typical attention span.

19. Teach the veteran/service member to break down tasks into meaningful units based on his/her demonstrated attention span.

20. Teach the veteran/service member to use timers or other cues to remind him/her to stay on task in an effort to reduce the time he/she may be distracted and off-task (see *Mastery of*

Your Adult ADHD—Therapist Guide by Safren, et al.).

10. Identify, challenge, and change self-talk that contributes to maladaptive feelings and actions. (21, 22)

21. Use cognitive therapy techniques to help the veteran/service member identify maladaptive self-talk (e.g., causing frustration, impulsivity, self-deprecation); challenge biases, and generate alternatives (or assign "Negative Thoughts Trigger Negative Feelings" in the *Adult Psychotherapy Homework Planner*, 2nd ed. by Jongsma).

22. Assign homework asking the veteran/service member to implement cognitive restructuring skills in relevant tasks; review and provide corrective feedback toward improving the skills.

11. Implement memory enhancing and compensatory strategies. (23, 24)

23. Assign and monitor memory-enhancing strategies for the veteran/service member (e.g., completing puzzles, reading short passages in books/magazines and discussing with someone what he/she read).

24. Assign and monitor memory compensatory strategies for the veteran/service member (e.g., keeping a notebook on hand at all times, making "to do" lists, utilizing mnemonics).

12. Reinforce behaviors that mitigate problems caused by attention/ concentration deficits. (25)

25. Encourage the veteran/service member to acknowledge and reward himself/herself for successes.

13. Inform chain of command of any duty restrictions as a result of attention/concentration deficits and side effects from medications. (26)

26. Encourage the service member to disclose any symptoms or side effects that could interfere with his/her performance and put the service member or other unit members at risk.

14. Effectively perform restricted duties as assigned by chain of command and ask to have limitations removed once deficits no longer impact functioning. (27, 28)

27. Instruct the service member to comply with duty restrictions if imposed and proactively seek out more responsibility when applicable.

28. Encourage the service member to provide weekly updates to his/her chain of command regarding progress.

15. Present for a follow-up evaluation as needed to assess for progress. (29)

29. Provide the veteran/service member with a scheduled follow-up to assess progress.

—. ______________________________

—. ______________________________

—. ______________________________

—. ______________________________

—. ______________________________

—. ______________________________

DIAGNOSTIC SUGGESTIONS

ICD-9-CM	*ICD-10-CM*	*DSM-5* Disorder, Condition, or Problem
314.00	F90.0	Attention-Deficit/Hyperactivity Disorder, Predominately Inattentive Presentation
314.01	F90.9	Unspecified Attention-Deficit/Hyperactivity Disorder
314.01	F90.8	Other Specified Attention-Deficit/Hyperactivity Disorder
294.9	R41.9	Unspecified Neurocognitive Disorder
296.90	F32.9	Unspecified Depressive Disorder
303.90	F10.20	Alcohol Use Disorder, Moderate or Severe
305.00	F10.10	Alcohol Use Disorder, Mild
304.30	F12.20	Cannabis Use Disorder, Moderate or Severe
305.20	F12.10	Cannabis Use Disorder, Mild
304.60	F18.20	Inhalant Use Disorder, Moderate or Severe (Inhalant Dependence)
305.90	F18.10	Inhalant Use Disorder, Mild (Inhalant Abuse)
305.50	F11.10	Opioid Use Disorder, Mild (Opioid Abuse)
________	________	______________________________
________	________	______________________________

BEREAVEMENT DUE TO THE LOSS OF A COMRADE

BEHAVIORAL DEFINITIONS

1. Verbalizes feelings of sadness, despair, anger, and/or confusion resulting from the loss of a fellow service member.
2. Experiences emotional numbness and a disconnection from others.
3. Reports physiological complaints such as vague pain, weakness, dizziness, and fatigue.
4. Avoids thinking or talking about the fellow service member.
5. Denies any negative impact on psychological well-being from the loss.
6. Exhibits a decrease in social involvement and occupational functioning.
7. Reports feelings of guilt over, and responsibility for, the death of a comrade.
8. Reports unpredictable waves of sadness, tearfulness, confusion, and/or poor concentration.
9. Exhibits unreasonable and unpredictable expressions of rage.

—. ____

____

—. ____

____

—. ____

____

LONG-TERM GOALS

1. Accept the loss and return to previous level of social and occupational functioning.
2. Think and talk about the individual without experiencing significant negative emotions and physical symptoms.

3. Eliminate feelings of guilt and self-loathing.

__. ____

____

__. ____

____

__. ____

____

SHORT-TERM OBJECTIVES

1. Describe the incident that led to the death of the comrade. (1, 2)

2. Describe in detail the nature of the bereavement response to the loss of the fellow comrade. (3)

3. Discuss the impact the loss has had on emotional well-being. (4, 5, 6)

THERAPEUTIC INTERVENTIONS

1. Actively build the level of trust with the veteran/service member through consistent eye contact, active listening, unconditional positive regard, and warm acceptance to help increase his/her ability to share painful thoughts and feelings.
2. Using empathy and compassion, support and encourage the veteran/service member to tell in detail the story of the loss.
3. Assess the veteran's/service member's type, intensity, and frequency of symptoms and the impact on social, occupational, and interpersonal functioning.
4. Engage the veteran/service member in a discussion about how the loss of his/her fellow comrade has impacted him/her emotionally; process the relevant content.
5. Discuss with the veteran/service member prior times in his/her life (loss or not loss-related) when he/she felt such a feeling of sadness or guilt.
6. Review past effective coping strategies that helped the

veteran/service member deal with the negative emotion.

4. Cooperate with a psychiatric evaluation to assess for the need for psychotropic medication. (7, 8)

7. Arrange for an evaluation for a prescription of psychotropic medication(s) if the veteran/service member requests it, if he/she is likely to be noncompliant with psychotherapy, or if occupational and social functioning are seriously impaired.

8. Monitor the veteran/service member for prescription compliance, side effects, and overall effectiveness of the medication; consult with the prescribing practitioner at regular intervals.

5. Acknowledge any substance use for the purpose of self-medicating grief symptoms. (9, 10)

9. Explore for the presence and degree of substance use by the veteran/service member in a dysfunctional attempt to deal with grief symptoms.

10. Refer the veteran/service member for a comprehensive substance use evaluation and treatment, if necessary.

6. Verbalize an understanding regarding the difference between uncomplicated and complicated bereavement. (11, 12)

11. Explain to the veteran/service member that bereavement is considered uncomplicated when symptoms are present (e.g., sadness, crying spells, grief), but are time-limited and have minimal impact on social and occupational functioning and are considered complicated when symptoms persist and seriously interrupt social and occupational activity.

12. Assist the veteran/service member in identifying symptoms that would lead him/her to believe that he/she was

experiencing complicated bereavement.

7. Identify what stages of grief have been experienced in the continuum of the grieving process. (13, 14)

13. Educate the veteran/service member about the five stages of grief (i.e., denial, anger, bargaining, depression, acceptance) and how it is not necessarily an all-or-none or stepwise progression.

14. Assist the veteran/service member in identifying which stage he/she is in or those stages he/she vacillates between.

8. Verbalize feelings of sadness to trusted individuals. (15)

15. Encourage the veteran/service member to acknowledge and express to trustworthy friends and family members his/her feelings of sadness related to the loss; process these experiences in session.

9. Verbalize feelings of anger. (16, 17)

16. Encourage the veteran/service member to acknowledge feelings of anger related to the loss; process feelings in session.

17. Assign the veteran/service member to read material on anger management (e.g., *Anger: Handling a Powerful Emotion in a Healthy Way* by Chapman, *Of Course You're Angry* by Rosselini, or *The Anger Control Workbook* by McKay).

10. Identify and replace feelings of shame and thoughts of guilt. (18, 19, 20, 21, 22)

18. Encourage the veteran/service member to acknowledge feelings of shame, as well as unrealistic and unwarranted thoughts of guilt related to the loss.

19. Assign the veteran/service member to keep a daily journal of automatic thoughts associated with guilt feelings (e.g., "Negative Thoughts Trigger Negative Feelings" in *Adult*

Psychotherapy Homework Planner, 2nd ed. by Jongsma, or "Daily Record of Dysfunctional Thoughts" in *Cognitive Therapy of Depression* by Beck, Rush, Shaw, and Emery); process the journal material to challenge guilty thinking patterns and replace them with reality-based thoughts.

20. Assign "behavioral experiments" in which guilt-inducing automatic thoughts are treated as hypotheses/ predictions, reality-based alternative hypotheses/ predictions are generated, and both are tested against the veteran's/service member's past, present, and/or future experiences.

21. Reinforce the veteran's/service member's positive, reality-based cognitive messages that enhance self-confidence and increase adaptive action (see "Positive Self-Talk" in the *Adult Psychotherapy Homework Planner*, 2nd ed. by Jongsma).

22. Assign the veteran/service member to read *Shame and Grace* by Smedes.

11. Verbalize an understanding that feelings of sadness, anger, shame, and guilt are normal grief reactions. (23, 24, 25)

23. Normalize the veteran's/service member's feelings and reaction by educating him/her on the common nature of such symptoms developed during grief reactions.

24. Instill a sense of recovery and growth and minimize "pathological" labels.

25. Educate the veteran/service member on how grief reactions differ between cultures, including the military culture.

12. Express feelings and thoughts that were not said while the fellow comrade was alive. (26, 27)

26. Assist the veteran/service member to articulate things he/she wishes he/she would have said to the fellow service member when he/she was alive; consider utilizing the empty chair technique or similar role-play to facilitate the expression of feelings.

27. Instruct the veteran/service member to write a letter detailing those things he/she wished he/she would have said to the fellow service member (or assign "A Letter to a Lost Loved One" in the *Adult Psychotherapy Homework Planner*, 2nd ed. by Jongsma); process the relevant content in session.

13. Talk with others that have experienced the loss of a fellow comrade. (28)

28. Encourage the veteran/service member to meet with a current service member or veteran that has experienced the loss of a fellow comrade; instruct the veteran/service member to inquire as to how the individual dealt with the loss.

14. Reflect on the purpose and meaning of life. (29)

29. Encourage the veteran/service member to use this opportunity to reflect on his/her purpose in life, as well as what is most important to him/her in life.

15. Develop and utilize spiritual resources as a means of handling grief. (30)

30. Encourage the veteran/service member to meet with spiritual resources (e.g., military chaplain, local minister) to assist with dealing with the loss.

16. Read materials/books on how to cope with sadness and deal with loss. (31, 32)

31. Assign the veteran/service member to read material on coping with depression (e.g., *The Feeling Good Handbook* by Burns, or *Mind Over Mood* by Greenberger and Padesky).

32. Instruct the veteran/service member to utilize bibliotherapy as a means of dealing with the loss (e.g., recommend *When Will I Stop Hurting?: Dealing with a Recent Death* by Kolf, *How Can It Be All Right When Everything Is All Wrong?* by Smedes, *Good Grief* by Westberg, or *Getting Through the Night: Finding Your Way After the Loss of a Loved One* by Price).

17. Develop a memorial to the fallen comrade. (33)

33. Encourage the veteran/service member to create a memorial (e.g., plaque, drawing/painting, tattoo) that honors the fallen comrade (or assign "Creating a Memorial Collage" in the *Adult Psychotherapy Homework Planner*, 2nd ed. by Jongsma).

—. ____________________

—. ____________________

—. ____________________

—. ____________________

—. ____________________

—. ____________________

DIAGNOSTIC SUGGESTIONS

ICD-9-CM	*ICD-10-CM*	*DSM-5* Disorder, Condition, or Problem
V62.82	Z63.4	Uncomplicated Bereavement
309.0	F43.21	Adjustment Disorder, With Depressed Mood
296.xx	F32.x	Major Depressive Disorder, Single Episode
296.xx	F33.x	Major Depressive Disorder, Recurrent Episode
305.00	F10.10	Alcohol Use Disorder, Mild
303.90	F10.20	Alcohol Use Disorder, Moderate or Severe
______	______	____________
______	______	____________

BORDERLINE PERSONALITY

BEHAVIORAL DEFINITIONS

1. Displays extreme emotional reactivity (anger, anxiety, or depression) that usually lasts from a few hours to a few days in response to a relatively minor stressor.
2. Exhibits a pattern of intense and chaotic interpersonal relationships.
3. Reports a marked identity disturbance.
4. Engages in impulsive behaviors that are potentially harmful to self and/or others.
5. Engages in recurrent suicidal gestures, threats, or self-mutilating behavior.
6. Reports chronic feelings of emptiness and boredom.
7. Displays frequent eruptions of intense and inappropriate anger.
8. Reports feelings of being unfairly treated and believes that others can't be trusted.
9. Views most issues in simple terms (e.g., right/wrong, black/white, trustworthy/deceitful) without regard for extenuating circumstances or complex situations.
10. Becomes very anxious with any hint of perceived abandonment in a relationship.
11. Frequently receives disciplinary action for disruptive behavior.
12. Reports threats of being dishonorably discharged from the military by superiors.
13. Has had frequent visits to military behavioral health professionals to discuss possibly being separated from the military for a personality disorder.
14. Displays a failure to function as a productive unit team member.

__. ____
____

__. ____
____

__. ____
____

LONG-TERM GOALS

1. Develop and demonstrate coping skills to deal with mood swings.
2. Develop the ability to control impulsive behavior.
3. Replace dichotomous thinking with the ability to tolerate ambiguity and complexity in people and issues.
4. Develop and demonstrate anger management skills.
5. Learn and practice interpersonal relationship skills.
6. Terminate self-damaging behaviors (such as substance abuse, sexual acting out, self-mutilation, and/or suicidal behaviors).
7. Eliminate disciplinary actions related to impulsive and disruptive behavior.

__. ____
____

__. ____
____

__. ____
____

SHORT-TERM OBJECTIVES

1. Discuss openly the history of difficulties that have led to seeking treatment. (1, 2, 3)

THERAPEUTIC INTERVENTIONS

1. Assess the veteran's/service member's experiences of distress and disability, identifying behaviors (e.g., parasuicidal acts, angry outbursts, overattachment), affect (e.g., mood swings, emotional overreactions, painful emptiness), and cognitions (e.g., biases such as dichotomous

thinking, overgeneralization, catastrophizing) that will become the targets of therapy.

2. Explore the veteran's/service member's history of abuse and/or abandonment, particularly in childhood years, and how it relates to his/her current functioning.

3. Validate the veteran's/service member's distress and difficulties as understandable given his/her particular circumstances, thoughts, and feelings.

2. Verbalize an accurate and reasonable understanding of the process of therapy and what the therapeutic goals are. (4, 5)

4. Orient the veteran/service member to dialectical behavior therapy (DBT), highlighting its multiple facets (e.g., support, collaboration, challenge, problem solving, skill-building) and discuss dialectical/biosocial view of borderline personality, emphasizing constitutional and social influences on its features (see *Cognitive-Behavioral Treatment of Borderline Personality* by Linehan).

5. Throughout therapy, ask the veteran/service member to read selected sections of books or manuals that reinforce therapeutic interventions (e.g., *Skills Training Manual for Treating BPD* by Linehan).

3. Verbalize a decision to work collaboratively with the therapist toward the therapeutic goals. (6)

6. Solicit from the veteran/service member an agreement to work collaboratively within the parameters of the DBT approach to overcome the behaviors, emotions, and cognitions that have been identified as causing problems in his/her life.

▼ 4. Verbalize any history of self-mutilative and suicidal urges and behavior. (7, 8, 9, 10)

7. Probe the nature and history of the veteran's/service member's self-mutilating behavior. ▼

8. Assess the veteran's/service member's suicidal gestures as to triggers, frequency, seriousness, secondary gain, and onset. ▼

9. Arrange for hospitalization, as necessary, when the veteran/service member is judged to be harmful to self; utilize a "buddy watch" when threat is less serious. ▼

10. Provide the veteran/service member with an emergency helpline telephone number or contact person (e.g., Chaplain, First Sergeant) that is available 24 hours a day. ▼

▼ 5. Promise to initiate contact with the therapist, helpline, or contact person if experiencing a strong urge to engage in self-harmful behavior. (11, 12)

11. Interpret the veteran's/service member's self-mutilation as an expression of the rage and helplessness that could not be expressed as a child victim of emotional abandonment or abuse; express the expectation that the veteran/service member will control the urge for self-mutilation. ▼

12. Elicit a promise (as part of a self-mutilation and suicide prevention contract) from the veteran/service member that he/she will initiate contact with the therapist, helpline, or contact person if a suicidal urge becomes strong and before any self-injurious behavior occurs; throughout the therapy process consistently assess the strength of the veteran's/service member's suicide potential. ▼

6. Reduce actions that interfere with participating in therapy. (13)

13. Continuously monitor, confront, and problem-solve the veteran's/service member's actions that threaten to interfere with the continuation of therapy such as missing appointments, noncompliance, and/or abruptly leaving therapy.

7. Cooperate with an evaluation by a prescribing practitioner for psychotropic medication and take medication, if prescribed. (14, 15)

14. Assess the veteran's/service member's need for medication (e.g., selective serotonin reuptake inhibitors) and arrange for prescription if appropriate.

15. Monitor and evaluate the psychotropic medication prescription compliance and the effectiveness of the medication on the veteran's/service member's level of functioning.

8. Reduce the frequency of maladaptive behaviors, thoughts, and feelings that interfere with attaining a reasonable quality of life. (16)

16. Use validation, dialectical strategies (e.g., metaphor, devil's advocate), and problem-solving strategies (e.g., behavioral and solution analysis, cognitive restructuring, skills training, exposure) to help the veteran/service member manage, reduce, or stabilize maladaptive behaviors (e.g., angry outbursts, binge drinking, abusive relationships, high-risk sex, uncontrolled spending, etc.), thoughts (e.g., all-or-nothing thinking, catastrophizing, personalizing), and feelings (e.g., rage, hopelessness, abandonment) (see *Cognitive-Behavioral Treatment of Borderline Personality* by Linehan).

9. Participate in a group (preferably) or individual personal skills development course. (17, 18)

17. Conduct group or individual skills training tailored to the veteran/service member's identified problem behavioral patterns (e.g., assertiveness for

abusive relationships, problem-solving and cognitive strategies for identifying and controlling financial, sexual, and other impulsivity). ▼

18. Use behavioral strategies to teach identified skills (e.g., instruction, modeling, advising), strengthen them (e.g., role-playing, exposure exercises), and facilitate incorporation into the veteran's/service member's everyday life (e.g., homework assignments). ▼

▼ 10. Verbalize a decreased emotional response to previous or current posttraumatic stress. (19)

19. After adaptive behavioral patterns and emotional regulation skills are evident, work with the veteran/service member on remembering and accepting the facts of the previous trauma, reducing denial and increasing insight into its effects, reducing maladaptive emotional and/or behavioral responses to trauma-related stimuli, and reducing self-blame. ▼

▼ 11. Identify, challenge, and replace biased, fearful self-talk with reality-based, positive self-talk. (20, 21, 22)

20. Explore the veteran's/service member's schema and self-talk that mediate his/her trauma-related and other fears (or assign "Negative Thoughts Trigger Negative Feelings" in the *Adult Psychotherapy Homework Planner*, 2nd ed. by Jongsma); identify and challenge biases, assisting him/her in generating thoughts that correct for the negative biases and build confidence. ▼

21. Assign the veteran/service member a homework exercise in which he/she identifies fearful self-talk and creates reality-based

alternatives; review and reinforce success, providing corrective feedback for failure (see "Journal and Replace Self-Defeating Thoughts" in the *Adult Psychotherapy Homework Planner*, 2nd ed. by Jongsma, or "Daily Record of Dysfunctional Thoughts" in *Cognitive Therapy of Depression* by Beck, Rush, Shaw, and Emery).

22. Reinforce the veteran's/service member's positive, reality-based cognitive messages that enhance self-confidence and increase adaptive action.

12. Participate in imaginal and/or *in vivo* exposure to trauma-related memories until talking or thinking about the trauma does not cause marked distress. (23, 24, 25)

23. Direct and assist the veteran/service member in constructing a hierarchy of feared and avoided trauma-related stimuli.

24. Direct imaginal exposure to the trauma in session by having the veteran/service member describe a chosen traumatic experience at an increasing, but personally-chosen level of detail; integrate cognitive restructuring and repeat until associated anxiety reduces and stabilizes; record the session and have the veteran/service member listen to it between sessions (see "Share the Painful Memory" in the *Adult Psychotherapy Homework Planner*, 2nd ed. by Jongsma, and *Posttraumatic Stress Disorder* by Resick and Calhoun); review and reinforce progress, problem-solve obstacles.

25. Assign the veteran/service member a homework exercise in which he/she does an exposure exercise and records responses or

listens to a recording of an in-session exposure (see *Posttraumatic Stress Disorder* by Resick and Calhoun); review and reinforce progress, problem-solve obstacles. ▽

▽ 13. Verbalize a sense of self-respect that is not dependent on others' opinions. (26)

26. Help the veteran/service member to value, believe, and trust in his/her evaluations of self, others, and situations and to examine them nondefensively and independent of others' opinions in a manner that builds self-reliance, but does not isolate the veteran/service member from others. ▽

▽ 14. Engage in practices that help enhance a sustained sense of joy. (27)

27. Facilitate the veteran's/service member's personal growth by helping him/her choose experiences that strengthen self-awareness, personal values, and appreciation of life (e.g., insight-oriented therapy, spiritual practices, or other relevant life experiences). ▽

▽ 15. Implement a pattern of thinking before action. (28, 29, 30)

28. Use modeling, role-playing, and behavioral rehearsal to teach the veteran/service member how to use "stop, listen, and think" before acting in several current situations. ▽

29. Review and process the veteran's/service member's use of "stop, listen, and think" before acting in day-to-day living and identify the positive consequences. ▽

30. Teach the veteran/service member problem-solving strategies involving defining a problem, generating options for addressing it, evaluating options, implementing a plan, and

re-evaluating/refining the plan (or assign "Plan Before Acting" in the *Adult Psychotherapy Homework Planner*, 2nd ed. by Jongsma).▽

16. Acknowledge intent and/or motivation to remain in the military. (31, 32)

31. Explore with the service member if it is his/her intent to remain in the military.

32. Discuss the implications of a discharge from the military based on a personality disorder.

__. ______________________

__. ______________________

__. ______________________

__. ______________________

__. ______________________

__. ______________________

DIAGNOSTIC SUGGESTIONS

ICD-9-CM	*ICD-10-CM*	*DSM-5* Disorder, Condition, or Problem
300.4	F34.1	Persistent Depressive Disorder
296.xx	F33.x	Major Depressive Disorder, Recurrent Episode
303.90	F10.20	Alcohol Use Disorder, Moderate or Severe
301.83	F60.3	Borderline Personality Disorder
301.9	F60.9	Unspecified Personality Disorder
______	______	______________________
______	______	______________________

BRIEF REACTIVE PSYCHOTIC EPISODE

BEHAVIORAL DEFINITIONS

1. Rapid onset of sensory (i.e., auditory, visual, olfactory, gustatory, somatic) hallucinations after a marked stressor (may or may not be combat/training related).
2. Rapid onset of bizarre thought content (e.g., delusions of persecution, nihilism, grandiosity, reference, erotomania, religiosity, control, infidelity, jealousy).
3. Strange and disorganized speech/thoughts (e.g., incoherence, derailment, looseness of associations, flight of ideas, neologisms, echolalia).
4. Strange and disorganized behavior (e.g., perseveration, inappropriate and odd dress, uncharacteristic disrespect to superiors, increased risky behavior).
5. Psychomotor abnormalities (e.g., excessive agitation, motor slowing).
6. Emotional agitation (e.g., short-tempered, increased anger and agitation, inappropriate physical aggression).
7. Social withdrawal and isolation.
8. Decrease in volition (i.e., lack of drive, motivation, and interest in goal-directed behavior).

—. ____

____

—. ____

____

—. ____

____

LONG-TERM GOALS

1. Eliminate or adequately control psychotic symptoms so that functioning can resume in a supervised environment.

2. Strengthen treatment alliance so that psychotropic medication is taken as prescribed.
3. Eliminate or adequately control positive and negative psychotic symptoms so that independent functioning can resume.
4. Accept the determination of the medical review board regarding eligibility for future service in the military.
5. Cooperate with ongoing psychiatric care in a Veterans Affairs healthcare center if discharge from active duty is necessary.

—. ____

____

—. ____

____

—. ____

____

SHORT-TERM OBJECTIVES

1. Obtain a complete history, including the type and severity of psychotic symptoms. (1, 2, 3, 4, 5)

THERAPEUTIC INTERVENTIONS

1. Demonstrate empathy and understanding toward the veteran/service member through active listening, questioning, and nonverbal behaviors.
2. Determine severity, history, and type of symptoms the veteran/service member is suffering from through the use of in-depth clinical interviewing and/or psychological testing.
3. Identify if the veteran's/service member's illness is a brief reactive episode or part of a previously dormant and chronic psychotic disorder.
4. Determine if the veteran's/service member's marked stressor was related to a combat, interpersonal, or some other environmental stressor in order to remove the stressor if possible.

5. Assess if the veteran's/service member's current psychotic episode is related to substance use (e.g., alcohol, amphetamines, caffeine, marijuana, ephedrine).

2. Family member, peer, or supervisor within the chain of command provides collateral information regarding past behavior. (6)

6. Explore the veteran's/service member's history of bizarre behavior, determining if there were any prior psychotic episodes.

3. Help the veteran/service member understand that symptoms are related to a mental illness. (7, 8)

7. Explain to the veteran/service member the nature of psychotic illness as a biological or genetic vulnerability or predisposition (diathesis) interacting with the environment and life events (stressors).

8. Educate the veteran/service member on options regarding future military service and brief psychotic illness.

4. Take psychotropic medications as prescribed. (9, 10, 11)

9. Refer the veteran/service member for an evaluation by a psychiatric practitioner in order to assess the need for psychotropic medication.

10. Provide education to the veteran/service member regarding side effects and additional treatment options.

11. Monitor medication compliance and refer the veteran/service member to a case manager or more structured setting if medication is not taken as prescribed.

5. Report decrease or elimination of positive psychotic symptoms (i.e., hallucinations and delusions). (12, 13, 14)

12. Monitor, reinforce and encourage the veteran/service member to continue taking psychotropic medication as prescribed.

13. Slowly and gently assist the veteran/service member in

confronting irrational beliefs through examining reality-based evidence.

14. Assist the veteran/service member in identifying internal vs. external sources of stimuli.

6. Gain more confidence and increase success in social interactions. (15, 16, 17)

15. Provide the veteran/service member opportunities for rewarding and nonthreatening social interactions.

16. Provide consistent reward and encouragement to the veteran/service member for positive social interactions.

17. Provide reassurance and empathy to the veteran/service member for failed social interactions.

7. Demonstrate improvement in cognition as evidenced by logical and understandable speech. (18)

18. Slowly and gently confront the veteran's/service member's illogical thinking and speech; reinforce logical and goal-directed thinking through role-playing and cognitive-behavioral techniques.

8. Demonstrate an understanding of the emotions and beliefs that support irrational thoughts and beliefs. (19, 20)

19. Explore the veteran's/service member's basic needs and emotions (e.g., fear, rejection, isolation) that contribute to the irrational thought.

20. Assist the veteran/service member in challenging irrational beliefs by presenting alternative explanations that are based in reality.

9. Family members provide emotional and social support in order to decrease chances of future psychotic episodes. (21, 22, 23)

21. Refer the veteran's/service member's family to family therapy so they can become educated on the veteran's/service member's illness.

22. Assist the family members in keeping strong expressed

emotions from interfering with the veteran's/service member's progress.

23. Teach the family members how not to convey mixed messages to the veteran/service member that tend to lead to relapse.

10. Family members focus on self-care in order to maintain and conserve personal emotional strength and perseverance. (24, 25)

24. Allow the family members to discuss their own feelings about the veteran's/service member's illness and how it impacts them.

25. Assist the family members in finding personal outlets that prevent burnout (e.g., support groups, hobbies, advocacy).

11. Accept the decision to leave military service if this is the determination by military medical authorities. (26, 27, 28, 29)

26. Initiate the process of a medical review of the veteran's/service member's fitness for duty in the military.

27. Assist the veteran/service member in processing and accepting the determination of the medical review board that he/she is not fit for military service due to his/her psychiatric condition.

28. Assist the veteran/service member with exploring vocational and living options as a civilian.

29. Refer the veteran/service member for vocational rehabilitation services.

12. Return to premorbid level of functioning and manage own basic Activities of Daily Living (ADLs). (12, 30)

12. Monitor, reinforce and encourage the veteran/service member to continue taking psychotropic medication as prescribed.

30. Assess the veteran's/service member's progress and overall ability in managing ADLs (e.g., paying bills, cooking, cleaning, hygiene).

13. Maintain consistent follow-up care with healthcare appointments. (31)

31. Ensure that the veteran/service member attends scheduled follow-up appointments with psychiatric, case management, psychotherapy, and medical services.

—. ______________________________

—. ______________________________

—. ______________________________

—. ______________________________

—. ______________________________

—. ______________________________

DIAGNOSTIC SUGGESTIONS

ICD-9-CM	*ICD-10-CM*	*DSM-5* Disorder, Condition, or Problem
298.8	F23	Brief Psychotic Disorder
295.40	F20.81	Schizophreniform Disorder
295.90	F20.9	Schizophrenia
292.xx	F19.259	Other (or Unknown) Substance Use Disorder, Moderate or Severe with Other (or Unknown) Substance-Induced Psychotic Disorder
297.1	F22	Delusional Disorder
296.xx	F31.xx	Bipolar I Disorder
296.89	F31.81	Bipolar II Disorder
296.xx	F32.x	Major Depressive Disorder, Single Episode
296.xx	F33.x	Major Depressive Disorder, Recurrent Episode
293.xx	F06.2	Psychotic Disorder Due to Another Medical Condition, With Delusions
293.82	F06.0	Psychotic Disorder Due to Another Medical Condition, With Hallucinations
301.0	F60.0	Paranoid Personality Disorder
310.22	F21	Schizotypal Personality Disorder
301.83	F60.3	Borderline Personality Disorder
________	________	______________________________
________	________	______________________________

CHRONIC PAIN AFTER INJURY

BEHAVIORAL DEFINITIONS

1. Complains of injury-related pain that is present most days of the week.
2. Reports a level of pain that makes it difficult to concentrate.
3. Displays grimacing or other pain-related facial expressions when moving around.
4. Reports an inability to fully participate in military training (e.g., wear body armor, ride in military vehicles for extended periods, perform physically strenuous routines) due to pain.
5. Reports being late for accountability formations and/or missing work due to severity of pain.
6. Uses over-the-counter and/or prescription pain medications on a regular basis.
7. Has developed a dependence on narcotic pain relievers as a result of trying to cope with chronic pain.
8. Uses alcohol and/or illicit drugs to minimize pain.
9. Dominates conversations with pain-related discussion.
10. Reports being repeatedly placed on physical limitation profiles by military healthcare providers.
11. Reports potential medical separation from service.

__. ____

____

__. ____

____

__. ____

____

LONG-TERM GOALS

1. Develop non-pharmacological pain management skills.
2. Alleviate pain to a degree that allows a return to previous level of social and occupational functioning.
3. Eliminate pain-related depressive symptoms.
4. Resolve any negative feelings about the injury responsible for the pain.
5. Increase aerobic and anaerobic fitness.
6. Accept that some level of pain and limitations may be life-long.

__. ____

____

__. ____

____

__. ____

____

SHORT-TERM OBJECTIVES

1. Describe the nature, history, severity, and impact of pain symptoms and service-related injury. (1, 2)
2. Complete a medical examination to assess for functional limitations and identify appropriate medical treatment options. (3)
3. Follow through with medical recommendations. (4, 5, 6)

THERAPEUTIC INTERVENTIONS

1. Assess the veteran's/service member's history of pain symptoms including duration, severity, and limitations that the symptoms cause.
2. Inquire about the veteran's/service member's precipitating injury and process any negative emotional content as a consequence of the injury.
3. Refer the veteran/service member to a physician who specializes in pain management.
4. Monitor the veteran's/service member's compliance with treatment recommendations.
5. Administer the Millon Behavioral Medicine Diagnostic (MBMD) to the veteran/service member to identify potential treatment adherence problems.

6. Problem-solve any treatment compliance problems with the veteran/service member.

4. Complete a psychological evaluation to determine the impact that pain has on emotional well-being. (7)

7. Administer the Millon Clinical Multiaxial Inventory-III (MCMI-III) or the Minnesota Multiphasic Personality Inventory-2 (MMPI-2) to the veteran/service member to assess for psychiatric symptoms related to pain.

EBT 5. Complete a psychiatric evaluation to determine if psychotropic medications are needed. (8)

8. Arrange for a psychiatric evaluation of the veteran/service member to determine if psychotropic medication is needed. EBT

EBT 6. Take medication as prescribed. (9)

9. Monitor the veteran's/service member's medication compliance, side effects, efficacy, and progress. EBT

EBT 7. Attend physical therapy appointment. (10, 11)

10. Arrange a physical therapy assessment and treatment recommendation appointment for the veteran/service member; monitor follow-through with treatment recommendations. EBT

11. Reinforce gains made by the veteran/service member in physical therapy such as increased mobility, decrease in pain, and overall physical functioning. EBT

EBT 8. Agree to a cognitive-behavioral program for managing pain. (12)

12. Explain to the veteran/service member the evidence supporting the use of cognitive-behavioral therapy for the management of chronic pain. EBT

EBT 9. Develop an understanding that thoughts and behaviors affect the pain experience. (13, 14, 15)

13. Explain to the veteran/service member the treatment rationale for cognitive-behavioral therapy for chronic pain management. EBT

14. Teach the veteran/service member to identify negative

cognitions that influence pain levels; assist the veteran/service member in developing more adaptive cognitions that mitigate pain symptoms.

15. Assign the veteran/service member to keep a daily log of thoughts and activities that worsen and mitigate pain symptoms; process log entries during session.

10. Verbalize an understanding of how the individual can take an active role in controlling pain. (16, 17)

16. Discuss the concept of learned helplessness and how it relates to exacerbation and continuation of chronic pain symptoms.

17. Explore periods during the veteran's/service member's military career where he/she took control over a situation and overcame an obstacle; apply this successful problem-solving approach to the current situation.

11. Learn to how recognize triggers that influence the pain experience. (18)

18. Teach the veteran/service member to keep a daily log of emotions, behaviors, situations, or environmental factors that influence his/her pain experience, focusing on the severity and durations of symptoms and what behaviors mitigate the pain experience; process the log entries in session.

12. Participate in biofeedback. (19)

19. Refer the veteran/service member to biofeedback training in order to reduce muscle tension and increase focus and self-efficacy.

13. Develop and implement self-care techniques for managing pain at home. (20, 21)

20. Teach the veteran/service member self-care techniques such as progressive muscle relaxation, diaphragmatic breathing, and imagery; identify situations at

home when techniques can be used.

21. Assign the veteran/service member to practice self-care techniques at home daily.

14. Tailor an exercise routine that takes into account physical limitations. (22, 23)

22. Refer the veteran/service member to a physical rehabilitation trainer/specialist to identify physical exercises that will increase physical fitness while minimizing pain and injury.

23. Encourage the service member to discuss alterations in his/her current unit's physical training program based on his/her limitations.

15. Discuss work accommodations with superiors. (24)

24. Encourage the service member to discuss needed accommodations in the work environment with his/her chain of command. (e.g., chair with more support, frequent breaks).

16. Strengthen support network. (25, 26)

25. Discuss the strengths and weaknesses of the veteran's/service member's current social support system; develop strategies to strengthen support system.

26. Refer the veteran/service member to a chronic pain support group.

17. Meet with military medical personnel if medical separation from service is recommended. (27, 28)

27. Encourage the service member to attend all medical separation appointments.

28. Explore opportunities for appeal if the service member does not agree with the medical separation finding (e.g., request a second opinion, consult with JAG or civilian attorney).

18. Meet with Veterans Affairs representative regarding

29. Identify the veteran's appropriate geographical region

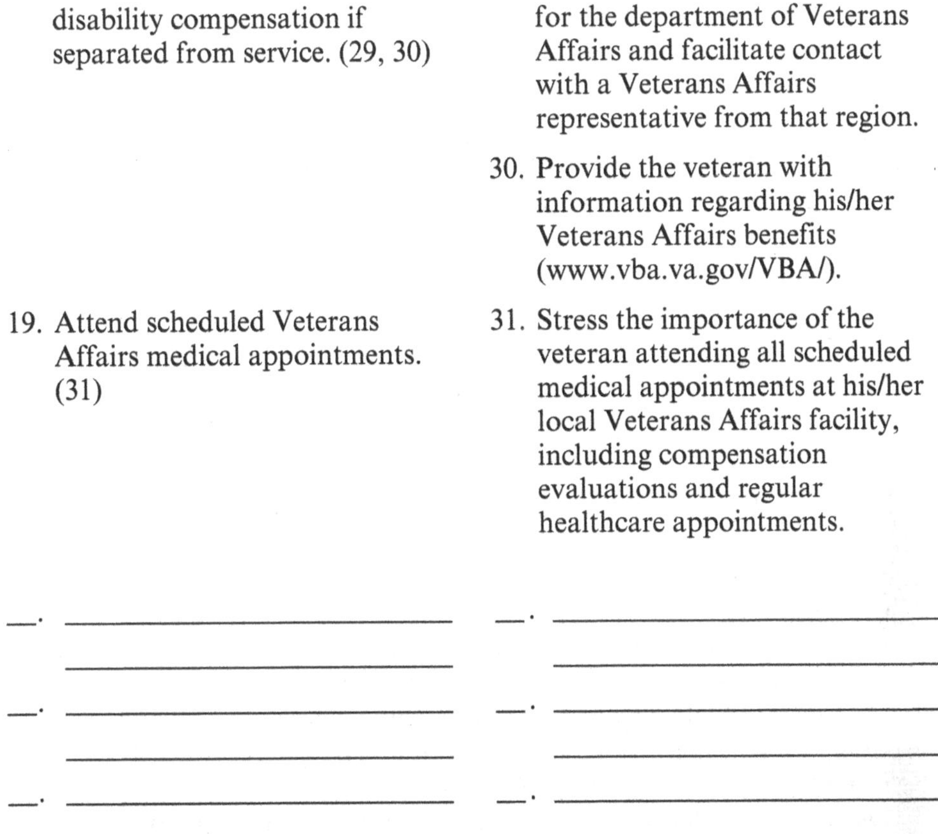

disability compensation if separated from service. (29, 30)

for the department of Veterans Affairs and facilitate contact with a Veterans Affairs representative from that region.

30. Provide the veteran with information regarding his/her Veterans Affairs benefits (www.vba.va.gov/VBA/).

19. Attend scheduled Veterans Affairs medical appointments. (31)

31. Stress the importance of the veteran attending all scheduled medical appointments at his/her local Veterans Affairs facility, including compensation evaluations and regular healthcare appointments.

__. ____________________

__. ____________________

__. ____________________

__. ____________________

__. ____________________

__. ____________________

DIAGNOSTIC SUGGESTIONS

ICD-9-CM	*ICD-10-CM*	*DSM-5* Disorder, Condition, or Problem
307.89	F54	Psychological Factors Affecting Other Medical Conditions
307.80	F45.1	Somatic Symptom Disorder, With Predominant Pain
300.81	F45.1	Somatic Symptom Disorder
296.xx	F32.x	Major Depressive Disorder, Single Episode
296.xx	F33.x	Major Depressive Disorder, Recurrent Episode
311	F32.9	Unspecified Depressive Disorder
311	F32.8	Other Specified Depressive Disorder
300.11	F44.x	Conversion Disorder
304.00	F11.20	Opioid Use Disorder, Moderate or Severe
305.50	F11.10	Opioid Use Disorder, Mild
301.9	F60.9	Unspecified Personality Disorder
________	________	____________________
________	________	____________________

COMBAT AND OPERATIONAL STRESS REACTION

BEHAVIORAL DEFINITIONS

1. Frequently verbalizes an intense fear associated with going on combat missions.
2. Becomes immobile during combat operations (i.e., freezes under fire).
3. Describes a hypervigilance in noncombat situations.
4. Demonstrates an increase in irritability and anger.
5. Complains of nonspecific physical symptoms.
6. Demonstrates a loss of confidence and abilities in combat skills.
7. Displays recent lapses of attention, concentration, and memory.
8. Verbalizes a loss of hope and faith in the mission, self, and/or the future.
9. Complains of sensory disturbances (e.g., loss of vision, touch, hearing).
10. Displays erratic and uncharacteristic behavior (e.g., emotional outbursts, fighting, illegal acts).
11. Presents with impaired speech or muteness.

__. ____

____

__. ____

____

__. ____

____

LONG-TERM GOALS

1. Return to full mission capability.
2. Restore confidence in combat abilities.
3. Restore a sense of hope, duty, and pride in the mission.

4. Eliminate physical and emotional factors that impede successful mission performance.

__. ____

____

__. ____

____

__. ____

____

SHORT-TERM OBJECTIVES

1. Describe the various symptoms that have developed in response to the combat/operational stress. (1, 2)

2. Describe how the current symptoms are impacting occupational functioning. (3, 4, 5)

THERAPEUTIC INTERVENTIONS

1. Explore the different signs and symptoms of combat/operational stress (e.g., fear, apathy, loss of confidence, irritability, sensory disturbances, etc.) experienced by the service member.

2. Interview the service member to assess for other explanations for the reported symptoms (e.g., psychiatric illness, traumatic brain injury, substance use).

3. Assess the severity of the service member's symptoms by utilizing brief self-report rating scales (e.g., PTSD Checklist–Military Version, Beck Depression Inventory–II, Beck Anxiety Inventory).

4. Gather collateral information from the service member's superiors (e.g., Squad Leader, Platoon Sergeant, First Sergeant) and peers regarding his/her occupational functioning.

5. Gather information regarding the impact of stress symptoms by observing the service member in his/her environment (e.g., observe

veteran/service member during training or while performing routine job duties).

3. If in the deployed setting, attend a specialized military restoration program. (6)

6. Remove the service member from his/her unit and place him/her in a restoration program for three to five days; monitor him/her for alleviation of stress symptom severity.

4. Identify and verbalize those symptoms that are expected and normal during and after stressful and dangerous missions. (7)

7. Educate the service member about the normal and expected symptoms of combat/operational stress and how some symptoms may be adaptive (e.g., hyperarousal, hypervigilance).

5. Acknowledge that combat/ operational stress symptoms are transient and that full recovery is expected. (8, 9)

8. Assist the service member in identifying prior episodes of combat/operational stress reactions and emphasize how he/she recovered from those episodes.

9. Educate the service member about the difference between severe psychiatric disorders (e.g., psychosis) and combat/ operational stress reactions.

6. Engage in restful and restorative sleep for two to three nights. (10, 11)

10. Ensure that the service member's basic physiological needs of rest and sleep are met by providing him/her a quiet and nonthreatening environment in which to relax.

11. If needed, coordinate the provision of medication for the purposes of initiating and maintaining the service member's sleep.

7. Replenish vital nutrients that maintain physical and emotional well-being. (12)

12. Ensure that the service member has the opportunity to eat nutritious foods and hydrate properly; monitor his/her maintenance of a pattern of consumption of a healthy diet.

8. Identify and replace negative and self-defeating thoughts that contribute to the combat/operational stress symptoms. (13, 14, 15, 16, 17)

13. Assist the service member in developing an awareness of his/her automatic thoughts that are consistent with fear or loss of competence schema.

14. Assign the service member to keep a daily log of automatic thoughts associated with fear about going on future missions and competence in his/her ability to defend himself/herself and others during combat (e.g., "Negative Thoughts Trigger Negative Feelings" in the *Adult Psychotherapy Homework Planner*, 2nd ed. by Jongsma); process the journal material to challenge distorted thinking patterns with reality based thoughts.

15. Assign behavioral experiments that challenge the service member's thoughts of professional incompetence and inadequacy (e.g., ask for an opinion about his/her abilities from someone he/she respects).

16. Reinforce the service member's positive cognitions that foster self-confidence and decrease fear and anxiety (see "Positive Self-Talk" in the *Adult Psychotherapy Homework Planner*, 2nd ed. by Jongsma).

17. Teach the service member to implement a thought-stopping technique (thinking of a stop sign and then a pleasant scene) for worries that have been addressed but persist (or assign "Making Use of the Thought-Stopping Technique" in the *Adult Psychotherapy Homework Planner*, 2nd ed. by Jongsma);

monitor and encourage the service member's use of the technique in daily life between sessions.

9. Learn and implement calming skills to reduce anxiety and manage stress symptoms. (18, 19, 20, 21)

18. Teach the service member relaxation skills (e.g., progressive muscle relaxation, guided imagery, slow diaphragmatic breathing) and how to discriminate between relaxation and tension; teach the client how to apply these skills to his/her daily life (e.g., *Progressive Relaxation Training* by Bernstein and Borkovec; *Treating GAD* by Rygh and Sanderson).

19. Assign the service member homework each session in which he/she practices relaxation exercises daily (or assign "Learning to Self-Soothe" in the *Addiction Treatment Homework Planner*, 4th ed. by Finley and Lenz; review and reinforce success while providing corrective feedback toward improvement.

20. Assign the service member to read about progressive muscle relaxation and other calming strategies in relevant books or treatment manuals (e.g., assign *Progressive Relaxation Training* by Bernstein and Borkovec or "Breathing Skills" in *Mastery of Your Anxiety and Panic—Workbook* by Barlow and Craske).

21. Use biofeedback techniques to facilitate the service member's success at learning relaxation skills.

10. Undergo gradual repeated imaginal exposure to the feared

22. Direct and assist the service member in constructing a

negative consequences predicted by worry and develop alternative reality-based predictions. (22, 23, 24, 25)

hierarchy of two to three spheres of worry related to combat situations for use in an exposure procedure (e.g., worry about failure to perform, or injury).

23. Select initial exposures that have a high likelihood of being a success experience for the service member; develop a plan for managing his/her negative affect engendered by exposure (e.g., deep breathing, muscle relaxation); mentally rehearse the procedure.

24. Ask the service member to vividly imagine the feared situation, holding them in mind until anxiety associated with them weakens (up to 30 minutes); generate reality-based alternatives to feared consequences and process them (see *Mastery of Your Anxiety and Panic—Therapist Guide*, 4th ed. by Craske and Barlow).

25. Assign the service member a homework exercise in which he/she does anxiety situation imaginal exposures and records responses (see *Mastery of Your Anxiety and Panic—Workbook* by Barlow and Craske; or *Generalized Anxiety Disorder* by Brown, O'Leary, and Barlow); review, reinforcing success and redirecting for failure.

11. Attend a stress management group. (26)

26. Refer the service member to a stress management group designed to teach individuals how to recognize and manage stress symptoms before the symptoms impact functioning.

12. Implement a regular exercise regimen as a stress prevention and reduction technique. (27)

27. Develop and reinforce the implementation of a regular physical exercise program by the service member.

13. Slowly take on military job duties as a method to reach full mission capability. (28, 29)

28. Assist the service member in identifying those job duties that are of a moderate level of stress and encourage him/her to begin working again.

29. Reinforce the service member's success in completing job responsibilities.

__. ____________________

__. ____________________

__. ____________________

__. ____________________

__. ____________________

__. ____________________

DIAGNOSTIC SUGGESTIONS

ICD-9-CM	*ICD-10-CM*	*DSM-5* Disorder, Condition, or Problem
V62.2	Z56.9	Other Problem Related to Employment
309.xx	F43.21	Adjustment Disorder, With Depressed Mood
309.xx	F43.22	Adjustment Disorder, With Anxiety
309.xx	F43.25	Adjustment Disorder, With Disturbance of Emotions and Conduct
308.3	F43.0	Acute Stress Disorder
309.81	F43.10	Posttraumatic Stress Disorder
300.11	F44.x	Conversion Disorder
300.82	F45.1	Somatic Symptom Disorder
300.xx	F68.10	Factious Disorder
______	______	____________________
______	______	____________________

CONFLICT WITH COMRADES

BEHAVIORAL DEFINITIONS

1. Frequently argues with fellow service members.
2. Displays a consistent pattern of confrontation with superiors.
3. Reports an inability to make friends in the military.
4. Exhibits a deficiency in problem-solving and interpersonal abilities with regard to confrontation.
5. Has a history of physical confrontations with peers and/or superiors.
6. Repeatedly subjected to disciplinary actions due to conflict with peers and/or superiors.
7. Displays a pervasive contempt and/or disdain for the military.
8. Reports feelings of being an outcast or misfit in his/her unit.

__. ____
____

__. ____
____

__. ____
____

LONG-TERM GOALS

1. Eliminate verbal and physical confrontations with military peers and/or superiors.
2. Develop adequate problem-solving and interpersonal skills related to managing conflicts.
3. Reports an elimination or decrease in disciplinary actions related to conflicts.
4. Develop an increased awareness of his/her role in the conflicts.
5. Learn to recognize escalating behaviors that lead to the conflicts.

__. ____
____

__. ____
____

__. ____
____

SHORT-TERM OBJECTIVES

1. Describe in detail the nature of the conflict with military peers and/or superiors. (1, 2)

2. Describe in detail oppositional and defiant behavior in childhood and adolescence. (3, 4)

3. Identify the impact that conflict with comrades has on mood. (5)

4. Identify the impact that conflict with comrades has on career. (6)

THERAPEUTIC INTERVENTIONS

1. Assess the frequency and severity of conflicts and the type of conflict (e.g., verbal, physical) that the service member is typically involved in.

2. Assess the typical precipitating event(s) (e.g., being told what to do, being teased) that seem to precede the service member's conflicts.

3. Explore the nature and extent of any oppositional and disruptive behavior that the service member engaged in during his/her childhood/adolescent years.

4. Ask the service member about previous mental health services for behavioral problems as a youth; compare and contrast past and current behaviors.

5. Assess the negative impact that conflict with military peers and/or supervisors has on the service member's mood, specifically does it perpetuate depression, worry, and/or agitation; process relevant content.

6. Assess the negative impact that conflict with military peers and/

or supervisors has on the service member's job performance, specifically has it caused being passed over for promotion and/or disciplinary actions against the service member such as Article 15's; process relevant content.

5. Report the presence of homicidal ideation directed toward comrade(s) during confrontations/altercations. (7, 8)

7. Assess the presence of homicidal ideation in the service member during conflicts with comrades.

8. Inform appropriate parties (military police, potential victim, chain of command) if a viable threat is identified.

6. Report alcohol, drug, and/or supplement use that may contribute to confrontations. (9, 10)

9. Complete a thorough substance use evaluation focusing on the service member's frequency and duration of use, type of substance used, and impact of substance use on mood and behavior (see the chapters on Substance Abuse/Dependence, Opioid Dependence, and Performance-Enhancing Supplement Use in this *Planner*).

10. Refer the service member for substance abuse/dependence treatment at his/her local base/post.

7. Cooperate with a psychiatric evaluation to determine if psychotropic medication is needed.(11, 12)

11. Refer the service member to a prescribing practitioner for psychotropic medication to assist with controlling his/her anger, mood swings, impulsiveness, and/or agitation that may be contributing to the confrontations.

12. Monitor the service member's medication compliance, side effects, and effectiveness; communicate pertinent information to the prescriber.

8. Discuss how conflict was handled in the service member's family of origin. (13, 14, 15)

13. Explore how the service member's parents/caretakers dealt with conflict in the home (e.g., yelling,

intimidation, talking); process the relevant material.

14. Assign the service member to develop a "lessons learned" list which includes positive and negative means of handling conflict that he remembers his parents/caretakers engaging in; process relevant material.

15. Assist the service member in visualizing himself/herself in the future as a parent and how he/she would do things differently than his/her parents/ caretakers.

9. Learn and implement adaptive problem-solving and conflict resolution skills. (16, 17, 18)

16. Assist the service member in identifying conflicts that can be handled through the use of open and honest verbal communication, appropriate nonverbal signals, and compromise and "swallowing" his/her pride.

17. Use the empty chair technique to assist the service member in practicing conflict resolution regarding a typical conflict with a military peer and/or superior; rehearse the technique until the service member feels comfortable with the confrontation.

18. Assign the service member to read and utilize "Applying Problem-Solving to Interpersonal Conflict" in the *Adult Psychotherapy Homework Planner*, 2nd ed. by Jongsma; process results in session.

10. Learn and implement anger management techniques. (19, 20, 21)

19. Assign the service member to keep a daily log of situations, individuals, and other events that create feelings of anger (or assign "Anger Journal" in the *Adult Psychotherapy Homework Planner*, 2nd ed. by Jongsma); review the log in session often.

20. Teach the service member how to recognize physical (clenching fists, tensing muscles) and behavioral (raising voice, threatening non-verbal behaviors) cues when he/she gets angry.

21. Teach the service member cognitive (replacing negative and hostile thoughts with positive ones) and behavioral (walk away from the situation, take a few deep breaths) strategies to avoid negative confrontations (or assign "Alternatives to Destructive Anger" in the *Adult Psychotherapy Homework Planner*, 2nd ed. by Jongsma).

11. Develop an understanding that thoughts influence our emotions and behaviors, including how anger develops and is expressed. (22, 23, 24, 25)

22. Explore the service member's self-talk that creates and maintains anger; assist him/her in replacing the maladaptive thoughts with alternate ones that allows him/her more options for understanding and reacting to the situation.

23. Teach the service member how to utilize "thought-stopping" as a means to interrupt thoughts that promote anger (or assign "Making Use of the Thought-Stopping Technique" in the *Adult Psychotherapy Homework Planner*, 2nd ed. by Jongsma).

24. Encourage the service member to visualize how he/she would feel if someone acted the way he/she did to someone he/she was close to (e.g., mother, boyfriend/girlfriend, sister); ask the service member to contemplate the difference between the two situations.

25. Reinforce the service member's success each time he/she reports

positive results utilizing cognitive techniques.

12. Develop outlets for relieving stress. (26)

26. Encourage the service member to increase time spent in activities that he/she finds relaxing and/or decreases perceived levels of tension and stress (e.g., exercising, hitting a punching bag, playing cards with friends).

13. Discuss personal views on the hierarchical structure of the military and if it is related to his/her conflicts. (27, 28)

27. Explore the service member's views about the hierarchical structure (i.e., chain of command) of the military and if he/she perceives a value in this type of organization.

28. Assign the service member to develop a list of rules and regulations that create anger and hostility (e.g., having to say "Yes, Sir" to someone he/she doesn't respect); assist the service member in developing simple and effective solutions for dealing with items on his/her list (when saying "Yes, Sir" to someone he/she doesn't respect, focus on respecting the rank and not the person).

14. Identify instances in the service member's personal life (e.g., spouse, parents, non-military friends) where conflict is a problem. (29)

29. Assist the service member in identifying other areas in his/her life where he/she has significant conflicts; draw parallels between work and personal life in order to illuminate a lifestyle pattern not confined to work and the military.

15. Accept consequences of behavior without further conflict. (30)

30. Encourage the service member to accept the consequences of his/her behavior without getting into verbal confrontations with superiors that could lead to more consequences and more confrontations; ask the question

"Would you rather do 50 push-ups for making a mistake or 100?"

16. Make amends to those that have been hurt or negatively impacted by behavior. (31)

31. Assist the service member in creating a list of people he/she has offended, disrespected, or assaulted and encourage him/her to offer an apology for his/her past behavior.

17. Acknowledge intent and/or motivation to remain in the military. (32)

32. Explore with the service member whether or not he/she wants to remain in the military or if his/her episodes of confrontation with comrades is a means to be separated/discharged from service; explore other options for leaving the military (e.g., hardship discharge, failure to adapt).

—. ______________________

—. ______________________

—. ______________________

—. ______________________

—. ______________________

—. ______________________

DIAGNOSTIC SUGGESTIONS

ICD-9-CM	*ICD-10-CM*	*DSM-5* Disorder, Condition, or Problem
V62.2	Z56.9	Other Problem Related to Employment
V71.01	Z72.811	Adult Antisocial Behavior
309.0	F43.21	Adjustment Disorder, With Depressed Mood
312.34	F63.81	Intermittent Explosive Disorder
312.30	F91.9	Unspecified Disruptive, Impulse-Control, and Conduct Disorder
301.7	F60.2	Antisocial Personality Disorder
301.83	F60.3	Borderline Personality Disorder
______	______	______________________
______	______	______________________

DEPRESSION

BEHAVIORAL DEFINITIONS

1. Reports depressed mood most days.
2. Reports change in appetite with or without weight gain.
3. Experiences a diminished interest in or enjoyment of activities.
4. Displays psychomotor agitation or retardation.
5. Complains of sleeplessness or hypersomnia.
6. Complains of a lack of energy.
7. Reports poor concentration and indecisiveness.
8. Exhibits a pattern of social withdrawal.
9. Reports suicidal thoughts and/or gestures.
10. Reports feelings of hopelessness, worthlessness, or inappropriate guilt.
11. Reports low self-esteem.
12. Acknowledges unresolved grief issues.
13. Experiences mood-related hallucinations or delusions.
14. Reports development or exacerbation of generalized physical aches and pains.
15. Reports a history of chronic or recurrent depression for which the veteran/service member has taken antidepressant medication, been hospitalized, or had outpatient treatment.

—. ______________________________

____

—. ______________________________

____

—. ______________________________

____

LONG-TERM GOALS

1. Alleviate depressed mood and return to previous level of effective functioning.
2. Recognize, accept, and cope with feelings of depression.
3. Develop healthy cognitive patterns and beliefs about self and the world that lead to alleviation and help prevent the relapse of depression symptoms.
4. Develop healthy work and social relationships that lead to alleviation and help prevent the relapse of depression symptoms.
5. Appropriately grieve the loss in order to normalize mood and to return to previous adaptive level of functioning.

—. ____

____

—. ____

____

—. ____

____

SHORT-TERM OBJECTIVES

1. Describe current and past experiences with depression, complete with its impact on function and attempts to resolve it. (1)
2. Verbally identify, if possible, the source of depressed mood. (2, 3)

THERAPEUTIC INTERVENTIONS

1. Assess the veteran's/service member's current and past mood episodes including their features, frequency, intensity, and duration (e.g., Clinical Interview supplemented by the *Inventory to Diagnose Depression* by Zimmerman, Coryell, Corenthal, and Wilson).
2. Ask the veteran/service member to make a list of what he/she is depressed about; process the list content.
3. Encourage the veteran/service member to share his/her feelings of depression in order to clarify them and gain insight as to causes.

3. Complete psychological testing to assess the depth of depression, the need for antidepressant medication, and suicide prevention measures. (4)

4. Arrange for the administration of an objective assessment instrument for evaluating the veteran's/service member's depression and suicide risk (e.g., Beck Depression Inventory-II and/or Beck Hopelessness Scale); evaluate results and give feedback to the veteran/service member.

4. Verbalize any history of suicide attempts and any current suicidal ideation. (5)

5. Explore the veteran's/service member's history and current state of suicidal ideation and behavior (see the chapter on Suicidal Ideation in this *Planner* if suicide risk is present).

5. State no longer having thoughts of self-harm. (6, 7, 8)

6. Assess and monitor the veteran's/service member's suicide potential.
7. Arrange for hospitalization, as necessary, when the veteran/ service member is judged to be harmful to self.
8. Coordinate a unit/buddy watch protocol with the service member's chain of command if increased risk of self-harm is present, but not to the level where hospitalization is required.

EBT 6. Take prescribed psychotropic medications responsibly at times ordered by prescribing practitioner. (9, 10)

9. Evaluate the veteran's/service member's possible need for psychotropic medication; arrange for a prescribing practitioner to give him/her a physical examination to rule out organic causes for depression, and assess need for antidepressant medication. EBT
10. Monitor and evaluate the veteran's/service member's psychotropic medication compliance, effectiveness, and side effects; communicate with prescribing practitioner. EBT

7. Identify and replace cognitive self-talk that is engaged in to support depression. (11, 12, 13, 14)

11. Assist the veteran/service member in developing an awareness of his/her automatic thoughts that reflect a depressogenic schemata.

12. Assign the veteran/service member to keep a daily journal of automatic thoughts associated with depressive feelings (e.g., "Negative Thoughts Trigger Negative Feelings" in the *Adult Psychotherapy Homework Planner,* 2nd ed. by Jongsma or "Daily Record of Dysfunctional Thoughts" in *Cognitive Therapy of Depression* by Beck, Rush, Shaw, and Emery); process the journal material to challenge depressive thinking patterns and replace them with reality-based thoughts.

13. Do "behavioral experiments" in which depressive automatic thoughts are treated as hypotheses/predictions, reality-based alternative hypotheses/ predictions are generated, and both are tested against the veteran's/service member's past, present, and/or future experiences.

14. Reinforce the veteran's/service member's positive, reality-based cognitive messages that enhance self confidence and increase adaptive action (see "Positive Self-Talk" in the *Adult Psychotherapy Homework Planner,* 2nd ed. by Jongsma).

8. Utilize behavioral strategies to overcome depression. (15, 16, 17)

15. Assist the veteran/service member in developing coping strategies (e.g., more physical exercise, less internal focus, increased social involvement,

more assertiveness, greater need sharing, more anger expression, etc.) for feelings of depression; reinforce success.

16. Engage the veteran/service member in "behavioral activation" by scheduling activities that have a high likelihood for pleasure and mastery (see "Identify and Schedule Pleasant Activities" in the *Adult Psychotherapy Homework Planner,* 2nd ed. by Jongsma); use rehearsal, role-playing, or role reversal, as needed, to assist adoption in the veteran's/service member's daily life; reinforce success.

17. Employ self-reliance training in which the veteran/service member assumes increased responsibility for routine activities (e.g., exercising, cooking, cleaning); reinforce success.

9. Identify important people in your life, past and present, and describe the quality, good and bad, of those relationships. (18)

18. Assess the veteran's/service member's "interpersonal inventory" of important past and present relationships and evidence of potentially depressive themes (e.g., loss and grief, interpersonal disputes, role transitions, and interpersonal deficits).

10. Verbalize any unresolved grief issues that may be contributing to depression. (19)

19. Explore the role of unresolved loss and grief issues as they contribute to the veteran's/service member's current depression (see Bereavement Due to the Loss of a Comrade chapter in this *Planner*).

11. Learn and implement problem-solving and/or conflict resolution skills to resolve interpersonal problems. (20, 21, 22)

20. Teach the veteran/service member conflict resolution skills (e.g., empathy, active listening, "I messages," respectful

communication, assertiveness without aggression, compromise) to help alleviate depression; use modeling, role-playing, and behavior rehearsal to work through several current conflicts. ▽

21. Help the veteran/service member resolve depression related to interpersonal problems through the use of reassurance and support, clarification of cognitive and affective triggers that ignite conflicts, and active problem-solving (or assign "Applying Problem-Solving to Interpersonal Conflict" in the *Adult Psychotherapy Homework Planner,* 2nd ed. by Jongsma). ▽

22. In conjoint sessions, help the veteran/service member resolve interpersonal conflicts. ▽

▽ 12. Implement a regular exercise regimen as a depression reduction technique. (23, 24)

23. Develop and reinforce a routine of physical exercise for the veteran/service member if a viable one is not currently in place. ▽

24. Instruct the service member to meet with a certified physical trainer at his/her local post/base to develop and reinforce a personal exercise program.

▽ 13. Learn and implement relapse prevention skills. (25)

25. Build the veteran's/service member's relapse prevention skills by helping him/her identify early warning signs of relapse, reviewing skills learned during therapy, and developing a plan for managing challenges. ▽

▽ 14. Increase assertive communication. (26)

26. Use modeling and/or role-playing to train the veteran/service member in assertiveness; if indicated and

available, refer him/her to an assertiveness training class/group for further instruction

15. Read books on overcoming depression. (27)

27. Recommend that the veteran/service member read self-help books on coping with depression (e.g., *Feeling Good* by Burns); process material read.

16. Show evidence of daily care for personal grooming and hygiene with minimal reminders from peers and superiors. (28)

28. Monitor and redirect the veteran/service member on daily grooming and hygiene.

17. Increasingly verbalize hopeful and positive statements regarding self, others, and the future (29, 30)

29. Assign the veteran/service member to write at least one positive affirmation statement daily regarding himself/herself and the future.

30. Teach the veteran/service member more about depression and to accept some sadness as a normal variation in feeling.

18. Express feelings of hurt, disappointment, shame, and anger that are associated with early life experiences. (31, 32)

31. Explore experiences from the veteran's/service member's childhood that contribute to the current depressed state.

32. Encourage the veteran/service member to share feelings of anger regarding pain inflicted on him/her in childhood that contribute to current depressed state.

19. Verbalize an understanding of the relationship between depressed mood and repression of feelings—that is, anger, hurt, sadness, and so on. (33)

33. Explain to the veteran/service member a connection between previously unexpressed (repressed) feelings of anger (and helplessness) and the current state of depression.

20. Return for a follow-up session to track progress, reinforce gains, and problem-solve barriers. (34)

34. Schedule a "booster session" for the veteran/service member for one to three months after therapy ends.

21. Develop an alternate plan of care/follow-up if deployment is pending. (35)

35. Identify behavioral health supports that will be available at the location where the service member will be deployed.

—. ____________________

—. ____________________

—. ____________________

—. ____________________

—. ____________________

—. ____________________

DIAGNOSTIC SUGGESTIONS

ICD-9-CM	*ICD-10-CM*	*DSM-5* Disorder, Condition, or Problem
309.0	F43.21	Adjustment Disorder, With Depressed Mood
296.xx	F31.xx	Bipolar I Disorder
296.89	F31.81	Bipolar II Disorder
300.4	F34.1	Persistent Depressive Disorder
301.13	F34.0	Cyclothymic Disorder
296.2x	F32.x	Major Depressive Disorder, Single Episode
296.3x	F33.x	Major Depressive Disorder, Recurrent Episode
295.70	F25.0	Schizoaffective Disorder, Bipolar Type
295.70	F25.1	Schizoaffective Disorder, Depressive Type
310.1	F07.0	Personality Change Due to Another Medical Condition
V62.82	Z63.4	Uncomplicated Bereavement
301.9	F60.9	Unspecified Personality Disorder
______	______	____________________
______	______	____________________

DIVERSITY ACCEPTANCE

BEHAVIORAL DEFINITIONS

1. Reports difficulty adjusting to and accepting the different cultural, racial, ethnic, and religious groups found in the military.
2. Exhibits a pervasive distrust of others from different cultural, racial, ethnic, and religious backgrounds.
3. Complains of feeling unsafe around dissimilar people.
4. Makes openly hostile, critical comments toward and about others from different backgrounds.
5. Reports an intentional desire to alienate and harm others from different backgrounds.
6. Engages in physical and verbal altercations with dissimilar people.
7. Avoids any social contact with fellow service members who come from different cultural, racial, religious, or ethnic backgrounds.
8. Refuses to communicate with or trust people from different backgrounds when they are supposed to be working together as a close-knit team, committed to protecting one another on military assignment.

—. ____

____

—. ____

____

—. ____

____

LONG-TERM GOALS

1. Become more accepting of and cooperative with others from different cultural, racial, ethnic, and religious backgrounds.
2. Base judgments about others on actions instead of cultural, racial, ethnic, and religious characteristics.
3. Refrain from hostile behavior toward people of diverse backgrounds.

4. Develop an appreciation for people that are dissimilar.
5. Demonstrate trust and respect toward others who come from different backgrounds and show that trust in military duty assignments as well as social contacts.

—. ____
____

—. ____
____

—. ____
____

SHORT-TERM OBJECTIVES

1. Describe in detail the nature of the discomfort and animosity felt toward individuals from different cultural, racial, ethnic, and religious backgrounds. (1)

2. Describe in detail the impact that beliefs about others from different backgrounds have on occupational functioning. (2, 3)

3. Verbalize more realistic cognitive reframes of beliefs about people

THERAPEUTIC INTERVENTIONS

1. Explore the extent and pervasiveness of the service member's feelings of discomfort and animosity toward others from different backgrounds; set limits on what type of disrespectful language will be tolerated in session.

2. Assess the extent that the service member's views and beliefs about others from different backgrounds have had on his/her job performance (e.g., individuals from other backgrounds not wanting work with him/her, hateful and disrespectful comments having resulted in demotion or lack of promotion).

3. Assess whether or not the service member's beliefs and actions have endangered the lives of other members of different cultural, racial, ethnic, and religious backgrounds (e.g., intentionally not providing cover or first aid in a combat situation).

4. Enter into a respectful and non-judgmental dialogue with the

from other cultures, races, ethnicities, and religions. (4, 5)

service member regarding his/her long-held beliefs about people from diverse backgrounds; use open-ended questions to elicit information and provide cognitive reframes when appropriate.

5. Assess whether or not the service member's views are products of his/her own thoughts, experiences, and reflections or a product of his/her adopting the beliefs of others (e.g., parents) during his/her upbringing; challenge these beliefs against reality versus stereotyping.

4. Articulate fears about being around others from different backgrounds. (6, 7)

6. Assist the veteran/service member in identifying his/her specific fears about being around people from diverse backgrounds.

7. Assist the veteran/service member in identifying irrational and illogical views related to the fears; use cognitive restructuring to assist with replacing his/her dysfunctional views.

5. Describe past positive experiences with individuals from diverse backgrounds. (8, 9)

8. Instruct the service member to create a list of positive experiences with individuals from diverse backgrounds.

9. Confront the service member on how if he/she had one positive experience with a person from a different background, then broad generalizations and judgments are not logical.

6. Actively seek out knowledge about different cultures, races, ethnic groups, and religions. (10, 11)

10. Instruct the service member to introduce himself/herself to at least one person from a different cultural, racial, ethnic, or religious background each day; process the experience, reinforcing adaptive responding.

11. Assist the service member in constructing a list of three

questions that focus on learning about culture, race, ethnicity, or religion; assign him/her to ask one individual from a different background each day these questions.

7. Verbalize an understanding of stereotypes and how they negatively impact individuals from different backgrounds. (12)

12. Explain the concept of stereotypes and provide examples of how stereotypes injure both individuals and entire groups; use a stereotype about the service member's own culture, race, ethnicity, or group to make the point.

8. Identify, challenge, and replace negative biases about individuals from different cultural, racial, ethnic, and religious backgrounds. (13, 14, 15)

13. Assist the service member in developing an awareness of his/her automatic thoughts that are consistent with a bigoted schema.

14. Assign the service member to keep a daily log of automatic thoughts associated with seeing others from different backgrounds as inferior or dangerous (or assign "Journal and Replace Self-Defeating Thoughts" in the *Adult Psychotherapy Homework Planner*, 2nd ed. by Jongsma); process the journal material to challenge distorted thinking patterns with reality-based thoughts.

15. Reinforce the service member's positive cognitions that foster openness and acceptance of people from diverse backgrounds.

9. Ask to be paired-up with someone from a different background for a training exercise. (16, 17)

16. Encourage the service member to request from his superiors that he be paired with someone from a different background for a training mission; explain to the service member that this will help develop trust and foster reliance on others.

17. Process and reinforce any of the service member's positive interaction experiences with

people different from him/her that serve to break down distorted beliefs about "them."

10. Develop a friendship with someone from a different background. (17, 18)

17. Process and reinforce any of the service member's positive interaction experiences with people different from him/her that serve to break down distorted beliefs about "them."

18. Encourage the service member to develop a friendship with someone from a different background.

11. Agree to professionally mentor someone from a different background. (17, 19)

17. Process and reinforce any of the service member's positive interaction experiences with people different from him/her that serve to break down distorted beliefs about "them."

19. Encourage the service member to ask his superiors to allow him to mentor a fellow comrade that is of a different culture, race, ethnicity, or religion.

__. ____________________

__. ____________________

__. ____________________

__. ____________________

__. ____________________

__. ____________________

DIAGNOSTIC SUGGESTIONS

ICD-9-CM	*ICD-10-CM*	*DSM-5* Disorder, Condition, or Problem
V62.4	Delete	
V62.2	Z56.9	Other Problem Related to Employment
309.0	F43.21	Adjustment Disorder, With Depressed Mood
301.7	F60.2	Antisocial Personality Disorder
301.0	F60.0	Paranoid Personality Disorder
______	______	____________________
______	______	____________________

FINANCIAL DIFFICULTIES

BEHAVIORAL DEFINITIONS

1. Amount of monthly bills is greater than monthly income, leading to increasing indebtedness.
2. Decrease in monthly income after returning from deployment (e.g., loss of hazard duty pay, loss of tax free status).
3. During deployment, assets were depleted and debt increased by a family member, friend, or other party responsible for managing finances.
4. Overdue debt creates a sense of hopelessness and helplessness.
5. Stress from overdue debts creates marital, family, work, and/or social conflict.
6. Demonstrates a long-term pattern of irresponsible and impulsive spending without considering financial, family, work, and social consequences.
7. Reprimanded by superiors due to not fulfilling financial obligations (e.g., spousal and child support, bill payment).
8. Lacks knowledge regarding effective money management.
9. Fears losing rank or being involuntarily separated from military service.
10. Reports of overdue debt are being made by creditors to credit bureaus, severely damaging credit rating.
11. Fears losing home ownership because of an inability to meet monthly mortgage payments.

—. ____

____

—. ____

____

—. ____

____

LONG-TERM GOALS

1. Establish a realistic budget that effectively balances income and expenses.
2. Regain legal control of finances (e.g., revoke power of attorney).
3. Regain sense of self-worth independent of material goods owned.
4. Gain insight into dynamics related to impulsive and irresponsible spending (e.g., family modeling, low self-esteem), leading to termination of poor money management.
5. Consistently apply effective money management techniques.
6. Reestablish trust and credibility with unit leaders.

__. ____
____

__. ____
____

__. ____
____

SHORT-TERM OBJECTIVES

1. Describe the details of the current financial situation. (1, 2, 3)
2. Describe the feelings associated with the current financial situation. (4, 5, 6)

THERAPEUTIC INTERVENTIONS

1. Assist the veteran/service member in openly discussing his/her financial difficulties while keeping in mind that the topic may evoke shame, embarrassment, and guilt.
2. Explore in detail the veteran's/service member's current financial situation.
3. Assist the veteran/service member in completing a list of all bills and assets focusing on which bills should be dealt with first (e.g., those over 30 days late or in default).
4. Assess the veteran/service member for the presence of clinically significant depressive and/or anxiety symptoms.

5. Explore the severity of the veteran's/service member's clinical symptoms and the need for treatment targeted at those symptoms; refer or treat for these conditions if they are present (see the chapters on Depression and Anxiety in this *Planner*).
6. Assess the veteran's/service member's level of suicide risk as a result of his/her financial situation; refer or treat for this condition if present (see the chapter on Suicidal Ideation in this *Planner*).

3. Identify financial hardships related to returning home from deployment. (7, 8)

7. Have the veteran/service member compare net income while deployed versus current net income; list expenses that will have to be cut to balance with the current income.
8. Have the veteran/service member list expenses that he/she has now that he/she didn't have while deployed (e.g., food, clothes, entertainment, rent); assist in planning how these expenses will be paid.

4. Take legal control of finances. (9, 10)

9. Encourage the veteran/service member to revisit his/her current power of attorney put in place prior to deployment.
10. Explore the option of revoking power of attorney if the individual(s) responsible for managing the veteran's/service member's finances does not have wise financial judgment or has stolen assets from the veteran/service member.

5. Inform the chain of command of current financial difficulties if deemed appropriate. (11)

11. Encourage the veteran/service member to inform his/her unit leadership of financial difficulties

if those difficulties will affect military duties.

6. Ask for financial assistance if necessary. (12, 13)

12. Refer the veteran/service member to the financial assistance program at his/her local base/post for a loan or assistance with food, clothing, or household items.

13. Explore with the veteran/service member whether family, friends, or religious organization could supply temporary financial support.

7. Meet with a military financial counselor on base/post in order to develop a budget that balances expenditures and income. (14, 15, 16, 17)

14. Refer the veteran/service member to a financial counselor at his/her local base/post to review expenses versus income and create a budget.

15. Assist the veteran/service member in creating a sound budget (or assign "Plan a Budget" in the *Adult Psychotherapy Homework Planner*, 2nd ed. by Jongsma); process the document upon completion.

16. Encourage the veteran/service member to adhere to the budget by making it part of his/her daily routine; review and monitor progress.

17. Encourage the veteran/service member to give a copy of his/her budget to a superior in his/her unit that he/she trusts.

8. Explore means of decreasing debt and expenditures. (18)

18. Encourage the veteran/service member to review current bills and determine if there are any "extras" that could be eliminated (e.g., cable, cell phone, magazine subscriptions).

9. Provide partner with specifics of the new budget and include

19. Encourage the veteran/service member to openly discuss his/her

him/her in all future financial decisions. (19, 20)

financial difficulties with his/her partner and to seek a team commitment to the new budget.

20. Encourage the veteran/service member to make future financial decisions in conjunction with his/her partner.

10. Keep weekly spreadsheets of all expenditures and income. (21)

21. Assist the veteran/service member with creating a basic budgeting spreadsheet and encourage him/her to review it weekly.

11. Identify personal traits that make irresponsible spending possible. (22, 23)

22. Explore the possibility that low self-esteem, feelings of loneliness, depression, and feelings of inadequacy may contribute to irresponsible financial behavior.

23. Assess the veteran/service member for any hypomanic or manic episodes that may contribute to impulsive spending; refer or provide treatment for this condition if present (see the chapters on Mania or Hypomania in the *Adult Psychotherapy Treatment Planner*, 4th ed. by Jongsma and Peterson).

12. Describe how the modeling of past family-of-origin behavior now impacts current financial situation. (24, 25)

24. Assist the veteran/service member in identifying irresponsible and impulsive spending patterns by those in his/her life while growing up; confront the need to develop a personal pattern which is responsible.

25. Explore the values and beliefs about money in the veteran's/service member's family of origin; assess together whether these values contribute to the problem and need to be reformulated.

13. Utilize cognitive-behavioral methods in controlling spending. (26, 27, 28, 29)

26. Encourage the veteran/service member to delay any new purchases over a predetermined amount for at least 48 hours.

27. Teach the veteran/service member to become more aware of his/her thoughts and emotions when he/she has the desire to make a new purchase; assist him/her in challenging maladaptive cognitions (e.g., "I need this item and I can add it to my credit card") and replacing them with adaptive cognitions (e.g., "I want this item, but my credit card balance is too high for me to add this cost now").

28. Teach the veteran/service member to create a pro and con list before any new purchase.

29. Role-play situations in which the veteran/service member is required to argue against the need to make a new purchase.

14. Explore means of increasing level of income. (30)

30. Review with the veteran/service member the potential benefit of acquiring a part-time job after duty hours to increase income.

15. Provide a report to chain of command regarding progress in alleviating financial problems. (31)

31. Encourage the veteran/service member to provide bi-monthly updates on financial progress to his unit leadership.

16. Meet with a military financial counselor in order to rebuild/strengthen credit worthiness. (32)

32. Refer the veteran/service member to a financial counselor at his/her local base/post in order to gain knowledge on how to improve his/her credit score.

17. Report specific incidents of financial decision making that had positive outcomes. (33)

33. Reinforce the veteran's/service member's positive outcomes through praise and acknowledgment.

18. Meet with the military legal department (i.e., Judge Advocate General) to determine if bankruptcy is appropriate. (34)

34. Refer the veteran/service member to a military attorney to explore the feasibility and impact of filing for bankruptcy.

__. ____________________

__. ____________________

__. ____________________

__. ____________________

__. ____________________

__. ____________________

DIAGNOSTIC SUGGESTIONS

ICD-9-CM	*ICD-10-CM*	*DSM-5* Disorder, Condition, or Problem
V62.89	Z60.0	Phase of Life Problem
309.0	F43.21	Adjustment Disorder, With Depressed Mood
296.xx	F31.1x	Bipolar I Disorder, Manic
296.89	F31.81	Bipolar II Disorder
296.xx	F32.x	Major Depressive Disorder, Single Episode
296.xx	F33.x	Major Depressive Disorder, Recurrent Episode
312.30	F91.9	Unspecified Disruptive, Impulse-Control, and Conduct Disorder
301.83	F60.3	Borderline Personality Disorder
301.7	F60.2	Antisocial Personality Disorder
______	______	____________________
______	______	____________________

HOMESICKNESS / LONELINESS

BEHAVIORAL DEFINITIONS

1. Complains of thoughts being dominated by missing family, friends, and/or previous home environment.
2. Reports a subclinical level of loneliness and emptiness.
3. Reports a constant focus on the desire to leave the military and return home to family.
4. Complains of feelings of helplessness, dread, and uncertainty related to living independently.
5. Displays clinically significant levels of anxiety and/or depression related to being separated from previous home environment.
6. Makes contact with family members as much as possible.
7. Almost never makes contact with family members because of fear of overwhelming homesickness.
8. Exhibits an inability to make new friends or to feel accepted in the new environment.
9. Complains of feeling distant, angry and/or resentful toward loved ones.
10. Reports being "picked on" by fellow comrades for his/her feelings of homesickness/loneliness.

__. ____
____

__. ____
____

__. ____
____

LONG-TERM GOALS

1. Reduce thoughts of home, family, and friends to a level that is not distressing.
2. Increase comfort and contentment with new environment.
3. Reduce feelings of loneliness/homesickness.
4. Increase social contacts and new friendships.
5. Eliminate symptoms of anxiety and depression related to being separated from the original home environment.

—. ____

—. ____

—. ____

SHORT-TERM OBJECTIVES

1. Describe the history and nature of the homesickness/loneliness. (1, 2, 3)
2. Complete psychological tests to assess depression and anxiety. (4)

THERAPEUTIC INTERVENTIONS

1. Establish rapport with the service member while creating an open and therapeutic environment.
2. Assess the service member's frequency, intensity, and duration of feelings of homesickness/loneliness and the impact on social, occupational, and interpersonal functioning.
3. Talk with the service member's first line supervisor (e.g., Squad Leader, Platoon Sergeant, First Sergeant) to assess the degree to which the homesickness/loneliness has impacted the service member's job performance.
4. Administer self-report measures to the service member (e.g., Beck Depression Inventory-II, Beck

Anxiety Inventory) to assess the depth and breadth of anxiety and depressive symptoms related to homesickness/loneliness.

3. Cooperate with an evaluation by a prescribing practitioner to assess for the need of psychotropic medication. (5, 6, 7)

5. Arrange for a psychiatric evaluation for the service member to determine if an antidepressant, anxiolytic, or hypnotic medication is needed.

6. Monitor the service member's medication compliance, side effects, and efficacy.

7. Inform the service member's chain of command if there are any duty restrictions while on medication, particularly those that place the service member or others at risk (e.g., operating heavy military equipment while taking medication that causes drowsiness).

4. Discuss feelings of homesickness/ loneliness in detail. (8, 9)

8. Explore in depth the service member's feelings about being in a new environment and how he/she feels about the military in general.

9. Assist the service member in creating a pro and con list related to his/her new environment and his/her newfound independence; process the list.

5. Verbalize an understanding that feelings of homesickness/ loneliness are a common experience among service members. (10, 11, 12)

10. Normalize the service member's feelings by explaining how separation can be difficult for anyone and that it is part of the developmental process between adolescence and adulthood.

11. Role-play a situation where the therapist and service member switch roles and the service member is asked to convince the therapist that what he/she is feeling is normal.

12. If appropriate within the current therapeutic relationship, share personal experiences with the service member regarding periods of homesickness/loneliness and how these feelings were coped with and overcome.

6. Elicit experiences of other service member's battles with homesickness/loneliness. (13, 14)

13. Assign the service member to talk with a superior that he/she respects, encouraging the service member to share his/her feelings about his/her homesickness/loneliness; encourage the service member to inquire about his/her superior's experience after leaving home for the first time.

14. Encourage the service member to talk with other fellow service members that he/she trusts about their emancipation experiences.

7. Identify, challenge, and replace dysfunctional self-talk that plays a role in creating and maintaining feelings of homesickness/loneliness. (15, 16, 17, 18)

15. Assist the service member in developing an awareness of his/her automatic thoughts that are consistent with a homesickness/loneliness schema; teach him/her how dysfunctional thoughts generate negative feelings (or assign "Negative Thoughts Trigger Negative Feelings" in the *Adult Psychotherapy Homework Planner*, 2nd ed. by Jongsma).

16. Assign the service member to keep a daily log of automatic thoughts associated with being homesick/lonely and an inability to be successful in a new environment (or assign "Journal and Replace Self-Defeating Thoughts" in the *Adult Psychotherapy Homework Planner*, 2nd ed. by Jongsma); process the journal material to challenge distorted thinking patterns with reality-based thoughts.

17. Reinforce the service member's positive cognitions that foster self-confidence and decrease feelings of homesickness/ loneliness (or assign "Positive Self-Talk" in the *Adult Psychotherapy Homework Planner*, 2nd ed. by Jongsma).

18. Teach the service member to implement a thought-stopping technique (think of a stop sign and then a pleasant scene) for negative thoughts that have been addressed but persist (or assign "Making Use of the Thought-Stopping Technique" in the *Adult Psychotherapy Homework Planner*, 2nd ed. by Jongsma); monitor and encourage the service member's use of the technique in daily life between sessions.

8. Honestly and openly discuss expectations about the military prior to his/her entering the military. (19, 20)

19. Explore the service member's expectations about the military before he/she enlisted (e.g., believed he/she would make a lot of friends, thought leaving home would be liberating).

20. Compare prior expectations with the service member's current reality while focusing on the importance of being flexible and adaptable (use the example of how the military instills an "adapt and overcome" mentality); review the service member's future expectations.

9. Verbalize and acknowledge successes in maintaining a positive and adaptive attitude. (21)

21. Reinforce the service member's successes in recognizing and correcting negative thoughts; provide periodic booster sessions focusing on the impact of cognitions on emotions.

10. Maintain contact with family and friends back home, while recognizing the importance of limits. (22, 23, 24)

22. Encourage the service member to maintain consistent contact with family and friends from his previous home environment, while explaining the importance of setting limits (e.g., not calling every day, keeping conversations brief).

23. Assist the service member in setting limits (e.g., creating a call schedule) if he/she has difficulty keeping contact to a minimum.

24. Help the service member sift through the type and amount of information that would be helpful to share with family and friends as a means of keeping connected with home.

11. Develop new social supports and utilize already existing social supports. (25, 26)

25. Explore reasons behind difficulties the service member has establishing new friendships and maintaining existing ones; explore automatic thoughts that trigger social anxiety (or assign "Restoring Socialization Comfort" in the *Adult Psychotherapy Homework Planner*, 2nd ed. by Jongsma).

26. Assign the service member to introduce himself/herself to three new people between sessions; acknowledge and reinforce success, redirect for failure.

12. Increase involvement in new social opportunities and challenges beyond what are typically comfortable. (27, 28, 29)

27. Assign the service member to attend social functions (e.g., parties, church socials) that tend to make him/her feel uncomfortable.

28. Teach the service member relaxation techniques (e.g., deep muscle release, positive imagery, diaphragmatic breathing) to cope with social anxiety.

29. Conduct two to three sessions of systematic desensitization focusing on reducing anxiety in social situations that make the service member feel uncomfortable.

13. Increase physical activity/exercise. (30)

30. Encourage the service member to exercise at least 30–45 minutes a day for five days a week as a means to improve mood and energy level.

14. Make plans to return home at specific periods throughout the year, allowing for a greater sense of control and self-determination. (31)

31. Assign the service member to create a travel schedule including dates to visit home, how long he/she will stay, who he/she will spend time with, and how he/she will handle intense feelings of sadness and despair once it is time to leave.

—. ____________________

—. ____________________

—. ____________________

—. ____________________

—. ____________________

—. ____________________

DIAGNOSTIC SUGGESTIONS

ICD-9-CM	*ICD-10-CM*	*DSM-5* Disorder, Condition, or Problem
309.0	F43.21	Adjustment Disorder, With Depressed Mood
V62.89	Z60.0	Phase of Life Problem
V62.2	Z56.9	Other Problem Related to Employment
296.xx	F32.x	Major Depressive Disorder, Single Episode
296.xx	F33.x	Major Depressive Disorder, Recurrent Episode
300.02	F41.1	Generalized Anxiety Disorder
301.6	F60.7	Dependent Personality Disorder
301.9	F60.9	Unspecified Personality Disorder
______	______	____________________
______	______	____________________

INSOMNIA

BEHAVIORAL DEFINITIONS

1. Complains of difficulty falling asleep.
2. Reports waking up throughout the night.
3. Complains of feeling unrefreshed after waking.
4. Complains of nightmares that cause sleep interruption.
5. Reports feeling tired throughout the day.
6. Displays physical effects of sleep deprivation (e.g., psychomotor retardation, muscle weakness).
7. Displays mental effects of sleep deprivation (e.g., decreased concentration, apathy, emotional lability).
8. Reports dozing off at inappropriate times (e.g., while driving, on missions, during meetings).
9. Reports excessive ruminations prior to bedtime.

—. ____

____

—. ____

____

—. ____

____

LONG-TERM GOALS

1. Restore restful sleep.
2. Decrease time to sleep onset.
3. Eliminate nighttime sleep interruptions.
4. Eliminate mental and physical side effects caused by sleep deprivation.
5. Increase alertness and concentration during the day.

__. ____
____

__. ____
____

__. ____
____

SHORT-TERM OBJECTIVES

1. Describe the history and details of insomnia. (1, 2, 3)

2. Complete self-report psychological measures to assess the impact of insomnia. (4)

3. Verbalize an understanding that poor sleep hygiene habits contribute to insomnia. (5, 6)

4. Practice healthy sleep hygiene behaviors. (7, 8)

THERAPEUTIC INTERVENTIONS

1. Assess the nature of the insomnia including the duration, frequency, severity of symptoms, and impact on current functioning.
2. Assess the veteran's/service member's current sleep hygiene practices.
3. Assess the veteran's/service member's views about sleep (e.g., is quantity more important than quality, how many hours does he/she need).
4. Administer the Insomnia Severity Index (ISI) and Sleep Impairment Index (SII) to the veteran/service member to assess problems with sleep latency, maintenance, and quality.
5. Explain to the veteran/service member how bad sleep habits create and maintain insomnia (e.g., watching television in bed).
6. Assign the veteran/service member to create a list of bad sleep habits that he/she has developed.
7. Instruct the veteran/service member on behavioral practices conducive to good sleep that include not using caffeine four

hours prior to bedtime, exercising in the mornings, not eating spicy meals/snacks prior to sleep, and removing cues to time that may promote "clock watching."

8. Assign the veteran/service member "Sleep Pattern Record" in the *Adult Psychotherapy Homework Planner*, 2nd ed. by Jongsma.

5. Verbalize an understanding that insomnia can be a conditioned response to the bedroom and bedroom behavior. (9, 10)

9. Explain the concept of stimulus control to the veteran/service member (see *Insomnia: A Clinician's Guide to Assessment and Treatment* by Morin and Espie).
10. Assign the veteran/service member to identify examples of stimulus conditioning in his/her life that create and maintain insomnia.

6. Implement appropriate stimulus control techniques. (11, 12)

11. Teach the veteran/service member stimulus control techniques (e.g., restrict time spent in bed, establish consistent sleep and wake time, go to bed only when sleepy, get out of bed if unable to fall asleep after 15 minutes, avoid daytime naps, only use the bed for sleep and sex).
12. Assist the veteran/service member in developing a plan for implementation of stimulus control techniques, keeping in mind obstacles such as decreased time given for sleep in the military and crowded and noisy barracks/home; monitor compliance and progress, making changes if needed.

7. Verbalize an understanding that high levels of arousal prior to bedtime contribute to insomnia. (13, 14, 15)

13. Explain to the veteran/service member how high levels of arousal interfere with sleep and that some psychiatric disorders

(e.g., posttraumatic stress disorder, nightmare disorder) can contribute to this elevated level of arousal.

14. Encourage the veteran/service member to decrease activities that create heightened arousal prior to bedtime (e.g., exercising before bedtime, arguing with significant other, thinking about upsetting past events).

15. Assist the veteran/service member in implementing strategies to counter high levels of arousal before bedtime (e.g., journaling, reading, listening to calming music, deep breathing, thought-stopping).

8. Identify, monitor, and change thoughts at bedtime that create charged emotions that maintain insomnia. (16, 17)

16. Explain to the veteran/service member the negative impact that ruminations and negative thinking have on sleep.

17. Teach the veteran/service member to challenge maladaptive cognitions that occur prior to bedtime and replace them with more adaptive ones; assign "Negative Thoughts Trigger Negative Feelings" in the *Adult Psychotherapy Homework Planner*, 2nd ed. by Jongsma.

9. Utilize thought-stopping techniques to counter intrusive and disruptive thoughts. (18)

18. Role-play thought stopping techniques in session (or assign "Making Use of the Thought-Stopping Technique" in the *Adult Psychotherapy Homework Planner*, 2nd ed. by Jongsma).

10. Complete a psychiatric evaluation to determine if psychotropic medications are needed. (19)

19. Refer the veteran/service member to a prescribing practitioner to assess whether he/she would benefit from medication to help with sleep onset and maintenance.

11. Take psychotropic medications as prescribed. (20)

20. Monitor medication compliance, side effects, efficacy, and progress.

12. Learn to manage nightmares that disrupt sleep patterns by utilizing imagery rehearsal techniques. (21)

21. Utilize Imagery Rehearsal Therapy with the veteran/service member to decrease frequency and intensity of nightmares (see the chapter on Nightmares in this *Planner*).

13. Complete a medical evaluation by a sleep medicine specialist to assess for the presence of sleep disordered breathing. (22)

22. Refer the veteran/service member to a sleep medicine specialist for a sleep study to assess for sleep disordered breathing (e.g., apnea).

14. Comply with recommendations from a sleep medicine specialist. (23)

23. Monitor the veteran's/service member's compliance with Continuous Positive Airway Pressure (CPAP) therapy; monitor effectiveness and progress.

15. Discuss possible risks with superiors that sleep disturbances may pose at work. (24)

24. Encourage the service member to discuss potential risks to self or others due to sleep problems (e.g., falling asleep on shooting range or while driving a military vehicle).

16. Develop a plan to avoid dozing off at work if sleep deprived. (25)

25. Assist the veteran/service member in developing strategies to keep from falling asleep during work activities (e.g., meetings, guard duty) such as standing up when he/she finds himself/herself nodding or when his/her eyes become heavy, using moderate amounts of caffeine prior to the activity, and moving his/her body position periodically.

17. Meet with military medical personnel if medical separation from service due to sleep disordered breathing/sleep apnea is recommended. (26, 27)

26. Encourage the service member to attend all medical separation appointments.

27. Explore opportunities for appeal if the service member does not agree with the medical separation finding (e.g., request a second opinion, consult with JAG or civilian attorney).

18. Meet with Veterans Affairs representative regarding disability compensation if separated from service. (28, 29)

28. Identify the veteran's appropriate geographical region for the department of Veterans Affairs and facilitate contact with a Veterans Affairs representative from that region.

29. Provide the veteran with information regarding his/her Veterans Affairs benefits (www.vba.va.gov/VBA/).

19. Attend scheduled Veterans Affairs medical appointments. (30)

30. Stress the importance of the veteran attending all scheduled medical appointments at his/her local Veterans Affairs facility.

—. ____________________

—. ____________________

—. ____________________

—. ____________________

—. ____________________

—. ____________________

DIAGNOSTIC SUGGESTIONS

ICD-9-CM	*ICD-10-CM*	*DSM-5* Disorder, Condition, or Problem
307.42	F51.01	Insomnia
307.44	F51.11	Hypersomnolence Disorder
307.47	F51.5	Nightmare Disorder
307.45	G47.xx	Circadian Rhythm Sleep-Wake Disorder
780.59	G47.33	Obstructive Sleep Apnea Hypopnea
780.59	G47.34	Idiopathic Hypoventilation
292.89	F19.282	Other (or Unknown) Substance-Induced Sleep Disorder
304.10	F13.20	Sedative, Hypnotic, or Anxiolytic Use Disorder, Moderate or Severe
305.40	F13.10	Sedative, Hypnotic, or Anxiolytic Use Disorder, Mild
307.47	F51.01	Unspecified Insomnia Disorder
307.47	F51.11	Unspecified Hypersomnolence Disorder
307.47	G47.9	Unspecified Sleep-Wake Disorder
______	______	____________________
______	______	____________________

MILD TRAUMATIC BRAIN INJURY

BEHAVIORAL DEFINITIONS

1. Reports neuropsychological and/or neurobehavioral changes secondary to a blunt force or acceleration/deceleration injury to the head without loss of consciousness or loss of consciousness less than 30 minutes.
2. Complains of cognitive symptoms including decreases in attention, concentration, and/or memory problems.
3. Complains of physical symptoms including headaches, dizziness, nausea, fatigue, insomnia, blurred vision, and/or disturbed balance and gait.
4. Complains of behavioral symptoms including irritability, loss of motivetion, sleep problems, and/or emotional and behavioral dysregulation.
5. Reports a negative impact on social, occupational, academic, and/or interpersonal functioning.

__. ____

__. ____

__. ____

LONG-TERM GOALS

1. Decrease memory, attention, and concentration deficits through adaptive strategies.
2. Reduce physical symptoms of mild traumatic brain injury.
3. Reduce behavioral symptoms of mild traumatic brain injury.
4. Reduce the level of daily distress caused by mild traumatic brain injury.

—. ____

____

—. ____

____

—. ____

____

SHORT-TERM OBJECTIVES

1. Describe the extent of impact on functioning and the nature of the traumatic brain injury. (1, 2, 3)

THERAPEUTIC INTERVENTIONS

1. Assess the extent of the veteran's/service member's problems from the mild traumatic brain injury including the impact on social, occupational, and interpersonal functioning.
2. Collect data from the veteran/ service member regarding the nature of the event including how the injury was sustained (e.g., fall, motor vehicle accident), if there was a period of loss of consciousness or posttraumatic amnesia, and if drugs and/or alcohol were involved.
3. Collect collateral information from the veteran's/service member's family, friends, and/or chain of command regarding changes in behavior, personality, or cognitive abilities since the injury.

2. Cooperate with a neurological evaluation. (4)

4. Refer the veteran/service member to a neurologist for a neurological examination.

3. Cooperate with a neuropsychological evaluation. (5, 6)

5. Refer the veteran/service member to a neuropsychologist for a comprehensive evaluation to assess for changes in memory, language, motor skills, executive

functioning, personality, attention/concentration, and information processing.

6. Review results of the neuropsychological evaluation with the veteran/service member if appropriate.

4. Verbalize an understanding of the neuropsychological and neurobehavioral consequences of mild traumatic brain injury. (7, 8)

7. Educate the veteran/service member about the typical symptoms of mild traumatic brain injury, how long the symptoms usually last, and what can be done to minimize the impact of those symptoms on daily functioning.

8. Provide the veteran/service member with the *Quick Guide—Patient/Family: Traumatic Brain Injury* published by the Department of Veterans Affairs (http://www1.va.gov/environagents/docs/TBI-handout-patients.pdf).

5. Verbalize an understanding of the importance of preventing a subsequent traumatic brain injury due to cumulative negative effects. (9)

9. Educate the veteran/service member on behaviors that can minimize the chances of sustaining a subsequent traumatic brain injury (e.g., wear seat belts and helmet while riding/driving in military vehicles, wear a helmet when riding a bicycle/motorcycle, don't drive under the influence of alcohol, illicit drugs, or certain prescription medications).

6. Cooperate with an occupational therapy evaluation. (10)

10. Refer the veteran/service member to an occupational therapist for an assessment of functional capacity and cognitive rehabilitation therapy; monitor follow-through on rehabilitation recommendations.

7. Develop and implement memory- enhancing strategies/techniques. (11, 12, 13, 14)

11. Assign the veteran/service member to utilize an event organizer/planner to keep track of medical appointments, work project deadlines, and other important information.

12. Encourage the veteran/service member to use a wristwatch alarm or other small alarm device to remind him/her of important appointments.

13. Encourage the veteran/service member to create a daily "to-do list" and check off each activity/ task once it has been completed.

14. Assist the veteran/service member in developing a daily routine that he/she can follow to decrease confusion.

8. Cooperate with a referral to a prescribing practitioner for a medication assessment for inattention. (15)

15. Refer the veteran/service member to a prescribing practitioner to assess for the appropriateness of medication to treat attention/concentration deficits.

9. Utilize behavioral and cognitive strategies to enhance attention and concentration. (16, 17, 18, 19)

16. Assign the veteran/service member to create a list of activities that he/she enjoys that can be done in brief increments of time (e.g., reading or playing video games for 10 minutes at a time); encourage the veteran/ service member to take breaks during tasks when he/she starts to feel overwhelmed.

17. Assign the veteran/service member to gradually increase time spent in enjoyable activities each week (e.g., increase time to 15 minutes first week, 20 minutes second week, etc.); maintain a graph of progress.

18. Assign the veteran/service member to utilize computer/video games that build attention/concentration (poker, solitaire, word puzzles).

19. Encourage the veteran/service member to talk with his family and/or friends regarding redirecting him/her during conversations if he/she wanders off topic.

10. Utilize behavioral, cognitive, and medical techniques/strategies to control impulsive and/or aggressive behavior. (20, 21, 22, 23)

20. Refer the veteran/service member to a prescribing practitioner to assess for the appropriateness of medication to treat his/her impulsivity and/or aggressiveness.

21. Assist the veteran/service member in exploring the negative impact of his/her impulsive and aggressive behavior on loved ones (or assign "Plan Before Acting" in the *Adult Psychotherapy Homework Planner*, 2nd ed. by Jongsma).

22. Instruct the veteran/service member to use time-out or "stop, think, react" as a means to think through his/her behavior instead of acting impulsively (or assign "Impulsive Behavior Journal" in the *Adult Psychotherapy Homework Planner*, 2nd ed. by Jongsma).

23. Teach the veteran/service member anger management techniques (e.g., count to 10 before reacting, deep breathing, monitoring automatic thoughts); reinforce the veteran's/service member's use of techniques.

11. Report an improvement in sleep quality and quantity. (24, 25, 26)

24. Refer the veteran/service member to a prescribing

practitioner to assess for the appropriateness of medication to treat his/her sleep difficulties.

25. Teach the veteran/service member healthy sleep hygiene behaviors such as not using caffeine four hours prior to bedtime, exercising in the mornings, not eating spicy meals/snacks prior to sleep, and removing cues to time that may promote "clock watching" (see the chapter on Insomnia in this *Planner*).

26. Assign the veteran/service member to complete the exercise "Sleep Pattern Record" in the *Adult Psychotherapy Homework Planner*, 2nd ed. by Jongsma.

12. Report a decrease in the frequency and intensity of posttraumatic headaches. (27, 28, 29)

27. Refer the veteran/service member to a prescribing practitioner to assess for the appropriateness of medication to treat his/her headaches.

28. Teach the veteran/service member how to recognize and avoid headache triggers (e.g., caffeine, dehydration, intense physical exercise).

29. Conduct EMG biofeedback to assist the veteran/service member in learning facial and neck muscle relaxation.

13. Attend and participate in a family session. (30)

30. Conduct a family session with the veteran/service member and his/her family focusing on education about mild traumatic brain injury, coping behaviors, and improving existing family supports.

14. Participate in Department of Veterans Affairs vocational

31. Provide information to the veteran/service member about

rehabilitation and educational programs. (31)

vocational rehabilitation programs provided by Department of Veterans Affairs (www.vba.va.gov/bln/vre/).

__. ____________________

____

__. ____________________

____

__. ____________________

____

__. ____________________

____

__. ____________________

____

__. ____________________

____

DIAGNOSTIC SUGGESTIONS

ICD-9-CM	*ICD-10-CM*	*DSM-5* Disorder, Condition, or Problem
294.9	R41.9	Unspecified Neurocognitive Disorder
294.0	G31.84	Mild Neurocognitive Disorder Due to Traumatic Brain Injury
293.83	F06.3x	Depressive Disorder Due to Another Medical Condition
780.xx	F51.01	Insomnia Disorder with Other Medical Comorbidity, Mild Neurocognitive Disorder Due to Traumatic Brain Injury
________	________	____________________
________	________	____________________

NIGHTMARES

BEHAVIORAL DEFINITIONS

1. Complains of distress resulting from repeated awakenings during sleep due to emotionally distressing dreams related to past combat experiences and/or content related to harm to self or loved ones.
2. Reports increased autonomic arousal, disorientation, recall of combat related dream content and negative affect after abrupt awakening.
3. Reports fragmented sleep throughout the night due to distressing dreams.
4. Experiences apprehension about falling asleep in order to avoid nightmares resulting in initial insomnia.
5. Complains of daytime hypersomnia due to fragmented sleep and initial insomnia.
6. Reports anxiety and dysphoria during the day, which is directly related to the prior nightmare episode.
7. Reports interpersonal difficulties with bedmate or roommate resulting from excessive movement and noise during mutual sleep periods (e.g., kicking, punching, crying, screaming).

—. ____

____

—. ____

____

—. ____

____

LONG-TERM GOALS

1. Eliminate distressing dreams.
2. Restore consolidated and uninterrupted sleep.
3. Eliminate anxiety about falling asleep.

4. Reduce daytime fatigue and excessive sleepiness.
5. Improve interpersonal difficulties with bedmate.

__. ____

____

__. ____

____

__. ____

____

SHORT-TERM OBJECTIVES

1. Describe the history and details of nightmare problems. (1, 2)

THERAPEUTIC INTERVENTIONS

1. Assess the extent of the veteran's/service member's nightmare problem to include collecting data on the frequency and intensity of the nightmares, the military experience that may have triggered the nightmares, and the level of emotional distress caused by the nightmares.
2. Request the veteran/service member to maintain a nightmare log for two weeks in order to document times of the night that nightmares occur, as well as record the feelings and images associated with the nightmares upon awakening.

2. Describe the history and patterns of sleep disturbances. (3)

3. Assess the nature of the veteran's/service member's associated sleep problems to include the number of nighttime awakenings, level of anxiety prior to sleep, bedtime routines, and level of daytime fatigue.

3. Describe other psychiatric symptoms. (4, 5)

4. Determine if the veteran's/service member's nightmares are consistent with normal reactions after returning from a combat deployment.

5. Assess the veteran/service member for psychiatric disorders that may be causing the nightmares (e.g., PTSD, ASD, or depression); refer for appropriate treatment/level of care.

4. Share history of medical problems. (6)

6. Assess the veteran/service member for history of neurological illness, traumatic brain injury, or past exposure to toxins; refer for medical evaluation if needed.

5. Share history of alcohol and drug use. (7)

7. Assess the degree that the veteran's/service member's alcohol and/or drug use causes or contributes to the problem; refer to substance dependence treatment if warranted.

6. Verbalize an understanding of how nightmares and sleep disturbances are connected. (8, 9)

8. Teach the veteran/service member about the concept of how fragmented sleep causes sleep problems and how nightmares promote fragmented, nonrestorative sleep.

9. Teach the veteran/service member about the concept of consolidated sleep and how quality of sleep is more important than quantity of sleep.

7. Practice good sleep hygiene behaviors. (10)

10. Instruct the veteran/service member on behavioral practices conducive to good sleep, which include not using caffeine four hours prior to bedtime, exercising in the mornings, getting out of bed if not able to fall asleep within 15 minutes, not eating spicy meals/snacks prior to sleep, and removing cues to time that may promote "clock watching."

8. Practice relaxation training exercises prior to bed and upon awakening from nightmares. (11)

11. Teach the veteran/service member relaxation techniques such as progressive muscle

relaxation, imagery and visualization, and meditation. ▽

▽ 9. Verbalize an understanding that nightmares can be viewed as a learned disorder and can be corrected through imagery. (12, 13)

12. Explain to the veteran/service member that nightmares can develop into a distinct disorder and can be considered a learned behavior similar to insomnia; nightmares can be conceptualized as a broken record that needs to be reset. ▽

13. Explain to the veteran/service member that nightmares are a form of imagery, and discuss how he/she is able to direct his/her images when conscious. ▽

▽ 10. Select a nightmare to change. (14, 15, 16, 17)

14. Instruct the veteran/service member to choose a nightmare that causes a level of distress of about 50 on a scale of 0–100 (0 = no distress and 100 = the most distress ever experienced). ▽

15. Encourage the veteran/service member to choose a nightmare and not a recurrent intrusive thought that occurs when awake. ▽

16. Instruct the veteran/service member to start with only one nightmare at a time in order to ensure that the veteran/service member fully understands the task and to prevent him/her from becoming overwhelmed. ▽

17. Instruct the veteran/service member not to rehearse the original nightmare to be changed since exposure is not necessary for improvement. ▽

▽ 11. Change the nightmare via imagery. (18, 19, 20)

18. Instruct the veteran/service member to change the nightmare any way he/she wishes (i.e., ask the veteran/service member to take a nightmare and replace the

distressing portion of the dream with a more positive or adaptive theme/outcome).

19. Provide examples to the veteran/service member if he/she has problems accessing new images (e.g., instead of seeing a friend injured by roadside bomb, imagine the friend making it through without injury).

20. Only provide suggestions to the veteran/service member and not the actual nightmare to be changed, as mastery and ownership may be an integral part of change.

12. Rehearse the new dream each day. (21, 22, 23)

21. Encourage the veteran/service member to rehearse the new dream twice a day for 20 minutes each time until the original nightmare disappears or is no longer distressing.

22. Instruct the veteran/service member to rehearse the new dream via writing if he/she is not able to utilize imagery effectively.

23. Assist the veteran/service member in selecting an additional nightmare to change once there has been resolution of the first nightmare; continue as needed.

13. Keep a prescribing practitioner appointment to evaluate for appropriateness of medication to decrease the intensity and frequency of nightmares and to assist with sleep if necessary. (24)

24. Refer the veteran/service member to a prescribing practitioner to whether the veteran/service member would benefit from an alpha-blocker, antidepressant, or sedative/hypnotic.

14. Report any over-the-counter medications used to help with sleep. (25)

25. Encourage the veteran/service member to report self-prescribed over-the-counter medications such as antihistamines and sleep aides.

15. Take medications as prescribed to assess effectiveness. (26)

26. Monitor the veteran's/service member's progress, compliance, and the side effects of prescribed medication.

16. Learn how to recognize side effects from medication that may interfere with training and mission status. (27)

27. Educate the veteran/service member on typical side effects (drowsiness, agitation, restlessness) that may interfere with military missions and increase risk of accidents.

17. Enter couples therapy to address problems related to the nightmares. (28, 29)

28. Encourage the veteran/service member and his/her partner to discuss feelings about the current situation.

29. Provide the veteran's/service member's partner educational information on nightmares and sleep disorders.

__. ____________________

__. ____________________

__. ____________________

__. ____________________

__. ____________________

__. ____________________

DIAGNOSTIC SUGGESTIONS

ICD-9-CM	*ICD-10-CM*	*DSM-5* Disorder, Condition, or Problem
307.47	F51.5	Nightmare Disorder
309.81	F43.10	Posttraumatic Stress Disorder
308.3	F43.0	Acute Stress Disorder
307.46	F51.4	Non-Rapid Eye Movement Sleep Arousal Disorder, Sleep Terror Type
307.42	F51.01	Insomnia
307.44	F51.11	Hypersomnolence Disorder
327.42	G47.52	Rapid Eye Movement Sleep Behavior Disorder
________	________	____________________
________	________	____________________

OPIOID DEPENDENCE

BEHAVIORAL DEFINITIONS

1. Demonstrates a pattern of opioid use leading to clinically significant impairment or distress.
2. Reports a need for markedly increased amounts of opioids to achieve the desired effect.
3. Presents with withdrawal symptoms characteristic of opioid dependence.
4. Verbalizes a persistent desire to cut down or control opioid use.
5. Spends a great deal of time trying to obtain opioids and recover from use.
6. Gives up important social, occupational, or recreational activities because of opioid use.
7. Engages in illegal activity to support the opioid habit (e.g., "doctor shopping" between both military and civilian physicians).
8. Opioid abuse continues despite significant negative occupational, financial, social, and familial consequence.
9. Abuses opioids in a maladaptive response to pain management.
10. Reports repeated lateness to morning accountability or physical training formations as a result of opioid use.

__. ____

____

__. ____

____

__. ____

____

LONG-TERM GOALS

1. Accept the powerlessness and unmanageability over opioids, and participate in a recovery-based program.
2. Withdraw from mood-altering substance, stabilize physically and emotionally, and then establish a supportive recovery plan.
3. Establish a sustained recovery, free from the use of all mood-altering substances.
4. Establish and maintain total abstinence while increasing knowledge of the disease and the process of recovery.
5. Acquire the necessary skills to maintain long-term abstinence from all mood-altering substances and live a life free of chemicals.

—. ______________________________

____

—. ______________________________

____

—. ______________________________

____

SHORT-TERM OBJECTIVES

THERAPEUTIC INTERVENTIONS

1. Cooperate with medical assessment and an evaluation of the necessity for pharmacological intervention. (1, 2)

1. Refer the veteran/service member to a military healthcare provider to perform a physical examination (include tests for HIV, hepatitis, and sexually transmitted diseases) and discuss the use of methadone, buprenorphine, and the abstinence-based model of opioid treatment.
2. Refer the veteran/service member to a military approved pharmacology-based maintenance/withdrawal program (e.g., methadone, buprenorphine).

2. Take prescribed medications as directed by the physician. (3,4)

3. Physician will monitor the effectiveness and side effects of medication, titrating as necessary.

4. Staff will administer prescribed medications and monitor for effectiveness and side effects.

3. Report acute withdrawal symptoms to the staff. (5)

5. Assess and monitor the veteran's/service member's condition during withdrawal, using a standardized procedure (e.g., Narcotic Withdrawal Scale) as needed.

4. Complete psychological testing or objective questionnaires for assessing opioid dependence. (6)

6. Administer to the veteran/service member psychological instruments designed to objectively assess opioid dependence (e.g., Substance Use Disorders Diagnostic Schedule-IV [SUDDS-IV], Substance Abuse Subtle Screen Inventory-3 [SASS-3]); give the client feedback regarding the results of the assessment.

5. Provide honest and complete information for a chemical dependence biopsychosocial history. (7)

7. Complete a thorough family and personal biopsychosocial history on the veteran/service member that has a focus on addiction (e.g., family history of addiction and treatment, other substances used, progression of substance abuse, consequences of abuse, problems in the military).

6. Attend didactic sessions and read assigned material in order to increase knowledge of addiction and the process of recovery. (8, 9, 10, 11)

8. Assign the veteran/service member to attend a chemical dependence didactic series to increase his/her knowledge of the patterns and effects of chemical dependence.

9. Require the veteran/service member to attend all chemical dependence didactics; ask him/her to identify several key points attained from each didactic and process these points with the therapist.

10. Assign the veteran/service member to read material on addiction (e.g., *Willpower's Not Enough* by Washton, *The*

Addiction Workbook by Fanning, or *Alcoholics Anonymous*); and process key points gained from the reading. ▽

11. Require the veteran/service member to read the book *Narcotics Anonymous* and gather five key points from it to process with the therapist. ▽

▽ 7. Attend group therapy sessions to share thoughts and feelings associated with, reasons for, consequences of, feelings about, and alternatives to addiction. (12, 13)

12. Assign the veteran/service member to attend group therapy. ▽

13. Direct group therapy that facilitates the veteran/service member sharing causes for, consequences of, feelings about, and alternatives to addiction. ▽

▽ 8. Verbally admit to powerlessness over mood-altering substances. (14)

14. Assign the veteran/service member to complete a Narcotics Anonymous (NA) Step One paper admitting to powerlessness over mood-altering chemicals, and present it in group therapy or to the therapist for feedback. ▽

▽ 9. List and discuss negative consequences resulting from or exacerbated by substance dependence. (15, 16, 17)

15. Ask the veteran/service member to make a list of the ways chemical use has negatively impacted his/her life (or assign "Substance Abuse Negative Impact versus Sobriety's Positive Impact" in the *Adult Psychotherapy Homework Planner*, 2nd ed. by Jongsma); process the list in individual or group sessions. ▽

16. Confront the veteran's/service member's use of denial to minimize the severity of, and negative consequences of, opioid abuse. ▽

17. Using the biopsychosocial history and the veteran's/service member's list of negative consequences of opioid abuse, assist him/her in understanding the need to stay in treatment. ▽

10. Verbalize recognition that mood-altering chemicals were used as the primary coping mechanism to escape from stress or pain, and resulted in negative consequences. (18)

11. List and discuss the negative emotions that were caused or exacerbated by substance dependence. (19)

12. List and discuss reasons to work on a plan for recovery from addiction. (20)

13. List lies used to hide substance dependence. (21, 22)

14. Verbalize ways a higher power can assist in recovery. (23)

15. Identify and accept the need for substance abuse treatment. (24)

18. Explore with the veteran/service member how his/her opioid use was used to escape from stress, physical and emotional pain, and boredom; confront the negative consequences of this pattern.

19. Probe the veteran's/service member's sense of shame, guilt, and low self-worth that has resulted from addiction and its consequences.

20. Assign the veteran/service member to write a list of reasons to be abstinent from addiction (or assign "Making Change Happen" or "A Working Recovery Plan" in the *Addiction Treatment Homework Planner*, 4th ed. by Finley and Lenz).

21. Help the veteran/service member see the dishonesty that goes along with addiction; ask him/her to list lies told to hide substance use.

22. Teach the veteran/service member why honesty is essential to recovery.

23. Teach the veteran/service member about the AA concept of a higher power and how this can assist in recovery (e.g., God can help with chronic pain or craving; regular prayer and meditation can reduce stress).

24. Conduct Motivational Interviewing to assess the veteran's/service member's stage of preparation for change; intervene accordingly, moving from building motivation, through strengthening the commitment to change, to participation in treatment (see *Motivational Interviewing*, 2nd ed. by Miller and Rollnick).

16. Identify realistic goals for substance abuse recovery. (25, 26, 27)

25. Assign the veteran/service member to meet with an AA/NA member who has been working the 12-Step program for several years and find out specifically how the program has helped him/her to stay sober; afterward, process the meeting.

26. Request that the veteran/service member write out basic treatment expectations (e.g., physical changes, social changes, emotional needs) regarding sobriety, and process these with the clinician.

27. Emphasize with the veteran/service member the goal of substance abuse recovery and the need for sobriety, despite lapses or relapses.

17. Verbalize a commitment to abstain from the use of mood-altering drugs. (28)

28. Develop an abstinence contract with the veteran/service member regarding the termination of the use of his/her drug; process the veteran's/service member's feelings related to the commitment.

18. Identify and make changes in social relationships that will support recovery. (29)

29. Review the negative influence of the veteran/service member continuing his/her alcohol-related friendships ("drug buddies") and assist him/her in making a plan to develop new sober relationships including "sobriety buddies"; revisit routinely and facilitate toward development of a new social support system.

19. Identify projects and other social and recreational activities that sobriety will now afford and that will support sobriety. (30, 31)

30. Assist the veteran/service member in planning social and recreational activities that are free from association with substance abuse; revisit routinely and facilitate toward development of a new set of activities.

31. Plan household, work-related, and/or other free-time projects

20. Verbalize how the living situation contributes to chemical dependence and acts as a hindrance to recovery. (32)

21. Make arrangements to terminate current living situation and move to a place more conducive to recovery. (33)

22. Identify the positive impact that sobriety will have on intimate and family relationships. (34)

23. Agree to make amends to significant others who have been hurt by a life dominated by substance abuse. (35, 36)

24. Participate in behavioral marital or family therapy to learn and implement ways to improve relations and communicate effectively. (37)

25. Learn and implement personal coping strategies to manage

that can be accomplished to build the veteran's/service member's self-esteem and self-concept as clean and sober.

32. Evaluate the role of the veteran's/service member's living situation in fostering a pattern of chemical dependence; process with the veteran/service member to help identify therapeutic changes.

33. Facilitate development of a plan for the veteran/service member to change his/her living situation to foster recovery; revisit routinely and facilitate toward accomplishing a positive change in living situation.

34. Assist the veteran/service member in identifying positive changes that will be made in family relationships during recovery.

35. Discuss the negative effects the veteran's/service member's substance abuse has had on family, friends, and work relationships and encourage a plan to make amends for such hurt.

36. Elicit from the veteran/service member a verbal commitment to make initial amends now to key individuals and further amends later or if working Steps Eight and Nine of an AA program.

37. Refer or provide behavioral couples or family therapy to improve relationship and communicate more effectively (see the chapter on Post-Deployment Reintegration in this *Planner*).

38. Teach the veteran/service member tailored coping

urges to lapse back into chemical use. (38)

strategies involving calming strategies (e.g., relaxation, paced breathing), thought-stopping, positive self-talk, and attentional focusing skills (e.g., distraction from urges, staying focused on behavioral goals of abstinence) to manage triggered urges to use chemical substances.

26. Identify, challenge, and replace destructive self-talk with positive, strength building self-talk. (39, 40)

39. Use Cognitive Therapy approaches to explore the veteran's/service member's schema and self-talk that weaken his/her resolve to remain abstinent; challenge the biases; assist him/her in generating realistic self-talk that correct for the biases and build resilience.

40. Rehearse situations in which the veteran/service member identifies his/her negative self-talk and generates empowering alternatives (or assign "Journal and Replace Self-Defeating Thoughts" in the *Adult Psychotherapy Homework Planner*, 2nd ed. by Jongsma); review and reinforce success.

27. Participate in gradual repeated exposure to triggers of urges to lapse back into chemical substance use. (41, 42)

41. Direct and assist the veteran/service member in construction of a hierarchy of urge-producing cues to use substances (or assign "Identifying Relapse Triggers and Cues" or "Relapse Prevention Planning" in the *Addiction Treatment Homework Planner*, 4th ed. by Finley and Lenz).

42. Select initial *in vivo* or role-played cue exposures that have a high likelihood of being a successful experience for the veteran/service member; facilitate coping and cognitive restructuring within and

after the exposure, use behavioral strategies (e.g., modeling, rehearsal, social reinforcement) to facilitate the exposure, review with the veteran/service member and group members, if done in group. ▼

▼ 28. Learn and implement personal skills to manage common day-to-day challenges and build confidence in managing them without the use of substances. (43, 44)

43. Assess the veteran's/service member's current skill in managing common everyday stressors (e.g., work, social, family role demands); use behavioral techniques (e.g., instruction, modeling, role-playing) to build social and/or communication skills to manage these challenges without the use of substances. ▼

44. Assign the veteran/service member to read about general social and/or communication skills in books or treatment manuals on building social skills (e.g., *Your Perfect Right* by Alberti and Emmons; *Conversationally Speaking* by Garner). ▼

▼ 29. Learn and implement pain management techniques as an alternative to coping through opioid use. (45, 46)

45. Explore the veteran's/service member's pain level associated with injury and assess his/her pattern of narcotic abuse to cope with pain. ▼

46. Teach or refer veteran/service member to a pain management program to learn alternatives to narcotic use for managing pain (see the chapter on Chronic Pain After Injury in this *Planner*). ▼

▼ 30. Implement relapse prevention strategies for managing possible future situations with high-risk for relapse. (47, 48, 49, 50)

47. Discuss with the veteran/service member the distinction between a lapse and relapse, associating a lapse with an initial, temporary, and reversible use of a substance and relapse with the decision to return to a repeated pattern of abuse. ▼

48. Identify and rehearse with the veteran/service member the management of future situations or circumstances in which lapses could occur.

49. Request that the veteran/service member identify feelings, behaviors, and situations that place him/her at a higher risk for substance abuse (or assign "Relapse Triggers" in the *Adult Psychotherapy Homework Planner*, 2nd ed. by Jongsma).

50. Instruct the veteran/service member to routinely use strategies learned in therapy (e.g., using cognitive restructuring, social skills, and exposure) while building social interactions and relationships (or assign "Aftercare Plan Components" in the *Adult Psychotherapy Homework Planner*, 2nd ed. by Jongsma).

31. Structure time and increase self-esteem by obtaining employment. (51)

51. Refer the veteran/service member to a supported employment program, or coach the veteran/service member on preparing for employment if leaving the military, searching for a job, and maintaining employment (see the chapter on Post-Deployment Reintegration in this *Planner*).

32. Verbalize that there are options to substance use in dealing with stress and in finding pleasure or excitement in life. (52, 53, 54)

52. Teach the veteran/service member the importance of getting pleasure out of life without using mood-altering substances.

53. Assign the veteran/service member in developing a list of pleasurable activities (see *Inventory of Rewarding Activities* by Birchler and Weiss or assign "Identify and Schedule Pleasant Activities" in the *Adult Psychotherapy Homework Planner*, 2nd ed. by

Jongsma); assign engagement in selected activities daily. ▽

54. Encourage the veteran/service member to establish a daily routine of physical exercise to build body stamina, self-esteem, and reduce depression (see *Exercising Your Way to Better Mental Health* by Leith). ▽

▽ 33. Verbalize the results of turning problems over to God each day. (55)

55. Using a Step Three exercise, teach the veteran/service member about the recovery concept of "turning it over;" then assign turning over problems to a higher power each day; ask the veteran/service member to record the event and discuss the results. ▽

▽ 34. Complete a re-administration of objective tests of opioid abuse as a means of assessing treatment outcome. (56)

56. Assess the outcome of treatment by re-administering to the veteran/service member objective tests of opioid dependence; evaluate the results and provide feedback to the veteran/service member. ▽

__. ____________________

__. ____________________

__. ____________________

__. ____________________

__. ____________________

__. ____________________

DIAGNOSTIC SUGGESTIONS

ICD-9-CM	*ICD-10-CM*	*DSM-5* Disorder, Condition, or Problem
304.00	F11.20	Opioid Use Disorder, Moderate or Severe
305.50	F11.10	Opioid Use Disorder, Mild
292.89	F11.22x	Opioid Use Disorder, Moderate or Severe with Opioid Intoxication
292.0	F11.23	Opioid Withdrawal
292.9	F11.89	Unspecified Opioid-Related Disorder
______	______	____________________
______	______	____________________

PANIC / AGORAPHOBIA

BEHAVIORAL DEFINITIONS

1. Complains of unexpected, sudden, debilitating panic symptoms (e.g., shallow breathing, sweating, heart racing or pounding, dizziness, depersonalization or derealization, trembling, chest tightness, fear of dying or losing control, nausea) that have occurred repeatedly resulting in persisting concern about having additional attacks.
2. Demonstrates marked avoidance of activities or environments due to fear of triggering intense panic symptoms, resulting in interference with performance of military duties.
3. Acknowledges a persistence of fear in spite of the recognition that the fear is unreasonable.
4. Acknowledges concern that panic symptoms will put self and others at risk.
5. Increasingly isolated self due to fear of traveling or leaving a "safe environment" such as home or base/post in the deployed environment.
6. Avoids public places or environments with large groups of people such as dining facilities, movies, shopping malls, and large military formations.

—. ____

____

—. ____

____

—. ____

____

LONG-TERM GOALS

1. Reduce the frequency, intensity, and duration of panic attacks.
2. Reduce the fear that panic symptoms will recur without the ability to manage them.
3. Reduce the fear that panic symptoms will endanger self or others.
4. Reduce the fear of triggering panic and eliminate avoidance of activities and environments thought to trigger panic.
5. Increase comfort in freely leaving home and/or base/post and being in a public environment.

__. ______________________________

____

__. ______________________________

____

__. ______________________________

____

SHORT-TERM OBJECTIVES

1. Describe the history and nature of the panic symptoms. (1, 2, 3, 4)

THERAPEUTIC INTERVENTIONS

1. Assess the veteran's/service member's frequency, intensity, duration, and history of panic symptoms, fear, and avoidance.
2. Assess the nature of any stimulus, thoughts, or situations that precipitate the veteran's/service member's panic (or assign "Monitoring My Panic Attack Experiences" in the *Adult Psychotherapy Homework Planner,* 2nd ed. by Jongsma).
3. Assess the impact the panic symptoms have had on the veteran's/service member's occupational and social functioning via standardized measures that allow serial measurement for the purpose of assessing progress (e.g., *OQ-45.2* by Burlingame, Lambert, and Reisinger).

4. Talk with the service member's first line supervisor (e.g., Squad Leader, Platoon Sergeant, First Sergeant) to assess the degree the anxiety symptoms have impacted the service member's job performance.

2. Complete psychological tests designed to assess the depth of agoraphobia and anxiety sensitivity. (5, 6)

5. Administer a fear survey to the veteran/service member to further assess the depth and breadth of agoraphobic responses (e.g., *The Mobility Inventory for Agoraphobia* by Chambless, Caputo, and Gracely).

6. Administer a measure of fear of anxiety symptoms to the veteran/service member to further assess its depth and breadth (e.g., *The Anxiety Sensitivity Index* by Reiss, Peterson, and Gursky).

3. Cooperate with an evaluation by a prescribing practitioner for psychotropic medication. (7, 8, 9)

7. Arrange for an evaluation for a prescription of psychotropic medication(s) to alleviate the veteran's/service member's symptoms.

8. Monitor the veteran/service member for prescription compliance, side effects, and overall effectiveness of the medication; consult with the prescribing practitioner at regular intervals.

9. Provide an update on the service member's condition, potential negative impacts on safety, and any occupational limitations while taking medication to his/her unit leadership.

4. Verbalize an accurate understanding of panic attacks and agoraphobia and their treatment. (10, 11)

10. Discuss with the veteran/service member how panic attacks are "false alarms" of danger, not medically dangerous, not a sign of weakness or craziness but are

common and often lead to unnecessary avoidance, embarrassment, and distress.

11. Assign the veteran/service member to read psycho-educational chapters of books or treatment manuals on panic disorders and agoraphobia (e.g., *Mastery of Your Anxiety and Panic—Workbook* by Barlow and Craske, *Don't Panic: Taking Control of Anxiety Attacks* by Wilson, or *Living with Fear* by Marks).

5. Verbalize an understanding of the rationale for treatment of panic. (12, 13)

12. Discuss how exposure serves as a means to desensitize learned fear, build confidence, and make him/her feel safer by building a new history of success experiences; use the example of how it's important to continue with combat missions after experiencing a personal threat from the enemy.

13. Discuss how changing thought patterns and eliminating cognitive errors decreases fear reactions and minimizes the severity, recurrence, and impact of panic symptoms; use the example of making one's self anxious via self-talk prior to attending a promotion board.

6. Implement calming and coping strategies to reduce overall anxiety and to manage panic symptoms. (14, 15)

14. Teach the veteran/service member progressive muscle relaxation as a daily exercise for general relaxation and train him/her in the use of coping strategies (e.g., staying focused on behavioral goals, muscle relaxation, diaphragmatic breathing, positive self-talk) to manage symptom attacks.

15. Teach the veteran/service member to keep focus on external stimuli and behavioral responsibilities during panic rather than being preoccupied with internal focus on physiological changes; use the example of how focusing on breathing and/or foot placement during running or marching deflects attention fatigue and pain.

7. Practice positive self-talk that builds confidence in the ability to endure anxiety symptoms without serious consequences. (16, 17)

16. Consistently reassure the veteran/service member of no connection between panic symptoms and heart attack, loss of control over behavior, or serious mental illness ("going crazy").

17. Use modeling and behavioral rehearsal to train the veteran/service member in positive self-talk that reassures him/her of the ability to endure anxiety symptoms without serious consequences (or assign "Positive Self-Talk" in the *Adult Psychotherapy Homework Planner*, 2nd ed. by Jongsma).

8. Identify, challenge, and replace biased, fearful self-talk with reality-based, positive self-talk. (18, 19, 20)

18. Explore the veteran's/service member's schema and self-talk that mediate his/her fear response, challenge the biases; assist him/her in replacing the distorted messages with self-talk that does not overestimate the likelihood of catastrophic outcomes nor underestimate the ability to cope with panic symptoms.

19. Explore the service member's beliefs about how his/her panic symptoms will cause the injury or death of himself or others on the battlefield (e.g., being

disabled by panic when under fire); emphasize how the service member is repetitiously trained in combat techniques and how muscle memory takes over during combat scenarios. ▼

20. Assign the veteran/service member a homework exercise in which he/she identifies fearful self-talk and creates reality-based alternatives (or assign "Journal and Replace Self-Defeating Thoughts" in the *Adult Psychotherapy Homework Planner,* 2nd ed. by Jongsma); review and reinforce success, providing corrective feedback for failure (see *10 Simple Solutions to Panic* by Antony and McCabe; *Mastery of Your Anxiety and Panic—Workbook* by Barlow and Craske). ▼

▼ 9. Undergo gradual repeated exposure to feared physical sensations until they are no longer frightening to experience. (21, 22)

21. Teach the veteran/service member a sensation exposure technique in which he/she generates feared physical sensations through exercise (e.g., breathes rapidly until slightly lightheaded, spins in chair briefly until slightly dizzy), then uses coping strategies (e.g., staying focused on behavioral goals, muscle relaxation, diaphragmatic breathing, positive self-talk) to calm himself/herself down; repeat exercise until anxiety wanes (see *10 Simple Solutions to Panic* by Antony and McCabe; *Mastery of Your Anxiety and Panic—Therapist Guide* by Craske and Barlow). ▼

22. Assign the veteran/service member a homework exercise in which he/she does sensation exposures and records (e.g., *Mastery of Your Anxiety and*

Panic—Workbook by Barlow and Craske; *10 Simple Solutions to Panic* by Antony and McCabe); review and reinforce success, providing corrective feedback for failure.

10. Undergo gradual repeated exposure to feared or avoided situations in which a panic attack and its negative consequences are feared. (23, 24, 25)

23. Direct and assist the veteran/service member in construction of a hierarchy of anxiety-producing situations associated with the phobic response; suggestions for the service member may include holding a rifle, riding in a military vehicle, or going on a combat mission where contact with the enemy is probable.

24. Select initial exposures that have a high likelihood of being a successful experience for the veteran/service member; develop a plan for managing the symptoms and rehearse the plan in imagination.

25. Assign the veteran/service member a homework exercise in which he/she does situational exposures and records responses (e.g., "Gradually Reducing Your Phobic Fear" in the *Adult Psychotherapy Homework Planner,* 2nd ed. by Jongsma; *Mastery of Your Anxiety and Panic—Workbook* by Barlow and Craske; *10 Simple Solutions to Panic* by Antony and McCabe); review and reinforce success, providing corrective feedback for failure.

11. Implement relapse prevention strategies for managing possible future anxiety symptoms. (26, 27, 28, 29)

26. Discuss with the veteran/service member the distinction between a lapse and relapse, associating a lapse with an initial and reversible return of symptoms, fear, or urges to avoid and relapse with the

decision to return to fearful and avoidant patterns.

27. Identify and rehearse with the veteran/service member the management of future situations or circumstances in which lapses could occur; review plan for managing lapses.

28. Instruct the veteran/service member to routinely use strategies learned in therapy (e.g., cognitive restructuring, exposure), building them into his/her life as much as possible.

29. Develop a "coping card" on which coping strategies and other important information (e.g., "pace your breathing," "focus on the task at hand," "you can manage it," and "it will go away") are written for the veteran's/service member's later use.

12. Verbalize the costs and benefits of remaining fearful and avoidant. (30)

30. Probe for the presence of secondary gain that reinforces the veteran's/service member's panic symptoms (e.g., not having to go on combat missions, ensure disability benefits aren't denied); discuss the long-term implications of this behavior.

13. Verbalize the separate realities of the irrationally feared object or situation and the emotionally painful experience from the past that has been evoked by the phobic stimulus. (31, 32, 33)

31. Clarify and differentiate between the veteran's/service member's current irrational fear and past emotional pain/trauma; be careful not to minimize or discount real potential future threats.

32. Encourage the veteran's/service member's sharing of feelings associated with past traumas through active listening, positive regard, and questioning.

33. Provide treatment to the veteran/service member for posttraumatic stress disorder if warranted.

14. Commit self to not allowing panic symptoms to take control of life and lead to a consistent avoidance of normal responsibilities. (34)

34. Support the veteran/service member in following through with military duties, family, and social activities rather than escaping or avoiding them to focus on panic.

15. Return for a follow-up session to track progress, reinforce gains, and problem-solve barriers. (35)

35. Schedule a "booster session" for the veteran/service member for one to three months after therapy ends.

16. Develop a plan of care if the service member is scheduled to deploy. (36, 37)

36. Assist the service member in identifying mental health resources at the location where he/she will be deployed.

37. Ensure that the service member has enough medication to get him/her through the deployment transition.

__. ____________________

__. ____________________

__. ____________________

__. ____________________

__. ____________________

__. ____________________

DIAGNOSTIC SUGGESTIONS

ICD-9-CM	*ICD-10-CM*	*DSM-5* Disorder, Condition, or Problem
300.01	F41.0	Panic Disorder
300.21	F40.00	Agoraphobia
300.22	F40.00	Agoraphobia
309.81	F43.10	Posttraumatic Stress Disorder
300.29	F40.xxx	Specific Phobia
______	______	____________________
______	______	____________________

PARENTING PROBLEMS RELATED TO DEPLOYMENT

BEHAVIORAL DEFINITIONS

1. Reports difficulties with parenting alone while partner is deployed.
2. Verbalizes feeling overwhelmed with caretaking responsibilities while partner is deployed.
3. Nondeployed parent reports insufficient income to adequately provide for the family.
4. Reports feelings of inadequacy as a parent.
5. Reports excessive guilt for leaving child due to deployment.
6. Nondeployed parent displays a lack of patience and hostility toward the child.
7. Verbalizes feelings of resentment and anger toward the deployed parent.
8. Nondeployed parent reports a lack of social, military, and community support regarding raising the child.
9. Child demonstrates an increase in oppositional and defiant behavior while the service member is deployed.
10. Child exhibits difficulty in family, academic, and social functioning related to the absence of the deployed parent.
11. Child demonstrates resentment toward either parent.

__. ____

____

__. ____

____

__. ____

____

LONG-TERM GOALS

1. Develop new parenting skills that will facilitate more effective parenting.
2. Obtain a greater sense of adequacy and competency in parenting.

3. Secure adequate financial resources necessary to sustain the family.
4. Resolve guilt issues surrounding leaving the child.
5. Develop family and community resources that can assist with deployment-related parenting challenges.
6. Seek educational and psychological assistance for the oppositional and defiant child.

—. ____
____

—. ____
____

—. ____
____

SHORT-TERM OBJECTIVES

1. Describe the status of the current parenting situation including the specific impact of the service member's deployment on the family. (1, 2, 3)
2. Identify major parenting problems and work toward their solution. (4, 5, 6, 7)

THERAPEUTIC INTERVENTIONS

1. Complete a comprehensive evaluation, taking into consideration the extent of the current problems and how things have changed in the family since the deployment; talk with both the nondeployed parent and the service member, if possible.
2. Ask the nondeployed parent to talk with other "stay behind" parents about how deployment has impacted their parenting abilities and family.
3. Ask the nondeployed parent to describe his/her expectations about being a "single" parent prior to the service member deploying.
4. Assign the nondeployed parent to create a list of parenting problems he/she is dealing with; rank them in order from most to least distressing.
5. Assist the nondeployed parent in identifying a problem with a moderate level of distress.

6. Assist the nondeployed parent in brainstorming possible solutions, deciding on a plan of action, and implementing a solution; monitor progress and make adjustments as necessary.
7. Reinforce successes and encourage the nondeployed parent to continue solving problems on his/her problem list.

3. Determine source of financial problems and develop a plan for meeting financial needs. (8, 9)

8. Assign the nondeployed parent and the service member to create a comprehensive list of expenditures and assets; make distinction between necessities and luxuries.
9. Encourage the nondeployed parent to meet with a military financial counselor on his/her local base/post.

4. Express feelings of inadequacy, helplessness, and frustration related to parenting. (10, 11)

10. Create a therapeutic environment that is conducive to open and honest expression of the nondeployed parent's feelings.
11. Normalize the nondeployed parent's feelings by drawing parallels to other clients' experiences and educating him/her on the normal and expected challenges of parenting.

5. Express feelings of resentment toward deployed parent. (12, 13, 14)

12. Encourage the nondeployed parent to acknowledge his/her resentment toward the service member; process the emotions.
13. Assist the nondeployed parent in identifying reasons for the resentment (e.g., feelings of loneliness, inadequacy, and helplessness).
14. Encourage the nondeployed parent to communicate his/her resentment to the service member in a nonthreatening and nonblaming manner; role-play the discussion with the

nondeployed parent prior to the actual conversation.

6. Verbalize an understanding of the impact deployment has on a child. (15, 16)

15. Assign the nondeployed parent to assist the child in discussing his/her feelings about the other parent being deployed.

16. Assign the nondeployed parent and the service member to read *Off to War: Voices of Soldiers' Children* by Ellis.

7. Acknowledge feelings of personal guilt related to leaving the child due to deployment. (17, 18)

17. If communication channels with the service member exist (e.g., email, telephone, webcam), assist the service member in communicating his/her guilt feelings about leaving; process the feelings.

18. Encourage the service member to speak with a behavioral health professional and/or chaplain in the deployed setting regarding his/her feelings.

8. Ask the deployed parent to take a more active role in parenting while deployed. (19)

19. Encourage the nondeployed parent to talk with the service member regarding taking a more active role in parenting while deployed (e.g., make joint decisions regarding major parenting issues, increase parental guidance during routine phone conversations); reaffirm that the service member must support the nondeployed parent in his/her decisions.

9. Verbalize an understanding of child development, particularly the impact of parental separation on the child. (20)

20. Assign the client to read *Ages and Stages: A Parent's Guide to Normal Childhood Development* by Schaefer and DiGeronimo.

10. Learn proven parenting techniques. (21, 22)

21. Assist the nondeployed parent in learning parenting techniques such as positive and negative reinforcement, natural and logical consequences, setting clear boundaries, consistently administering and following through with consequences, and "time out."

22. Ask the nondeployed parent and the service member to read and utilize parenting training manuals (e.g., *The Parent's Handbook: Systematic Training for Effective Parenting* by Dinkmeyer, McKay, and Dinkmeyer).

11. Implement proven techniques daily. (23)

23. Assign the nondeployed parent to implement parenting techniques and record progress (or assign "Using Reinforcement Principles in Parenting" in the *Adult Psychotherapy Homework Planner*, 2nd ed. by Jongsma); provide constructive feedback during session.

12. Identify and utilize community supports that can assist with parenting responsibilities. (24)

24. Assist the nondeployed parent in identifying community resources on and off post/base (church, family resource center, Big Brothers/Big Sisters) that can assist with parenting responsibilities and care of the child); reinforce the parent when he/she asks for help.

13. Identify and utilize family and friends that can assist with parenting responsibilities. (25)

25. Assist the nondeployed parent in identifying family members and friends that can assist with babysitting, shopping, etc.; reinforce the parent when he/she asks for help.

14. Coordinate psychological services for the child. (26, 27)

26. Make an appointment with a child psychologist or other behavioral health professional trained in treating childhood behavior problems.

27. Reinforce the parent for attending family sessions when appropriate.

15. Meet with the child's teacher(s) to discuss the current situation with the child. (28)

28. Ask the parent to make an appointment with the child's teacher(s) to provide background information about the child's problem and ask the teacher(s) to keep him/her updated regarding progress and the child's behavior.

16. Develop personal stress relief activities/behaviors.(29)

29. Encourage the nondeployed parent to engage in activities that he or she enjoys and that relieve stress (e.g., exercising, going to the movies, meeting friends for coffee).

17. Verbalize a sense of increased abilities, effectiveness, and confidence in parenting. (30, 31, 32)

30. Provide ongoing support and encouragement to the parent regarding implementing and following through with new parenting strategies and providing corrective feedback as needed.

31. Schedule "booster" sessions for the nondeployed parent while the service member is deployed.

32. Schedule a family session after the service member returns from deployment in order to discuss re-deployment parenting issues such as the need to parent as a team (or assign "Parenting as a Team" in the *Adult Psychotherapy Homework Planner*, 2nd ed. by Jongsma).

__. ________________________

__. ________________________

__. ________________________

__. ________________________

__. ________________________

__. ________________________

DIAGNOSTIC SUGGESTIONS

ICD-9-CM	*ICD-10-CM*	*DSM-5* Disorder, Condition, or Problem
V61.20	Z62.820	Parent-Child Relational Problem
309.24	F43.22	Adjustment Disorder, With Anxiety
309.28	F43.23	Adjustment Disorder, With Mixed Anxiety and Depressed Mood
V61.10	Z63.0	Relationship Distress with Spouse or Intimate Partner
______	______	________________
______	______	________________

PERFORMANCE-ENHANCING SUPPLEMENT USE

BEHAVIORAL DEFINITIONS

1. Demonstrates a pattern of performance-enhancing supplement use leading to clinically significant impairment.
2. Reports continued use of performance-enhancing supplements despite negative health, social, and occupational consequences.
3. Exhibits increased agitation, anger, and aggression subsequent to performance-enhancing supplement use.
4. Reports the emergence of anxiety, depressive, and/or psychotic symptoms subsequent to performance-enhancing supplement use.
5. Reports failing a random urinalysis conducted by his/her unit.

—. ____
____

—. ____
____

—. ____
____

LONG-TERM GOALS

1. Refrain from use of all over-the-counter and illegally obtained performance-enhancement supplements.
2. Return to previous level of physical and emotional health.
3. Increase physical stamina and performance through non-supplement use.

—. ____

____

—. ____

____

—. ____

____

SHORT-TERM OBJECTIVES

1. Describe the history and details of the performance-enhancement supplement use. (1, 2)
2. Cooperate with a medical and psychiatric evaluation. (3)
3. Follow through with any medical recommendations and advice. (4)
4. Verbalize an understanding of the negative health consequences that performance-enhancing supplements can cause. (5, 6)

THERAPEUTIC INTERVENTIONS

1. Assess the nature of the supplement use including duration, frequency, impact on current functioning, and type of performance-enhancement supplements used (e.g., anabolic steroids, creatine, ephedra).
2. Assess the veteran's/service member's views about performance-enhancement supplements (e.g., they carry no health risks, all athletes use them).
3. Refer the veteran/service member to a military or Veterans Affairs medical and/or psychiatric practitioner to evaluate for any negative physical and emotional health consequences associated with performance-enhancement supplement use.
4. Monitor the veteran's/service member's compliance with medical, psychiatric, and/or dietary recommendations.
5. Educate the veteran/service member on the potential negative health consequences of performance-enhancing supplements.

6. Assign the veteran/service member to research the effects of performance-enhancement supplements online through reputable Internet sources (e.g., WebMD, National Institutes of Health).

5. Dispose of all performance-enhancing supplements. (7)

7. Assign the veteran/service member to dispose of all performance-enhancement supplements; discourage him/her from giving them to a friend.

6. Describe in detail the reasons for taking performance-enhancing supplements. (8, 9, 10)

8. Assign the veteran/service member to create a list of reasons why he/she used performance-enhancement supplements; process the list in session.

9. Assist the veteran/service member in identifying temporary positive feelings that performance-enhancement supplement use created.

10. Explore with the veteran/service member where he/she learned about performance-enhancement supplement use (e.g., another service member, friend, or family member); process relevant material.

7. Verbalize an understanding that many people use performance-enhancing supplements to overcome perceived weaknesses. (11, 12, 13)

11. Educate the veteran/service member about the pervasive view in the military and civilian world that strength, power, and beauty should be obtained at any cost.

12. Assign the veteran/service member to create a list of his/her strengths; process list in session.

13. Assist the veteran/service member in countering his/her perceived weaknesses by assigning environmental

experiments (e.g., ask friends, superiors, fellow service members if they view the veteran/service member as having particular weaknesses).

8. Disclose perceived flaws in physical stamina, strength, and abilities. (13, 14, 15)

13. Assist the veteran/service member in countering his/her perceived weaknesses by assigning environmental experiments (e.g., ask friends, superiors, fellow service member if they view the veteran/service member as having particular weaknesses).
14. Assign the veteran/service member to create a list of his/her perceived flaws in stamina, strength, and abilities; process list in session.
15. Explore origins of these perceived flaws (e.g., family, criticism by superiors) and what factors maintain these perceptions (e.g., maladaptive thoughts, critical superior).

9. Express feelings of inadequacy and insecurity related to perceived physical limitations. (16, 17, 18)

16. Create a therapeutic environment that is conducive to open and honest expression of the veteran's/service member's feelings of inadequacy and insecurity; process feelings in session.
17. Challenge the veteran's/service member's feelings of inadequacy and insecurity by creating adaptive cognitions to replace maladaptive ones (or assign "Journal and Replace Self-Defeating Thoughts" in the *Adult Psychotherapy Homework Planner*, 2nd ed. by Jongsma).
18. Assist the veteran/service member in identifying evidence

that does not support his/her views of inadequacy (e.g., scored a perfect score at the shooting range, finished in top 10 percent on physical fitness test).

10. Acknowledge connection between peer pressure and performance-enhancing supplement use. (19, 20, 21)

19. Educate the veteran/service member on the significant influence peer pressure can have on behavior.

20. Assign the veteran/service member to list times in his/her life that peer pressure influenced him/her.

21. Assist the veteran/service member in developing methods to combat peer pressure (e.g., create a new social network, learn to anticipate peer pressure before it happens).

11. Increase physical exercise as a means to naturally enhance stamina and strength. (22)

22. Assign the veteran/service member to engage in physical activity at least five days per week that focuses on aerobic and anaerobic fitness.

12. Discuss treatment plan and goals related to remaining abstinent from performance-enhancing supplements. (23, 24)

23. Encourage the service member to discuss his/her goals for treatment with his/her chain of command

24. Encourage the service member to keep his/her chain of command updated on progress; ask for assistance in remaining abstinent from performance-enhancement supplements if needed.

13. Pass a random urinalysis. (25)

25. Arrange for the veteran/service member to submit to random urine testing for the presence of supplements; acknowledge and reinforce the veteran's/service member's passing of a random urinalysis.

__. ____________________ __. ____________________

__. ____________________ __. ____________________

__. ____________________ __. ____________________

DIAGNOSTIC SUGGESTIONS

ICD-9-CM	*ICD-10-CM*	*DSM-5* Disorder, Condition, or Problem
305.90	F19.10	Other (or Unknown) Substance Use Disorder, Mild
292.89	F19.229	Other (or Unknown) Substance Use Disorder, Moderate or Severe with Other (or Unknown) Substance Intoxication
292.1	F19.259	Other (or Unknown) Substance Use Disorder, Moderate or Severe with Other (or Unknown) Substance-Induced Psychotic Disorder
292.84	F19.24	Other (or Unknown) Substance Use Disorder, Moderate or Severe with Other (or Unknown) Substance-Induced Depressive Disorder
292.89	F19.280	Other (or Unknown) Substance Use Disorder, Moderate or Severe with Other (or Unknown) Substance-Induced Anxiety Disorder
292.9	F19.99	Unspecified Other (or Unknown) Substance-Related Disorder
300.7	F45.22	Body Dysmorphic Disorder

PHOBIA

BEHAVIORAL DEFINITIONS

1. Describes a persistent and unreasonable fear of a specific object or situation often found or encountered in the military that promotes avoidance behaviors because an encounter with the phobic stimulus provokes an immediate anxiety response.
2. Avoids the phobic stimulus/feared environment or endures it with distress, resulting in interference of military duties and/or social functioning.
3. Avoids specific phobias that may be specific to or required for military service (e.g., use of gas mask, fear of flying, fear of being submerged under water).
4. Acknowledges a persistence of fear despite recognition that the fear is unreasonable.
5. Develops negative feelings about self due to inability to overcome fear and pressure from superiors and fellow service members.
6. Demonstrates no evidence of a panic disorder.

__. ____

____

__. ____

____

__. ____

____

Most of the content of this chapter (with only slight revisions) originates from A. E. Jongsma, Jr., L. M. Peterson, and T. J. Bruce, *The Complete Adult Psychotherapy Treatment Planner,* 4th ed. (Hoboken, NJ: John Wiley & Sons, 2006).

LONG-TERM GOALS

1. Reduce fear of the specific stimulus object or situation that previously provoked phobic anxiety.
2. Reduce phobic avoidance of the specific object or situation, leading to comfort and independence in moving around in the environment.
3. Eliminate negative feelings about self caused by difficulty in overcoming feared object/situation.
4. Eliminate interference in military duties and remove distress from feared object or situation.

—. ____

____

—. ____

____

—. ____

____

SHORT-TERM OBJECTIVES

1. Describe the history and nature of the phobia(s), complete with impact on functioning and attempt to overcome it. (1, 2, 3, 4)

THERAPEUTIC INTERVENTIONS

1. Explore and identify the objects or situations that precipitate the veteran/service member's phobic fear; keep in mind that phobias most commonly seen in military personnel that are related to military service are fear of enclosed spaces, flying, and restricted breathing/suffocation.
2. Assess the client's fear and avoidance, including the focus of fear, types of avoidance (e.g., distraction, escape, dependence on others), development, and disability.
3. Assess the impact the phobic symptoms have had on the veteran's/service member's occupational and social functioning via standardized measures that allow serial measurement for the purpose of

assessing progress (e.g., *OQ-45.2* by Burlingame, Lambert, and Reisinger).

4. Talk with the service member's first line supervisor (e.g., Squad Leader, Platoon Sergeant, First Sergeant) to assess the degree that the phobic symptoms have impacted the service member's job performance.

2. Complete psychological tests designed to assess features of the phobia. (5)

5. Administer a self-report measure to the veteran/service member (e.g., from *Measures for Specific Phobia* by Antony) to further assess the depth and breadth of phobic responses.

EB 3. Cooperate with an evaluation by a prescribing practitioner for psychotropic medication. (6, 7, 8)

6. Arrange for an evaluation for a prescription of psychotropic medication(s) if the veteran/service member requests it, if he/she is likely to be noncompliant with gradual exposure, or if occupational and social functioning is seriously impaired. EB

7. Monitor the veteran/service member for prescription compliance, side effects, and overall effectiveness of the medication; consult with the prescribing practitioner at regular intervals. EB

8. Provide an update to the service member's unit leadership on his/her condition, potential negative impacts on safety, and any occupational limitations while taking medication. EB

EB 4. Verbalize an accurate understanding of information about phobias and their treatment. (9, 10, 11)

9. Discuss with the veteran/service member how phobias are very common, a natural but irrational expression of our fight or flight response, are not a sign of weakness, but cause unnecessary

distress, embarrassment, and disability.

10. Discuss with the veteran/service member how phobic fear is maintained by a "phobic cycle" of unwarranted fear and avoidance that precludes positive, corrective experiences with the feared object or situation, and how treatment breaks the cycle by encouraging these experiences (see *Mastery of Your Specific Phobia—Therapist Guide* by Craske, Antony, and Barlow; or *Specific Phobias* by Bruce and Sanderson).

11. Assign the veteran/service member to read psycho-educational chapters of books or treatment manuals on specific phobias (e.g., *Mastery of Your Specific Phobia—Client Manual* by Antony, Craske, and Barlow; *The Anxiety and Phobia Workbook* by Bourne; *Living with Fear* by Marks).

5. Verbalize an understanding of the cognitive, physiological, and behavioral components of anxiety and its treatment. (12, 13, 14)

12. Discuss with the veteran/service member how phobias involve perceiving unrealistic threats, bodily expressions of fear, and avoidance of what is threatening that interact to maintain the problem (see *Mastery of Your Specific Phobia—Therapist Guide* by Craske, Antony, and Barlow; or *Specific Phobias* by Bruce and Sanderson); use the example of how someone with a fear of needles may react during the initial inoculation process in basic training.

13. Discuss with the veteran/service member how changing thought patterns and eliminating cognitive errors decreases phobic

reactions and minimizes the severity, recurrence, and impact of anxiety symptoms. ▽

14. Discuss with the veteran/service member how exposure serves as a means to desensitize learned fear, build confidence, and make them feel safer by building a new history of success experiences (see *Mastery of Your Specific Phobia—Therapist Guide* by Craske, Antony, and Barlow; or *Specific Phobias* by Bruce and Sanderson); use the example of how superiors make subordinates practice in front of mock promotion boards before attending the actual board. ▽

▽ 6. Learn and implement calming skills and coping strategies to reduce and manage anxiety symptoms. (15, 16, 17, 18)

15. Teach the veteran/service member anxiety management skills (e.g., staying focused on behavioral goals, muscle relaxation, diaphragmatic breathing, positive self-talk) to address anxiety symptoms that may emerge during encounters with phobic objects or situations. ▽

16. Teach the veteran/service member to keep focus on external stimuli and behavioral responsibilities during phobic reaction rather than being preoccupied with internal focus on physiological changes; use the example of how focusing on breathing and/or foot placement during running or marching deflects attention fatigue and pain. ▽

17. Assign the veteran/service member a homework exercise in which he/she practices daily calming skills; review and reinforce success, providing corrective feedback for failure. ▽

18. Use biofeedback techniques to facilitate the veteran/service member's success at learning calming skills. ▼

▼ 7. Learn and implement applied tension skills. (19, 20)

19. Teach the veteran/service member applied tension in which he/she tenses neck and upper torso muscles to curtail blood flow out of the brain to help prevent fainting during encounters with phobic objects or situations involving blood, injection, or injury (see "Applied Tension, Exposure *In Vivo*, and Tension-only in the Treatment of Blood Phobia" in *Behaviour Research and Therapy* by Ost, Fellenius, and Sterner). ▼

20. Assign the veteran/service member a homework exercise in which he/she practices daily applied tension skills; review and reinforce success, providing corrective feedback for failure. ▼

▼ 8. Identify, challenge, and replace biased, fearful self-talk with positive, realistic, and empowering self-talk. (21, 22, 23)

21. Explore the veteran's/service member's schema and self-talk that mediate his/her fear response; challenge the biases; assist him/her in replacing the distorted messages with reality-based, positive self-talk. ▼

22. Assign the veteran/service member a homework exercise in which he/she identifies fearful self-talk and creates reality-based alternatives (or assign "Journal and Replace Self-Defeating Thoughts" in the *Adult Psychotherapy Homework Planner,* 2nd ed. by Jongsma); review and reinforce success, providing corrective feedback for failure. ▼

23. Use behavioral techniques (e.g., modeling, corrective feedback,

imaginal rehearsal, social reinforcement) to train the veteran/service member in positive self-talk that prepares him/her to endure anxiety symptoms without serious consequences (or assign "Positive Self-Talk" in the *Adult Psychotherapy Homework Planner,* 2nd ed. by Jongsma). ▽

▽ 9. Undergo repeated exposure to feared or avoided phobic objects or situations. (24, 25, 26)

24. Direct and assist the veteran/service member in construction of a hierarchy of anxiety-producing situations associated with the phobic response; suggestions for the service member may include wearing the gas mask without the hood or wearing it for only a few seconds at a time and gradually increase time worn or sit in a helicopter while it's running, but not take off. ▽

25. Select initial exposures that have a high likelihood of being a successful experience for the veteran/service member; develop a plan for managing the symptoms and rehearse the plan. ▽

26. Assign the veteran/service member a homework exercise in which he/she does situational exposures and records responses (see "Gradually Reducing Your Phobic Fear" in *Adult Psychotherapy Homework Planner,* 2nd ed. by Jongsma; *Mastery of Your Specific Phobia—Client Manual* by Antony, Craske, and Barlow; *Living with Fear* by Marks); review and reinforce success or provide corrective feedback toward improvement. ▽

▽ 10. Implement relapse prevention strategies for managing possible future anxiety symptoms. (27, 28, 29, 30)

27. Discuss with the veteran/service member the distinction between a lapse and relapse, associating a lapse with a temporary and

reversible return of symptoms, fear, or urges to avoid and relapse with the decision to return to fearful and avoidant patterns.

28. Identify and rehearse with the veteran/service member the management of future situations or circumstances in which lapses could occur; review plan for managing lapses.

29. Instruct the veteran/service member to routinely use strategies learned in therapy (e.g., cognitive restructuring, exposure), building them into his/her life as much as possible.

30. Develop a "coping card" on which coping strategies and other important information (e.g., "you're safe," "pace your breathing," "focus on the task at hand," "you can manage it," "stay in the situation," and "let the anxiety pass") are written for the veteran's/service member's later use.

11. Verbalize the costs and benefits of remaining fearful and avoidant. (31)

31. Probe for the presence of secondary gain that reinforces the veteran's/service member's phobic actions through escape or avoidance mechanisms (e.g., not having to go on combat missions, ensure disability benefits aren't denied); discuss the long-term implications of this behavior.

12. Verbalize the separate realities of the irrationally feared object or situation and the emotionally painful experience from the past that has been evoked by the phobic stimulus. (32, 33)

32. Clarify and differentiate between the veteran's/service member's current irrational fear and past emotional pain/trauma; be careful not to minimize or discount real potential future threats.

33. Encourage the veteran's/service member's sharing of feelings

associated with past traumas through active listening, positive regard, and questioning.

13. Commit self to not allowing phobic fear to take control of life and lead to a consistent avoidance of normal responsibilities and activities. (34, 35)

34. Support the veteran/service member in following through with military duties, family, and social activities rather than escaping or avoiding them.

35. Ask the veteran/service member to list several ways his/her life will be more satisfying or fulfilling (e.g., getting promoted, going back to work) as he/she manages his/her symptoms of anxiety and continues normal responsibilities.

14. Return for a follow-up session to track progress, reinforce gains, and problem-solve barriers. (36)

36. Schedule a "booster session" for the veteran/service member for one to three months after therapy ends.

15. Develop a plan of care if the service member is scheduled to deploy. (37, 38)

37. Assist the service member in identifying mental health resources at the location where he/she will be deployed.

38. Ensure that the service member has enough medication to get him/her through the deployment transition.

—. ____________________

—. ____________________

—. ____________________

—. ____________________

—. ____________________

—. ____________________

DIAGNOSTIC SUGGESTIONS

ICD-9-CM	*ICD-10-CM*	*DSM-5* Disorder, Condition, or Problem
300.29	F40.xxx	Specific Phobia

PHYSIOLOGICAL STRESS RESPONSE–ACUTE

BEHAVIORAL DEFINITIONS

1. Complains of excessive physiological arousal with or without the presence of an identified trigger.
2. Complains of an excessive startle response.
3. Reports an increase in agitation and irritability.
4. Complains of difficulty initiating and/or maintaining sleep.
5. Reports sensory sensitivity accompanied by exaggerated behaviors intended to detect threats.
6. Reports a constant monitoring/scanning of the environment to detect a threat.
7. Reports difficulty concentrating.
8. Complains of exhaustion after periods of arousal.
9. Reports medical problems related to chronic stress.

__. ____

____

__. ____

____

__. ____

____

LONG-TERM GOALS

1. Decrease hypervigilance and hyperarousal to levels that are manageable.
2. Eliminate agitation, irritability, and sleep disturbances.
3. Eliminate excessive scanning and monitoring of nonthreatening environments.
4. Prevent development of posttraumatic stress disorder.
5. Improve physical health.

__. ____
____

__. ____
____

__. ____
____

SHORT-TERM OBJECTIVES

1. Describe in detail the history and nature of the hyperarousal symptoms. (1, 2)

2. Complete psychological testing. (3, 4)

3. Cooperate with a psychiatric evaluation to assess the need for psychotropic medication. (5, 6, 7)

THERAPEUTIC INTERVENTIONS

1. Assess the veteran's/service member's type, intensity, and frequency of hyperarousal symptoms and the impact on his/her social, occupational, and interpersonal functioning.
2. Talk with the service member's first line supervisor (e.g., Squad Leader, Platoon Sergeant, First Sergeant) to assess the degree the hyperarousal symptoms have impacted the service member's job performance.
3. Administer self-report measures to assist with differential diagnosis (e.g., MMPI-2, PTSD Checklist-Military Version).
4. Provide feedback to the veteran/service member regarding his/her testing results.
5. Arrange for an evaluation for a prescription of psychotropic medication(s) if the veteran/service member requests it, if he/she is likely to be noncompliant with psychotherapy, or if occupational and social functioning is seriously impaired.
6. Monitor the veteran/service member for prescription compliance, side effects, and overall effectiveness of the medication;

consult with the prescribing practitioner at regular intervals.

7. Provide an update to the service member's unit leadership on his/her condition, potential negative impacts on safety, and any occupational limitations while taking medication.

4. Cooperate with a medical evaluation to assess current level of physical health. (8)

8. Encourage the veteran/service member to see a physician in order to assess for any negative impact that stress has had on the veteran's/service member's physical health (e.g., high blood pressure, consistent heart arrhythmias).

5. Describe in detail any substance use history, particularly related to self-medicating increased physiological arousal. (9)

9. Assess the veteran's/service member's pattern of substance use, paying particular attention to maladaptive patterns of use.

6. Participate in substance abuse/dependence treatment as indicated. (10, 11)

10. Refer the veteran/service member to chemical dependency treatment if appropriate.

11. Encourage the veteran/service member to attend a 12-step program (e.g., Alcoholics Anonymous) at least three times a week for three months.

7. Describe any trauma incident related to the onset of the hypervigilance. (12)

12. Sensitively explore the trauma that the veteran/service member has experienced, allowing him/her to relate as much detail as he/she is comfortable with initially (or assign "Describe the Trauma" or "Share the Painful Memory" in the *Adult Psychotherapy Homework Planner*, 2nd ed. by Jongsma).

8. Verbalize an understanding of the typical reaction when exposed to a traumatic stressor. (13, 14)

13. Educate the veteran/service member about common reactions after exposure to a traumatic event (e.g., increased startle response, insomnia, nightmares, mood changes).

14. Normalize the veteran's/service member's experience and symptoms; encourage the veteran/service member to seek a higher level of care if symptoms do not remit or cause clinically significant distress in functioning.

9. Verbalize an understanding that cognitions contribute to the maintenance of fear, hypervigilance, and hyperarousal. (15)

15. Explain to the veteran/service member the concept of how thoughts impact our feelings and behavior, particularly in maintaining fear and threat assessment; use an example from the veteran's/service member's everyday life.

10. Identify, challenge, and replace negative and self-defeating thoughts that contribute to the increased levels of arousal. (16, 17, 18)

16. Assist the veteran/service member in developing an awareness of his/her automatic thoughts that are consistent with maintaining the view that the world is a hostile and dangerous place.

17. Assign the veteran/service member to keep a daily log of automatic thoughts associated with themes of threat and vulnerability (e.g., "Negative Thoughts Trigger Negative Feelings" in the *Adult Psychotherapy Homework Planner*, 2nd ed. by Jongsma); process the journal material to challenge distorted thinking patterns with reality-based thoughts.

18. Reinforce the veteran's/service member's positive cognitions that foster a sense of safety and security and decrease hyperarousal and hypervigilance (see "Positive Self-Talk" in the *Adult Psychotherapy Homework Planner*, 2nd ed. by Jongsma).

11. Implement deep breathing techniques. (19)

19. Teach the veteran/service member diaphragmatic breathing; assign the veteran/

service member to practice twice a day for 10 minutes each time, for at least one week.

12. Implement progressive muscle relaxation. (20)

20. Teach the veteran/service member progressive muscle relaxation; assign the veteran/service member to practice twice a day for 15 minutes each time, for at least one week.

13. Participate in imaginal exposure therapy as a method of decreasing physiological arousal. (21, 22, 23)

21. Assist the service member in constructing a hierarchy of memories/events that create significant levels of physiological arousal when visualized; create a range from little arousal to intense arousal.

22. Select and implement an initial exposure that will allow the greatest chances for the veteran's/service member's success (e.g., moderately arousing); instruct the veteran/service member to utilize previously learned breathing and relaxation exercises to counter anxiety and arousal level.

23. Assign the veteran/service member a homework exercise that allows him/her to practice imaginal exposure between sessions; review progress weekly (or assign "Gradually Reducing Your Phobic Fear" in the *Adult Psychotherapy Homework Planner*, 2nd ed. by Jongsma).

14. Implement and practice sleep hygiene techniques to combat sleep difficulties. (24, 25, 26)

24. Educate the veteran/service member about how increased levels of arousal promote insomnia.

25. Instruct the veteran/service member on behavioral practices conducive to good sleep, which include not using caffeine four hours before going to bed and removing cues to time that may promote "clock watching" (see

the chapter on Insomnia in this *Planner*).

26. Assign the veteran/service member the "Sleep Pattern Record" exercise in the *Adult Psychotherapy Homework Planner*, 2nd ed. by Jongsma.

15. Verbalize an understanding that coexisting disorders/conditions (e.g., panic, pain) may contribute to hyperarousal. (27)

27. Educate the veteran/service member on how other conditions can make an individual more sensitive and aware of arousal levels, which can lead to greater distress.

16. Participate with treatment for panic symptoms. (28)

28. Provide treatment for panic symptoms if appropriate (see the chapter on Panic/Agoraphobia in this *Planner*).

17. Participate with treatment for pain. (29)

29. Provide treatment for pain symptoms if appropriate (see the chapter on Chronic Pain After Injury in this *Planner*).

—. ______________________________

—. ______________________________

—. ______________________________

—. ______________________________

—. ______________________________

—. ______________________________

DIAGNOSTIC SUGGESTIONS

ICD-9-CM	*ICD-10-CM*	*DSM-5* Disorder, Condition, or Problem
300.00	F41.9	Unspecified Anxiety Disorder
309.81	F43.10	Posttraumatic Stress Disorder
308.3	F43.0	Acute Stress Disorder
300.6	F48.1	Depersonalization/Derealization Disorder
300.15	F44.89	Other Specified Dissociative Disorder
300.15	F44.9	Unspecified Dissociative Disorder
305.00	F10.10	Alcohol Use Disorder, Mild
303.90	F10.20	Alcohol Use Disorder, Moderate or Severe
______	______	______________________
______	______	______________________

POST-DEPLOYMENT REINTEGRATION PROBLEMS

BEHAVIORAL DEFINITIONS

1. Complains of difficulty adjusting to being home after deployment.
2. Reports feeling overwhelmed with family, social, and occupational responsibilities.
3. Experiences increased conflict with significant other.
4. Complains of feeling disconnected from family and friends.
5. Displays an increase in anger, irritability, and aggressiveness toward family, friends, and strangers.
6. Reports conflicted feelings about being home and a desire to return to the deployed setting.
7. Expresses feeling increased financial strain.
8. Complains of significant sleep and mood disturbances.

__. ____

____

__. ____

____

__. ____

____

LONG-TERM GOALS

1. Acclimate to the return to home, friends, family, and community from deployment.
2. Reestablish and strengthen connections with significant other and children.
3. Return to previous level of social and occupational functioning prior to deployment.

4. Eliminate or minimize the impact of post-deployment sleep and mood changes.
5. Begin preparation for next deployment, change of duty station, or career change.

__. ______________________________

__. ______________________________

__. ______________________________

SHORT-TERM OBJECTIVES

1. Describe in detail the nature of the post-deployment problems. (1, 2)

2. Attend recommended and required post-deployment reintegration briefings and activities. (3, 4, 5)

THERAPEUTIC INTERVENTIONS

1. Establish a therapeutic relationship with the service member that conveys an attitude of understanding and recognition of the challenges service members deal with after deployment.
2. Assess the service member's type, intensity, and frequency of post-deployment concerns and the impact on social, occupational, and interpersonal functioning.
3. Encourage the service member to attend required unit post-deployment briefings and evaluations (e.g., Chaplain's brief, combat stress control/ mental health brief, post-deployment health assessment); process his/her reactions to these briefings.
4. Assist the service member in maintaining a positive attitude about required briefings and evaluations by explaining that the briefings and evaluations are

provided to assist with post-deployment reintegration by preventing social and emotional problems and increasing life satisfaction.

5. Explain to the service member the importance of answering thoughtfully and honestly during post-deployment evaluations (e.g., helps identify current and potential problems, documents service connected problems/disabilities).

3. Ease back into previous life in a slow and thoughtful manner. (6, 7)

6. Encourage the service member to take his/her time with regard to becoming reacquainted with his/her predeployment life; discuss the implications of moving too fast (e.g., burning self out, alienating others).

7. Assist the service member in creating a "to do list" that prioritizes needs based on importance and difficulty; encourage the service member to handle issues with greater chances of success and ease in order to build confidence.

4. Assume household responsibilities slowly while being respectful and understanding of significant other's needs. (8, 9, 10)

8. Explain to the service member the importance of not moving too fast and being aware of his/her significant other's feelings when reassuming household responsibilities such as paying bills and being the primary disciplinarian with the children.

9. Discuss with the service member how abrupt disruption and change can worsen things in a family with pre-existing high levels of stress.

10. Invite the service member's significant other for a couples'

session; create a household responsibilities agreement between the couple that describes individual and joint duties.

5. Set time and access limits with friends and family. (11)

11. Instruct the service member to set limits with his/her extended family and friends (e.g., limit time and access) as a means to focus on immediate family.

6. Refrain or limit drinking for the first six months after returning from deployment. (12, 13)

12. Educate the service member on how alcohol can worsen personal and family stress by increasing problems and decreasing coping abilities.

13. Refer the service member for a substance abuse evaluation if deemed necessary; review results and reinforce recommendations made by substance abuse treatment professional.

7. Verbalize an understanding that his/her significant other has changed since the service member has been gone on deployment. (10, 14, 15)

10. Invite the service member's significant other for a couples' session; create a household responsibilities agreement between the couple describing individual and joint duties.

14. Explain to the service member that his/her partner may have developed a greater sense of independence as a result of taking on more responsibilities and new roles while the service member was deployed; process any fears or anxieties related to this realization.

15. Instruct the service member to discuss with his/her significant other ways in which his/her significant other has changed/ grown during the service member's absence (or assign "How Can We Meet Each Other's Needs and Desires?" or

"Positive and Negative Contributions to the Relationship: Mine and Yours" in the *Adult Psychotherapy Homework Planner*, 2nd ed. by Jongsma).

8. Verbalize an understanding that the children have changed/matured. (16, 17, 18)

16. Assist the service member in creating a comparison list of where his/her children were developmentally when he/she left and where they are now.

17. Assign the service member to read material on child development (e.g., *Ages and Stages: A Parent's Guide to Normal Childhood Development* by Schaefer and DiGeronimo, and/or *Your Child's Growing Mind: Brain Development and Learning from Birth to Adolescence* by Healy); process readings and answer any questions the service member may have.

18. Assign the service member to read material on effective childrearing techniques (e.g., *The Parent's Handbook: Systematic Training for Effective Parenting* by Dinkmeyer, McKay, and Dinkmeyer, or *Parenting with Love and Logic* by Cline and Fay) if he/she is having difficulty managing behavioral problems with his/her children.

9. Verbalize an understanding that the parenting style of the service member's significant other may have changed while the service member was deployed. (19, 20)

19. Explain to the service member that a parent may change parenting styles (e.g., indulgent to authoritarian) due to being the only parent while the service member is deployed or to meet the developmental needs of the children.

20. Encourage the service member to be flexible with parenting styles

and negotiate parenting roles and responsibilities in the family (or assign "Learning to Parent as a Team" in the *Adult Psychotherapy Homework Planner*, 2nd ed. by Jongsma); conduct a couples' session if necessary.

10. Identify financial hardships related to returning home from deployment. (21, 22, 23)

21. Have the service member compare net income while deployed versus current net income; list expenses that will have to be cut to balance with the current income.

22. Have the service member list expenses that he/she has now that he/she didn't have while deployed (e.g., food, clothes, entertainment, rent); assist in planning how these expenses will now be paid (or assign "Plan a Budget" in the *Adult Psychotherapy Homework Planner*, 2nd ed. by Jongsma).

23. Refer the service member to the financial assistance program at his/her local base/post for a loan or assistance with food, clothing, or household items.

11. Postpone discussions about career changes until after adjustment to being back from deployment has occurred. (24)

24. Encourage the service member to postpone discussion about career changes (e.g., leaving the military, moving to a different base/post) until the stress level has decreased in the family and routines have returned to normal.

12. Gradually take over everyday driving responsibilities. (25)

25. Educate the service member about road rage and the challenges of adjusting to driving in a nonhostile environment; instruct the service member to initially allow his significant other to drive when possible.

13. Focus on the positive aspects of returning home from deployment. (26)

26. Assist the service member in creating a list of the positive aspects of returning from deployment (e.g., more time with family, out of harm's way, less restriction of travel).

14. Utilize civilian-based support resources if necessary. (27)

27. Refer the service member and his family to Military One Source for individual and family counseling by a civilian provider, legal and educational counseling, and financial planning (1-800-342-9647).

—. ______________________

—. ______________________

—. ______________________

—. ______________________

—. ______________________

—. ______________________

DIAGNOSTIC SUGGESTIONS

ICD-9-CM	*ICD-10-CM*	*DSM-5* Disorder, Condition, or Problem
V62.2	Z56.9	Other Problem Related to Employment
309.0	F43.21	Adjustment Disorder, With Depressed Mood
V61.10	Z63.0	Relationship Distress with Spouse or Intimate Partner
V61.20	Z62.820	Parent-Child Relational Problem
307.42	F51.01	Insomnia
307.44	F51.11	Hypersomnolence Disorder
______	______	______________________
______	______	______________________

POSTTRAUMATIC STRESS DISORDER (PTSD)

BEHAVIORAL DEFINITIONS

1. Has been exposed to a traumatic event involving actual or perceived threat of death or serious injury.
2. Reports response of intense fear, helplessness, or horror to the traumatic event.
3. Experiences disturbing and persistent thoughts, images, and/or perceptions of the traumatic event.
4. Experiences frequent nightmares.
5. Describes a reliving of the event, particularly through dissociative flashbacks.
6. Displays significant psychological and/or physiological distress resulting from internal and external clues that are reminiscent of the traumatic event.
7. Intentionally avoids thoughts, feelings, or discussions related to the traumatic event.
8. Intentionally avoids activities, places, people, or objects (e.g., up-armored vehicles) that evoke memories of the event.
9. Inability to remember various important aspects of the traumatic event.
10. Displays a significant decline in interest and engagement in activities.
11. Experiences feelings of detachment or distance from others.
12. Experiences an inability to experience loving feelings.
13. Reports a sense of a foreshortened future.
14. Experiences disturbances in sleep.
15. Experiences intense anger and irritability.
16. Reports difficulty concentrating as well as feelings of sadness and guilt.
17. Reports hypervigilance and an exaggerated startle response.
18. Refuses to participate in combat and training missions.
19. Engages in a pattern of substance abuse.
20. Acknowledges a desire to separate from the military.
21. Reports feelings of letting his/her fellow comrades, unit, and country down.

22. Acknowledges increased marital and family conflict.
23. Acknowledges increased interpersonal conflict with friends, fellow comrades, and superiors.
24. Reports thoughts of suicide or homicide.
25. Engages in eruptions of verbal and/or physical violence or threats of violence with little or no provocation.

—. ______________________________

____

—. ______________________________

____

—. ______________________________

____

LONG-TERM GOALS

1. Eliminate or reduce the negative impact trauma-related symptoms have on social, occupational, and family functioning.
2. Return to the level of psychological functioning prior to exposure to the traumatic event.
3. Eliminate avoidance of persons, places, activities, and objects that are reminiscent of the traumatic event.
4. Think about or openly discuss the traumatic event with others without experiencing significant psychological or physiological distress.
5. Regain confidence in abilities as an effective Solider, Sailor, Airman, Marine, or Coast Guardsman.
6. Regain the "warrior" mentality.

—. ______________________________

____

—. ______________________________

____

—. ______________________________

____

SHORT-TERM OBJECTIVES

1. Describe in detail the history and nature of the PTSD symptoms. (1, 2)

THERAPEUTIC INTERVENTIONS

1. Within an atmosphere of warm acceptance, informed active listening, and unconditional

positive regard, explore and assess the veteran's/service member's type, intensity, and frequency of PTSD symptoms and the impact on his/her social, occupational, and interpersonal functioning (or assign "How the Trauma Affects Me" in the *Adult Psychotherapy Homework Planner*, 2nd ed. by Jongsma).

2. Talk with the service member's first line supervisor (e.g., Squad Leader, Platoon Sergeant, First Sergeant) to assess the degree to which the PTSD symptoms have impacted the service member's job performance.

2. Cooperate with psychological testing. (3, 4)

3. Administer self-report measures to assist with differential diagnosis and to assess the severity of PTSD symptoms and the impact on functioning (e.g., MMPI-2, Personality Assessment Inventory, PTSD Checklist–Military Version).

4. Provide feedback to the veteran/service member regarding his/her testing results.

3. Acknowledge any substance use for the purpose of self-medicating PTSD symptoms. (5, 6)

5. Assess the presence and degree of substance use by the veteran/service member to deal with PTSD symptoms.

6. Refer the veteran/service member for a comprehensive substance use evaluation and treatment, if necessary.

4. Cooperate with a psychiatric evaluation to assess for the need for psychotropic medication. (7, 8, 9)

7. Arrange for an evaluation for a prescription of psychotropic medication(s) (e.g., SSRI medications) if the veteran/service member requests it, if he/she is likely to be noncompliant with psychotherapy, or if

occupational and social functioning are seriously impaired.

8. Monitor the veteran/service member for prescription compliance, side effects, and overall effectiveness of the medication; consult with the prescribing practitioner at regular intervals.

9. Provide an update to the service member's unit leadership on his/her condition, potential negative impacts on safety, and any occupational limitations while taking medication.

5. Describe the precipitating traumatic event in detail. (10)

10. Assist the veteran/service member in describing the details of the traumatic event (most significant event if there are more than one); encourage the veteran/service member to be aware of as many details of the event as possible while focusing on how he/she felt before the event, at the time of the event, and after it was over (e.g., anxiety, dread, shame, guilt, disgust), the most vivid parts of the recollection, and any sounds or smells that he/she remembers; process the emotions associated with retelling of this story (frequent retelling is a form of exposure therapy).

6. Verbalize an understanding of PTSD and the differences between PTSD and combat stress reaction. (11, 12)

11. Educate the veteran/service member on PTSD including symptoms, causes, prognosis, and available treatments (see www.ncptsd.va.gov).

12. Educate the veteran/service member about the differences between PTSD (e.g., collection of specific, often chronic symptoms that significantly impact social and occupational functioning and

that requires treatment) and combat stress reaction (e.g., brief emotional, behavioral, and/or physical reactions to a combat stressor that is expected to resolve on its own or with minimal intervention).

7. Verbalize an understanding of the treatment rationale for PTSD. (13, 14)

13. Educate the veteran/service member about how effective treatments for PTSD utilize virtual reality, imaginal, and *in vivo* exposure techniques to desensitize an individual's fears, and cognitive restructuring to assist the individual in viewing the world in a much less dangerous manner.

14. Assign the veteran/service member to review information on cognitive restructuring, exposure therapy, and relaxation training in *Reclaiming Your Life from a Traumatic Experience: A Prolonged Exposure Treatment Program Workbook* by Rothbaum, Foa, and Hembree.

8. Learn and utilize relaxation and calming strategies. (15, 16)

15. Teach the veteran/service member diaphragmatic breathing, assigning him/her to practice twice a day for 10 minutes each time; encourage implementation of this technique when anxiety or stress rises.

16. Teach the veteran/service member progressive muscle relaxation, assigning him/her to practice twice a day for 15 minutes each time; urge use of this technique when PTSD symptoms develop.

9. Verbalize an understanding that cognitions contribute to the maintenance of fear and avoidance. (17)

17. Explain to the veteran/service member the concept of how thoughts impact our feelings and behavior, particularly in

maintaining fear and reinforcing avoidance of perceived threats; use an example that relates to his/her situation (e.g., a person's up-armored vehicle was hit with an improvised explosive device, and every time he/she sees an up-armored vehicle he/she remembers the past traumatic event, assumes he/she will get attacked again, and avoids all up-armored vehicles). EBT

EBT 10. Identify, challenge, and replace negative and self-defeating fearful thoughts that contribute to avoidance. (18, 19, 20)

18. Assist the veteran/service member in developing an awareness of his/her automatic thoughts that are consistent with maintaining the view that the world is a hostile and dangerous place and injury and death is inevitable. EBT

19. Assign the veteran/service member to keep a daily log of automatic thoughts associated with themes of threat and danger (e.g., "Negative Thoughts Trigger Negative Feelings" in the *Adult Psychotherapy Homework Planner*, 2nd ed. by Jongsma); process the journal material to challenge distorted thinking patterns with reality-based thoughts. EBT

20. Reinforce the veteran's/service member's positive cognitions that foster a sense of safety and security and decrease fearful and avoidance behavior (see "Positive Self-Talk" in the *Adult Psychotherapy Homework Planner*, 2nd ed. by Jongsma). EBT

EBT 11. Participate with Prolonged Exposure treatment. (21, 22, 23, 24)

21. Educate the veteran/service member about the common reactions to trauma and the causes of posttraumatic symptoms. EBT

22. Utilize imaginal or virtual reality exposure as a way to recount/relive the emotional experience for an extended period of time (e.g., 60–90 minutes; see *Prolonged Exposure Therapy for PTSD: Emotional Processing of Traumatic Experiences—Therapist Guide* by Foa, Hembree, and Rothbaum). EBT

23. Utilize *in vivo* exposure as a way to gradually expose the person to objects, situations, and places that create significant anxiety for the veteran/service member (see *Prolonged Exposure Therapy for PTSD: Emotional Processing of Traumatic Experiences—Therapist Guide* by Foa, Hembree, and Rothbaum). EBT

24. Provide psychoeducation, exposure, and cognitive treatments once or twice weekly in 90-minute sessions for approximately three months or until an acceptable level of symptom remission is reached; provide follow-up booster sessions as needed. EBT

EBT 12. Learn and implement thought stopping to manage intrusive unwanted thoughts. (25)

25. Teach the veteran/service member thought-stopping in which he/she internally voices the word "stop" and/or imagines something representing the concept of stopping (e.g., a stop sign or light) immediately upon noticing unwanted trauma or otherwise negative, unwanted thoughts (or assign "Making Use of the Thought-Stopping Technique" in the *Adult Psychotherapy Homework Planner*, 2nd ed. by Jongsma). EBT

13. Cooperate with eye movement desensitization and reprocessing (EMDR) to reduce the impact of negative emotions associated with the trauma. (26)

14. Implement relapse prevention strategies for managing possible future trauma-related symptoms. (27, 28, 29, 30)

15. Utilize writing as a means of exposure to the recollections/ memories of the trauma. (31)

26. Provide brief EMDR treatmen or refer the veteran/service member to a clinician trained in EMDR to reduce the emotional reactivity to the trauma and reduce PTSD symptoms.

27. Discuss with the veteran/service member the distinction between a lapse and relapse, associating a lapse with an initial and reversible return of symptoms, fear, or urges to avoid and relapse with the decision to return to fearful and avoidant patterns.

28. Identify and rehearse with the veteran/service member the management of future situations or circumstances in which lapses could occur.

29. Instruct the veteran/service member to routinely use strategies learned in therapy (e.g., using cognitive restructuring, social skills, and exposure) while building social interactions and relationships.

30. Develop a "coping card" or other reminder on which coping strategies and other important information (e.g., "pace your breathing," "focus on the task at hand," "you can manage it," and "it will go away") are recorded for the veteran's/service member's later use.

31. Instruct the veteran/service member to utilize writing about the trauma as a method of exposure (or assign "Share the Painful Memory" in the *Adult Psychotherapy Homework Planner*, 2nd ed. by Jongsma) if other exposure approaches are too difficult.

16. Cooperate with Imagery Rehearsal Therapy as an adjunctive treatment to target persistent nightmares. (32)

32. Utilize Imagery Rehearsal Therapy as an adjunctive treatment for nightmares along with exposure-based treatments for PTSD (see the Nightmares chapter in this *Planner*).

17. Practice good sleep hygiene behaviors. (33)

33. Instruct the veteran/service member on behavioral practices conducive to good sleep that include not using caffeine four hours prior to bedtime, exercising in the mornings, getting out of bed if not able to fall asleep within 15 minutes, not eating spicy meals/snacks prior to sleep, and removing cues to time that may promote "clock watching" (see the chapter on Insomnia in this *Planner*).

18. Cooperate with group therapy for PTSD. (34)

34. Conduct or refer the veteran/service member to group therapy that includes other veterans/service members suffering from PTSD and that focuses on managing and living with PTSD.

19. Cooperate with conjoint or family therapy. (35)

35. Conduct or refer the veteran/service member to conjoint or family therapy in order to educate his/her family on PTSD and increase family support and family functioning.

20. Implement a regular exercise regimen as a way to reduce stress and anxiety. (36)

36. Develop and reinforce the implementation of a regular physical exercise program by the veteran/service member.

21. Meet with military medical personnel if medical separation from service is recommended. (37, 38)

37. Encourage the service member to attend all medical separation appointments.

38. Explore opportunities for appeal if the service member does not agree with the medical separation finding (e.g., request a second opinion, consult with JAG or civilian attorney).

22. Meet with a Veterans Affairs representative regarding disability compensation if separated from service. (39, 40)

39. Identify the veteran's Veterans Affairs appropriate geographical region and facilitate contact with a Veterans Affairs representative from that region.

40. Provide the veteran with information regarding his/her Veterans Affairs benefits (www.vba.va.gov/VBA/).

23. Attend scheduled Veterans Affairs medical appointments. (41)

41. Stress the importance of the veteran attending all scheduled medical appointments at his/her local Veterans Affairs facility, including compensation evaluations and regular healthcare appointments.

—. ____________________

—. ____________________

—. ____________________

—. ____________________

—. ____________________

—. ____________________

DIAGNOSTIC SUGGESTIONS

ICD-9-CM	*ICD-10-CM*	*DSM-5* Disorder, Condition, or Problem
309.81	F43.10	Posttraumatic Stress Disorder
308.3	F43.0	Acute Stress Disorder
300.6	F48.1	Depersonalization/Derealization Disorder
300.15	F44.9	Unspecified Dissociative Disorder
300.15	F44.89	Other Specified Dissociative Disorder
305.00	F10.10	Alcohol Use Disorder, Mild
303.90	F10.20	Alcohol Use Disorder, Moderate or Severe
300.02	F41.1	Generalized Anxiety Disorder
296.2x	F32.x	Major Depressive Disorder, Single Episode
296.3x	F33.x	Major Depressive Disorder, Recurrent Episode
V65.2	Z76.5	Malingering
301.83	F60.3	Borderline Personality Disorder
______	______	____________________
______	______	____________________

PRE-DEPLOYMENT STRESS

BEHAVIORAL DEFINITIONS

1. Complains of feeling overwhelmed with the amount of preparation involved prior to deployment.
2. Reports an uncharacteristic emotional withdrawal from loved ones.
3. Exhibits a decline in communication with loved ones.
4. Complains of decreased feelings of intimacy toward loved ones.
5. Complains of anxiety and fear related to be being injured during deployment.
6. Reports anxiety about the "unknown" of the deployment.
7. Complains of significant worry related to finances while deployed.
8. Reports guilt about leaving loved ones behind.

—. ____

____

—. ____

____

—. ____

____

LONG-TERM GOALS

1. Feel comfortable about level of pre-deployment preparation reached.
2. Decreased anxiety surrounding injury and/or death during deployment.
3. Restore previous levels of intimacy and closeness with loved ones.
4. Feel confident with financial plan in place prior to deployment.

—. ____

____

—. ____

____

—. ____

____

SHORT-TERM OBJECTIVES

1. Describe in detail the nature of the pre-deployment stress. (1, 2, 3)

2. Identify and discuss the nature of the anxiety related to the actual deployment. (4)

THERAPEUTIC INTERVENTIONS

1. Assess the degree of pre-deployment stress that the service member is under and what makes the stress level higher or lower.

2. Assign the service member to create a list of all pre-deployment stressors that he/she is dealing with (e.g., financial concerns, insecurity regarding loss of intimate relationship, fear of injury or death, etc.); rate them from most to least stressful.

3. Encourage the service member to choose a pre-deployment problem/stressor of a moderate level of stress and apply the Military Problem Solving Process to his/her current situation (e.g., recognize and define the problem, gather facts and make assumptions, define end states or goals and establish criteria for success, develop possible solutions, analyze and compare possible solutions, select and implement solutions, analyze solutions for effectiveness).

4. Assess the degree of pre-deployment anxiety related to the deployment including fear and apprehension about being injured, doubts about being able to be away from loved ones for an

extended period of time, and the loss of privacy.

3. Acknowledge that fear and anxiety are normal and expected reactions prior to deployment. (5, 6, 7)

5. Normalize the service member's fears by reassuring him/her that most service members feel this way at some point prior to deployment; if necessary, focus treatment on relief from generalized anxiety (see the chapter on Anxiety in this *Planner*).

6. Assign the service member to talk with other service members preparing for deployment, as well as those that have returned from deployment, about these feelings.

7. Encourage the service member to meet with his/her unit Chaplain to address any spiritual concerns he/she may have about the deployment.

4. Identify community and family supports that can assist the family while the service member is deployed. (8, 9)

8. Assist the service member in identifying and contacting community and family supports that could assist the family during difficult times; reinforce the service member's courage in asking for help.

9. Provide the service member with the phone number for Military OneSource (1-800-342-9647); encourage the service member to give the number to his loved ones.

5. Develop a clear and realistic financial plan that both parties feel comfortable with. (10, 11, 12, 13)

10. Refer the service member to a financial counselor at his/her local base/post to assist with creating a budget (or assign "Plan a Budget" in the *Adult Psychotherapy Homework Planner*, 2nd ed. by Jongsma).

11. Encourage the service member to include his significant other in the financial planning and ensure that he/she is supportive of the final budget; develop contingencies for unexpected financial hardships.

12. Encourage the service member to adhere to the budget by making it part of his/her daily routine; assign him/her to review the budget with his/her significant other weekly for the first few months of the deployment.

13. Educate the service member about the Servicemembers Civil Relief Act (SCRA) and how he/she may qualify for reduced interest rates and payment deferments.

6. Spend excess free time from work with family. (14, 15, 16)

14. Encourage the service member to avoid the temptation to spend free time with friends or in activities that only he/she enjoys.

15. Assign the service member to participate in activities that involve the entire family such as going to the beach or spending time at the park (or assign "When Can We Be Together?" in the *Brief Family Therapy Homework Planner* by Bevilacqua and Dattilio).

16. Assist the service member in setting clear boundaries with extended family and friends regarding visiting and social obligations in the weeks leading up to deployment.

7. Address any unresolved marital/relationship issues prior to deployment. (17, 18)

17. Explore any unresolved marital/relationship problems that may resurface during the deployment (or assign "How Can We Meet Each Other's Needs and Desires?" in the *Adult*

Psychotherapy Homework Planner, 2nd ed. by Jongsma).

18. Conduct a couple's/marital session for the purpose of resolving identified problems while keeping in mind that the number of meetings may be limited.

8. Increase communication with loved ones as a means to strengthen intimacy. (19, 20)

19. Encourage the service member to increase levels of verbal and physical affection during the weeks preceding deployment.

20. Encourage the service member to reassure his/her significant other of his commitment and love of him/her.

9. Reduce alcohol intake. (21)

21. Educate the service member on how alcohol use can increase anxiety and stress, disrupt sleep, decrease sexual performance, and create anger and resentment within the family; monitor alcohol intake for abuse.

10. Discuss expectations and realities regarding communication while deployed. (22, 23, 24)

22. Assign the service member to research the availability and primary modes of communication used where he/she will be deployed (e.g., level of access to Internet and telephone); inform family of findings.

23. Instruct the service member to create a "communication calendar" in collaboration with his/her family detailing what days and times he/she will call, email, or write; inform loved ones that times may change due to unforeseen circumstances.

24. Direct the service member to explain to his/her family that if he/she is not heard from for a while this does not mean that he/she has been injured or killed, but is most likely due to

communication "blackouts" or downed networks.

11. Develop a plan of how to recognize birthdays, anniversaries, and graduations for loved ones. (25)

25. Encourage the service member to preorder gifts/flowers for special occasions such as a child's birthday or wedding anniversary, allowing for delivery to his/her loved one while deployed.

12. Develop a system that will help a young child to understand how long the parent will be gone. (26, 27)

26. Educate the service member on the fact that young children may not understand the concept of how long six months or a year is to wait while his/her parent is deployed.

27. Create visual aides that assist the child in keeping track of when the parent will be home (e.g., place 365 pieces of his/her favorite candy in a jar, allowing one piece to be taken out every day for a one-year deployment).

13. Ensure that the service member's will, power-of-attorney, and other important documents are up-to-date and accessible. (28, 29, 30)

28. Direct the service member to visit the military legal department (i.e., Judge Advocate General) at his/her local base/post to review and update his/her will and/or power-of-attorney; include spouse/legal guardian in this process.

29. Encourage the service member to consider creating a limited power-of-attorney (e.g., sell a vehicle, manage specific bills) as opposed to a general power-of-attorney, which offers little protection for the service member during separation, divorce, or other extreme situations.

30. Encourage the service member to renew or cancel contracts and leases that will expire or continue to be active during the deployment (e.g., apartment, cellular telephone).

14. Identify and locate all important documents that may be needed by the service member or family members during the deployment. (31)

15. Renew medication prescriptions and get enough refills to last for at least 90 days. (32)

16. Locate and disseminate emergency contact information. (33)

__. ____________________

__. ____________________

__. ____________________

31. Instruct the service member to compile all important documents (e.g., birth certificates, immunizations, medical records, passports, etc.), make copies, and provide a copy to his/her spouse or legal representative and take a copy with him/her on deployment.

32. Direct the service member to schedule an appointment with his/her primary care provider in order to get refills on his/her medication to prevent him/her from running out during the transition phase between leaving his/her stateside unit and settling in to the deployment location.

33. Provide the service member with the appropriate American Red Cross crisis contact number so that his/her family will know how to get in touch with him/her during an emergency.

__. ____________________

__. ____________________

__. ____________________

DIAGNOSTIC SUGGESTIONS

ICD-9-CM	*ICD-10-CM*	*DSM-5* Disorder, Condition, or Problem
V62.2	Z56.9	Other Problem Related to Employment
309.0	F43.21	Adjustment Disorder, With Depressed Mood
300.02	F41.1	Generalized Anxiety Disorder
300.00	F41.9	Unspecified Anxiety Disorder

SEPARATION AND DIVORCE

BEHAVIORAL DEFINITIONS

1. Reports thoughts of ending the marriage (or relationship, if not married).
2. Moved out of the home to establish separate living arrangements due to dissatisfaction with the relationship.
3. Initiated legal proceedings for separation, divorce, and/or child custody.
4. Reports confusion about how to best deal with the feelings and welfare of the children.
5. Acknowledges anger, hurt, and fear regarding breaking the partnership and having to face life as a single person.
6. Reports spiritual conflict over the breaking of marriage vows.
7. Complains of depression and exhibits withdrawal as part of the grief process related to the loss of the relationship.
8. Reports uncertainty about remaining in the military due to the risk of being separated from children and partner as a result of a change of duty station move.

__. ____

____

__. ____

____

__. ____

____

LONG-TERM GOALS

1. Evaluate the possibility of resolving the differences and review the pros and cons of remaining married.
2. Consistently uphold "the best interests of the children" as paramount and act accordingly, regardless of the final fate of the marriage.
3. Resolve the initial confusion and turmoil of separation.
4. Learn to cope with the varied losses that separation entails.
5. Mourn the end of the relationship adequately to facilitate cooperation in reaching a fair divorce agreement.
6. Reduce conflict, hurt, and angry feelings between partners.
7. Establish and maintain healthy co-parenting practices.
8. Rediscover affectionate feelings and renew commitment to each other to work toward resolution of conflicts.
9. Make a decision regarding staying in or leaving the military when possible.

__. ____

____

__. ____

____

__. ____

____

SHORT-TERM OBJECTIVES

1. Each partner verbalizes facts and feelings regarding own emotional stability, physical health, vocational satisfaction, and any religious conflicts regarding divorce. (1)
2. If significant emotional, medical, or vocational problems predate the serious relationship conflicts, agree to postpone the divorce or separation decision until the other issues have been resolved. (2)

THERAPEUTIC INTERVENTIONS

1. Assess each partner's emotional and physical health, vocational stability, and religious conflict over divorce.
2. If significant extramarital problems exist, encourage each partner to postpone the decision about separation until after those problems have been addressed.

3. Verbally acknowledge that there is no interest in conjoint or individual counseling to improve the marriage, but only interest in pre-divorce treatment. (3)	3. Establish the type of treatment that will be conducted by describing and having partners agree to (a) conjoint marital therapy, (b) individual marital treatment, or (c) pre-divorce treatment.
4. Cooperate with psychological testing to assess the degree of acceptance of the decision to divorce. (4)	4. Assess the steps each partner has taken toward divorce by administering the Marital Status Inventory by Weiss and Cerreto, and interviewing each partner about his/her sense of hope and vision for the future.
5. Describe the origination, development, and present state of the relationship. (5, 6, 7)	5. Assess the developmental stage of the marriage (i.e., early marriage, couple with young children, long-term marriage).
	6. Assess the history of the marriage (e.g., recent changes in respective partners' happiness with relationship, their expectations for the marriage, and thoughts about divorce.)
	7. Assess partners' current satisfaction with the relationship, using interview and self-report instruments (e.g., Relationship Satisfaction Questionnaire by Burns; Marital Adjustment Test by Lock and Wallace; or Dyadic Adjustment Scale by Spanier).
6. Describe any suspicions regarding the other partner having had an affair. (8)	8. Assess the presence or suspicion of affairs in relationship.
7. Verbalize any incidents of physical, sexual, or emotional abuse or intimidation by other partner. (9)	9. Assess for incidents of violence or intimidation in the relationship.
8. List the members of each partner's extended family who have broken committed	10. Review the extended family history in regard to divorce and have each partner verbalize how

relationships, and discuss the impact that this history may have on a decision to divorce. (10)

9. Identify any cultural, ethnic, or religious beliefs that my have a bearing on a decision to divorce; verbalize a resolution of such conflicts. (11)

10. Verbalize any marital problems that are related to one or both partners being in the military. (12)

11. Have each partner identify how he/she behaved in ways that improved the relationship, and how he/she behaved in ways that harmed the relationship. (13)

12. List the pros and cons of the available options—continuing the relationship, separation, and divorce. (14)

13. Verbalize empathy for each other while each partner states how divorce will impact personal and social life, immediate and extended family relationships, and spirituality. (15)

14. Each partner verbalizes a dedication to being sensitive to the children's thoughts, needs, and feelings during this time of insecurity. (16, 17, 18)

this history may be affecting the decision to divorce.

11. Ask each partner to identify his/her subcultural identification and its influence on attitudes about divorce (e.g., ethnicity, religious identification); facilitate a resolution of conflict between behavior and beliefs.

12. Ask each partner to describe how the military has impacted the marriage; process content and problem-solve, when possible.

13. Ask each partner to turn to the other and express in what ways self has (a) contributed to the downfall of the relationship, and (b) in what ways he/she has attempted to make the relationship work.

14. Ask both partners to verbalize their points of view on (a) the pros and cons of preserving the relationship, and (b) the pros and cons of separation or divorce.

15. Ask each partner to verbalize the implications of divorce in the following areas: (a) personal, (b) family (including children), (c) religious, and (d) social. Have the other partner paraphrase the first person's statements in each area to increase understanding and empathy between the two partners.

16. Sensitize the partners to the upheaval that children face by having them discuss the anticipated effects on their children.

17. Assign parents to read *How to Help Your Child Overcome Your Divorce* by Benedek and Brown; *The Parent's Book About Divorce* by Gardner; and/or *Mom's House, Dad's House* by Ricci.

18. Have partners verbally contract with each other and with the therapist that all decisions in the divorce and separation process will be made with the "best interests of the children" as the paramount concern.

15. Agree on how and what to tell the children regarding the impending divorce; practice the disclosures. (19)

19. Using role-playing techniques have the partners rehearse telling the children together about the divorce. Have them explain that (a) they both love the children very much, (b) they plan to divorce, (c) the divorce is not the children's fault, (d) there is nothing the children can do to get parents back together, and (e) they will both continue to love and see the children.

16. Report on the experience of telling the children about the divorce, and agree on what further explanation or support may be necessary. (19, 20)

19. Using role-playing techniques have the partners rehearse telling the children together about the divorce. Have them explain that (a) they both love the children very much, (b) they plan to divorce, (c) the divorce is not the children's fault, (d) there is nothing the children can do to get parents back together, and (e) they will both continue to love and see the children.

20. Review the experience of parents telling the children of the divorce or separation and probe the needs for further explanation or support; press for agreement on this issue.

17. Each partner identify how he/she has allowed own anger to get out of control, causing unnecessary pain to the other; agree to the need for better control. (21, 22, 23, 24, 25)

21. Ask each partner to describe times when his/her own anger was destructive to the other partner.

22. Clarify for the couple the role of the therapist; to (a) aid the family in making the separation or divorce transition, and (b) help both partners deal with the turbulent emotions experienced during this process. Emphasize that the therapist's role is to serve the best interests of all family members; however, he/she will not be a mediator or judge.

23. Teach partners to recognize the gradations of anger and to take steps to cool down (e.g., practice relaxation and deep-breathing exercises, take time-out for 15 minutes, go for a walk) before self-control becomes eroded.

24. Ask each partner to identify hot topics and practice in-session cognitive rehearsal about how to cope with such topics adaptively.

25. Have both partners practice time-out (agree to a pause in the conversation when anger begins to elevate) while discussing an emotional topic in session.

18. Each partner exercise anger control skills (e.g., identifying escalating level of anger, using time-out techniques, refocusing on problem at hand) to negotiate the future of the relationship and parenting without screaming, intimidating, or evoking fear. (23, 24, 25)

23. Teach partners to recognize the gradations of anger and to take steps to cool down (e.g., practice relaxation and deep-breathing exercises, take time-out for 15 minutes, go for a walk) before self-control becomes eroded.

24. Ask each partner to identify hot topics and practice in-session cognitive rehearsal about how to cope with such topics adaptively.

	25. Have both partners practice time-out (agree to a pause in the conversation when anger begins to elevate) while discussing an emotional topic in session.
19. Agree to whether and when one partner will move out; negotiate the terms and conditions of the separation. (26)	26. Facilitate discussion and decision making, pending legal advice, regarding whether and when one partner will move out of the house; if an in-house separation is financially necessary, negotiate the terms and conditions.
20. Clarify new boundaries by establishing the new goals of the altered relationship, the new prescriptions and proscriptions. (27)	27. Facilitate a written agreement between the partners stipulating what forms of contact are acceptable (e.g., planning around children's activities) and what are prohibited (e.g., sexual intimacies), as well as the goals of the new relationship (e.g., to provide the children with safe, healthy home environments; support each other as parent to the children; etc.).
21. Each partner constructively express his/her emotional pain about the decline of the relationship and verbalize new short- and long-term goals for personal life. (28)	28. Using individual sessions as needed, allow each partner to express his/her anger, disappointment, and disapproval over what has happened; balance these expressions of hurt with an elicitation of his/her goals for coping with short-term and long-term situations with the other partner and children.
22. Verbalize an understanding of the differences between litigation, arbitration, and mediation as means of dissolving the marriage; agree to one choice. (29)	29. Educate partners regarding the three choices available for dissolving the marriage: (a) litigation, which is an adversarial legal process; (b) arbitration, in which a third party, whom each partner typically helps choose, makes decisions regarding property and custody; and (c)

mediation, in which the partners come to their own agreement, with the help of a trained mediator.

23. Develop a co-parenting agreement that is in the best interest of the children and deals with the children's residence, emotional support, financial support, and custody and visitation. (30)

30. Facilitate the development of a co-parenting agreement in which the partners pledge that (a) the children's primary residence will be established in their best interests; (b) neither parent will belittle the other and his/her family members in front of the children; (c) parents will avoid placing the children in loyalty conflicts; and (d) the parents agree regarding terms of financial support for the children.

24. Have each partner outline a plan for how to increase his/her social life and strengthen his/her social and spiritual support system. (31)

31. Using individual sessions, assist each partner in developing a varied social network (e.g., asking others to socialize; beginning or increasing involvement in club, community, volunteer, and/or church activities; dating).

25. Cooperate with bringing children to sessions in order to listen to them express their emotional reactions and needs. (32)

32. Conduct parent-child sessions, when necessary, to ensure that the children's emotional needs are being attended to.

26. Accept and follow-through on referral to divorce and single parent support groups. (33)

33. Encourage partners to attend local divorce therapy groups and/or self-help groups (e.g., Parents without Partners).

27. Verbalize the effect divorce has had on religious beliefs and practices. (34)

34. Assess whether the divorce has affected either partner's religious and spiritual connections, and assist in problem solving if he/she has difficulty reestablishing connections (e.g., switching parishes, investigating churches that welcome divorced members).

28. Decide on whether staying or leaving the military is in the best interest of the children and marriage. (35)

35. Encourage both partners to decide if remaining in the military (one or both if a dual military couple) is worth the strain that it puts on the relationship.

__. ____________________

__. ____________________

__. ____________________

__. ____________________

__. ____________________

__. ____________________

DIAGNOSTIC SUGGESTIONS

ICD-9-CM	*ICD-10-CM*	*DSM-5* Disorder, Condition, or Problem
309.0	F43.21	Adjustment Disorder, With Depressed Mood
305.00	F10.10	Alcohol Use Disorder, Mild
303.90	F10.20	Alcohol Use Disorder, Moderate or Severe
296.xx	F32.x	Major Depressive Disorder, Single Episode
296.xx	F33.x	Major Depressive Disorder, Recurrent Episode
300.4	F34.1	Persistent Depressive Disorder
300.02	F41.1	Generalized Anxiety Disorder
V61.10	Z63.0	Relationship Distress with Spouse or Intimate Partner
995.81	T74.11XA	Spouse or Partner Violence, Physical, Confirmed, Initial Encounter
995.81	T74.11XD	Spouse or Partner Violence, Physical, Confirmed, Subsequent Encounter
301.6	F60.7	Dependent Personality Disorder
301.83	F60.3	Borderline Personality Disorder
________	________	____________________
________	________	____________________

SEXUAL ASSAULT BY ANOTHER SERVICE MEMBER

BEHAVIORAL DEFINITIONS

1. Complains of thoughts being dominated by the sexual assault.
2. Reports extreme emotional response when thinking or talking about the assault.
3. Reports feeling betrayed by his/her fellow service member(s).
4. Reports a general distrust for all service members.
5. Reports anger and resentment toward his/her unit, superiors, and the military.
6. Displays an inability to be intimate with others.
7. Complains of an inability to enjoy sexual contact with a chosen partner.

—. ____

—. ____

—. ____

LONG-TERM GOALS

1. Emotionally and cognitively resolve the issue of being sexually assaulted.
2. Discuss and think about the sexual assault without having an extreme emotional reaction.
3. Regain a sense of trust for fellow service members, unit, and military.
4. Increase capacity for intimacy and sexual contact in relationships.

—. ____

__. ____

____

__. ____

____

SHORT-TERM OBJECTIVES

1. Describe in detail the sexual assault. (1, 2)

2. Complete a psychiatric evaluation to determine if psychotropic medication is warranted. (3, 4)

3. Identify support systems that can aid in recovery from the sexual assault. (5, 6, 7, 8, 9)

THERAPEUTIC INTERVENTIONS

1. Ask the service member to share as much of the details of the assault as he/she is comfortable with; assess the nature of the sexual assault against the service member including how long ago the assault happened, if he/she knew the perpetrator, status of the criminal investigation, the strength of avoidance behaviors, and the overall psychological health of the service member (or assign "Picturing the Place of the Abuse" in the *Adult Psychotherapy Homework Planner*, 2nd ed. by Jongsma).
2. Assess the impact the sexual assault has had on the service member's social, occupational, and interpersonal functioning.
3. Refer the service member to a psychiatric prescribing practitioner to assess if psychotropic medication is needed to assist with sleep onset and maintenance and/or depressive and anxiety symptoms.
4. Monitor the service member's medication compliance, side effects, effectiveness, and progress.
5. Assist the service member in identifying and contacting community and family supports that could assist him/her in

recovery from the sexual assault; reinforce service member's courage in asking for help.

6. Assist the service member in making contact with his/her military sexual assault victim's advocate.
7. Encourage the service member to talk with his/her unit Chaplain for spiritual guidance and comfort.
8. Assist the service member in locating a support group, in-person or online, which consists of other service members who have been sexually assaulted.
9. Provide the service member with phone number for Military One Source for free confidential counseling from a civilian behavioral healthcare provider: 1-800-342-9647.

4. Identify and discuss the nature and extent of the feelings surrounding the sexual assault. (10, 11)

10. Create a supportive and compassionate therapeutic environment and encourage the service member to openly and honestly share his/her feelings about the sexual assault; be aware of any personal feelings and comments that may be construed as judgmental.
11. Encourage the service member to discuss how the perpetrator being a fellow service member influences his/her reaction to the sexual assault; process relevant material.

5. Decrease feelings of guilt and shame related to the sexual assault. (12, 13, 14)

12. Assign the service member to read literature on dealing with guilt and shame (e.g., *Healing the Shame That Binds You* by Bradshaw; *The Gift of Guilt: 10 Steps to Freedom from Guilt, Forever* by Miller); process important material.

13. Assist the service member in identifying any beliefs held, related to self-blame, for the sexual assault; compassionately and respectfully challenge those beliefs.

14. Identify and discuss how military culture may unknowingly blame the female victim for the sexual assault (e.g., "Women don't belong in the military"; "It's her fault for wanting to be around men all the time").

6. Express feelings about the perpetrator including the future possibility of forgiveness for him/her. (15, 16, 17)

15. Assign the service member to write a letter to the perpetrator detailing how he/she has impacted the service member's life (or assign "A Blaming Letter and a Forgiving Letter to Perpetrator" in the *Adult Psychotherapy Homework Planner*, 2nd ed. by Jongsma); assist the service member in deciding whether or not to destroy the letter, keep for future reference, or send to the perpetrator.

16. Assist the service member in planning for a face-to-face meeting with the perpetrator if so desired; inform chain of command if the service member decides to meet face-to-face.

17. Utilizing the empty chair technique, role-play the confrontation scenario until the service member feels comfortable with the process.

7. Increase level of trust with others as evidenced by increased social involvement and sharing of personal information. (18)

18. Encourage the service member to gradually increase his/her contact with others; once the service member becomes comfortable with someone, encourage him/her to share intimate details about himself/herself with the person; gradually increase the sharing if

the person is determined to be trustworthy.

8. Verbalize an understanding that not all service members are capable of sexual assault. (19, 20, 21)

19. Assign the service member to create a list of all positive interactions with other service members that he/she can recall.
20. Assign the service member to gradually become more involved in social interactions with service members of the opposite sex.
21. Teach the service member relaxation techniques (imagery, progressive muscle relaxation) that he/she can use prior to or during social interactions.

9. Increase level of intimacy with loved ones. (22, 23)

22. Encourage the service member to share his/her positive feelings about an individual with the person.
23. Encourage the service member to share intimate details about the sexual assault with someone he/she trusts; process the results in session.

10. Increase enjoyment of sexual contact with partner. (24, 25)

24. Encourage the service member to discuss his/her concerns about sexual intimacy with his/her partner.
25. Encourage the service member to gradually increase the level of sexual contact with his/her partner as the service member feels comfortable (e.g., start with hugging, moving on to kissing, and so on).

11. Cooperate with Military Police regarding investigation. (26)

26. Educate the service member on the criminal investigation process; encourage the service member to fully cooperate with the investigation.

12. Communicate with chain of command regarding status of the case. (27)

27. Encourage the service member to keep his/her chain of command informed of the status and progress of the criminal investigation.

13. Make the decision to either remain or leave the military. (28)

28. Assign the service member to create a pro and con list regarding his/her continued military service; process the list in session.

14. Regain a sense of power and control over life. (29)

29. Reinforce the service member's views, statements, and behaviors that are consistent with self-efficacy theory (e.g., one is capable of performing in a manner that is conducive to attaining goals).

15. Identify self as a survivor and not a victim. (30)

30. Reinforce with the service member how viewing one's self as a survivor creates a greater sense of control vs. seeing one's self as a victim.

__. ____________________

__. ____________________

__. ____________________

__. ____________________

__. ____________________

__. ____________________

DIAGNOSTIC SUGGESTIONS

ICD-9-CM	*ICD-10-CM*	*DSM-5* Disorder, Condition, or Problem
995.83	T74.21XA	Spouse or Partner Violence, Sexual, Confirmed, Initial Encounter
995.83	T74.21XD	Spouse or Partner Violence, Sexual, Confirmed, Subsequent Encounter
995.83	T74.21XA	Adult Sexual Abuse by Nonspouse or Nonpartner, Confirmed, Initial Encounter
995.83	T74.21XD	Adult Sexual Abuse by Nonspouse or Nonpartner, Confirmed, Subsequent Encounter
308.3	F43.0	Acute Stress Disorder
309.81	F43.10	Posttraumatic Stress Disorder
296.xx	F32.x	Major Depressive Disorder, Single Episode
296.xx	F33.x	Major Depressive Disorder, Recurrent Episode
300.02	F41.1	Generalized Anxiety Disorder
300.00	F41.9	Unspecified Anxiety Disorder
301.82	F60.6	Avoidant Personality Disorder
301.6	F60.7	Dependent Personality Disorder
________	________	____________________
________	________	____________________

SHIFT WORK SLEEP DISORDER

BEHAVIORAL DEFINITIONS

1. Reports difficulty adjusting to a consistent sleep schedule due to frequent shift rotations and/or working night shifts.
2. Complains of an inability to sleep during the day when not working, creating a sleep debt.
3. Complains of excessive daytime sleepiness related to work schedule.
4. Exhibits difficulty concentrating due to excessive sleepiness and fatigue.
5. Complains of a lack of energy and motivation as a consequence of sleep deprivation.
6. Reports an increase in disciplinary actions, errors, and/or accidents at work.
7. Reports an increase in utilizing "sick call."

__. ____
____

__. ____
____

__. ____
____

LONG-TERM GOALS

1. Develop and adapt to a sleep schedule that promotes adequate quantity and quality of sleep.
2. Report feeling rested and refreshed after sleep period.
3. Eliminate cognitive, emotional, and physical symptoms associated with sleep deprivation.
4. Report an absence of negative occupational and social effects of sleep deprivation.

5. Report an overall satisfaction with work and sleep schedule.

—. ____

____

—. ____

____

—. ____

____

SHORT-TERM OBJECTIVES

1. Describe the history and details of the current sleep problems. (1, 2, 3, 4)

2. Report current use of alcohol, and/or illicit prescription or over-the-counter drugs used to counter sleep disturbances. (5, 6, 7)

THERAPEUTIC INTERVENTIONS

1. Assess the nature of the veteran's/service member's sleep disturbance, including sleep latency time, disruption of sleep, amount of time slept, and subjective ratings of fatigue, sleepiness, and impact on functioning.

2. Assess the veteran's/service member's sleep pattern including bedtime routine, sleep hygiene behaviors, and nutritional/health habits.

3. Assign the veteran/service member to maintain a sleep diary documenting sleep patterns, thoughts, feelings, and behavior associated with sleeping.

4. Interview collateral sources (e.g., superiors, coworkers, family members) that can verify the impact that the shift work and related sleep disturbances negatively impact occupational and social functioning.

5. Assess the impact alcohol and/or drug use has on the veteran's/service member's current sleep difficulties.

6. Educate the veteran/service member on the negative effects

substances have on sleep patterns and sleep architecture.

7. Encourage the veteran/service member to discontinue all non-prescribed substance use until he/she is evaluated by a medical healthcare provider.

3. Report any mood disturbances related to sleep difficulties. (8)

8. Assess the impact that sleep deprivation has on the veteran's/service member's mental health to include depressive, anxiety, and psychotic symptoms.

4. Decrease the number of night shifts worked in a row. (9, 10)

9. Explain to the veteran/service member that decreasing the number of night shifts worked in a row can help minimize disruptions in sleep.

10. Encourage the veteran/service member to talk with his/her supervisor regarding making alternate work schedule arrangements.

5. Cooperate with a medication evaluation to determine if psychotropic medications are needed. (11)

11. Refer the veteran/service member to a prescribing practitioner to assess whether he/she would benefit from medication to improve sleep quality, increase sleep quantity, decrease depressive and anxiety symptoms, and increase alertness during working hours.

6. Take psychotropic medications as prescribed. (12)

12. Monitor the veteran/service member for medication compliance, side effects, and efficacy.

7. Practice healthy sleep hygiene behaviors. (13, 14)

13. Instruct the veteran/service member on behavioral practices conducive to good sleep that include not using caffeine four hours prior to bedtime, exercising in the mornings, not eating spicy meals/snacks prior to sleep, and removing cues to time that may promote "clock watching."

14. Assign the veteran/service member "Sleep Pattern Record" in the *Adult Psychotherapy Homework Planner*, 2nd ed. by Jongsma.

8. Implement appropriate stimulus control techniques. (15, 16)

15. Teach the veteran/service member stimulus control techniques (e.g., restrict time spent in bed, establish consistent sleep and wake time, go to bed only when sleepy, get out of bed if unable to fall asleep after 15 minutes, avoid daytime naps, only use the bed for sleep and sex).

16. Assist the veteran/service member in developing a plan for implementation of stimulus control techniques, keeping in mind obstacles such as decreased time given for sleep in the military and crowded and noisy barracks/home; monitor compliance and progress and make changes if needed.

9. Learn and implement calming skills for use at bedtime. (17, 18)

17. Teach the veteran/service member relaxation skills (e.g., progressive muscle release, slow diaphragmatic breathing); teach application of these skills to facilitate relaxation and sleep at bedtime.

18. Refer the veteran/service member for conduct biofeedback training to strengthen a successful relaxation response.

10. Identify, challenge, and replace self-talk associated with sleep disturbance. (19, 20)

19. Explore the veteran's/service member's schema and self-talk that mediate his/her emotional responses counterproductive to sleep (e.g., fears, worries of sleeplessness), challenging the negative biases; assist him/her in replacing the distorted messages with reality-based alternatives and positive self-talk that will increase

the likelihood of establishing a sound sleep pattern. ▽

20. Assign the veteran/service member a homework exercise in which he/she identifies targeted self-talk and creates reality-based alternatives (or assign "Negative Thoughts Trigger Negative Feelings" in the *Adult Psychotherapy Homework Planner*, 2nd ed. by Jongsma). ▽

▽ 11. Implement a thought-stopping technique to dismiss thoughts counterproductive to sleep. (21)

21. Assign the veteran/service member to implement the thought-stopping technique on a daily basis and at night to dismiss thoughts counterproductive to sleep (or assign "Making Use of the Thought-Stopping Technique" in the *Adult Psychotherapy Homework Planner*, 2nd ed. by Jongsma). ▽

12. Prepare for an approaching shift change. (22)

22. Instruct the veteran/service member to prepare for an approaching shift change by gradually shifting his/her bedtime and wake time back by one to two hours several days to a week before the change.

13. Minimize the impact that daylight has on circadian rhythm while driving home during the day from work. (23)

23. Assign the veteran/service member to wear dark wrap-around sunglasses during his/her drive home from work during the day.

14. Set consistent times to complete personal errands (e.g., shopping, going to the bank) during the day. (24)

24. Encourage the veteran/service member to attend to personal errands and responsibilities during specified times during the day; encourage errands be kept to a minimum and saved for days off.

15. Develop a consistent sleep schedule that applies to work and non-work days. (25)

25. Encourage the veteran/service member to not revert back to a nighttime sleep schedule over the weekend or a night off as this can cause more difficulties.

16. Create a sleeping environment that is void of light. (26)

26. Instruct the veteran/service member to create a light-free sleeping environment by blacking out windows, sealing door cracks, and/or wearing a night mask.

17. Create a noise/disturbance-free sleeping environment. (27)

27. Instruct the veteran/service member to minimize noise and disruptions by turning off the telephone ringer, asking family members to be quiet, removing pets from the immediate area, etc.

18. Take steps to increase alertness during work hours. (28, 29, 30, 31)

28. Instruct the veteran/service member to utilize moderate amounts of caffeine to promote wakefulness.

29. Instruct the veteran/service member to take brief naps during breaks or lunch if allowed.

30. Instruct the veteran/service member to maintain a consistent caloric intake as a way to keep his/her metabolism steady.

31. Encourage the veteran/service member to take brief walks throughout the night or engage in some type of physical activity.

__. ____________________________

__. ____________________________

__. ____________________________

__. ____________________________

__. ____________________________

__. ____________________________

DIAGNOSTIC SUGGESTIONS

ICD-9-CM	*ICD-10-CM*	*DSM-5* Disorder, Condition, or Problem
307.45	G47.xx	Circadian Rhythm Sleep-Wake Disorder
309.0	F43.21	Adjustment Disorder, With Depressed Mood
V62.2	Z56.9	Other Problem Related to Employment
______	______	______________________
______	______	______________________

SOCIAL DISCOMFORT

BEHAVIORAL DEFINITIONS

1. Reports an overall pattern of social anxiety, shyness, or timidity that presents itself in most social situations.
2. Exhibits hypersensitivity to the criticism or disapproval of others.
3. Reports no close friends or confidants outside of first-degree relatives.
4. Avoids situations that require a degree of interpersonal contact.
5. Verbalizes a reluctance to be involved in social situations out of fear of saying or doing something foolish or of becoming emotional in front of others.
6. Displays debilitating performance anxiety and/or avoidance of required social performance demands.
7. Reports increased heart rate, sweating, dry mouth, muscle tension, and shakiness in social situations.
8. Complains of being "passed over" for promotions due to poor performance related to high anxiety during promotion board interviews.

__. ____

____

__. ____

____

__. ____

____

LONG-TERM GOALS

1. Interact socially without undue fear or anxiety.
2. Participate in social performance requirements without undue fear or anxiety.
3. Develop the essential social skills that will enhance the quality of relationship life.
4. Develop the ability to form relationships that will enhance recovery support system.
5. Reach a personal balance between solitary time and interpersonal interaction with others.
6. Improve performance on military activities (e.g., promotion boards) that have an impact on military career progression.

__. ____
____

__. ____
____

__. ____
____

SHORT-TERM OBJECTIVES

1. Describe the history and nature of social fears and avoidance. (1, 2, 3)
2. Complete psychological tests designed to assess the nature and severity of social anxiety and avoidance. (4)

THERAPEUTIC INTERVENTIONS

1. Establish rapport with the veteran/service member toward building a therapeutic alliance.
2. Assess the veteran's/service member's frequency, intensity, duration, and history of panic symptoms, fear, and avoidance.
3. Assess the nature of any stimulus, thoughts, or situations that precipitate the veteran's/service member's social fear and/or avoidance.
4. Administer a measure of social anxiety to the veteran/service member to further assess the depth and breadth of social fears and avoidance (e.g., *The Social Interaction Anxiety Scale and/or*

Social Phobia Scale by Mattick and Clarke).

3. Cooperate with an evaluation by a prescribing practitioner for psychotropic medication. (5, 6)

5. Arrange for an evaluation for the veteran/service member for a prescription of psychotropic medications.

6. Monitor the veteran/service member for prescription compliance, side effects, and overall effectiveness of the medication; consult with the prescribing practitioner at regular intervals.

4. Participate in small group therapy for social anxiety. (7)

7. Enroll the veteran/service member in a small (closed enrollment) group for social anxiety (see "Shyness" in *The Group Therapy Treatment Planner*, 2nd ed. by Paleg and Jongsma; or "Social Anxiety Disorder" by Turk, Heimberg, and Hope in *Clinical Handbook of Psychological Disorders* by Barlow [Ed.]).

5. Verbalize an accurate understanding of the vicious cycle of social anxiety and avoidance. (8, 9)

8. Discuss with the veteran/service member how social anxiety derives from cognitive biases that overestimate negative evaluation by others, undervalue the self, distress, and often lead to unnecessary avoidance.

9. Assign the veteran/service member to read psychoeducational chapters of books or treatment manuals on social anxiety that explain the cycle of social anxiety and avoidance and the rationale for treatment (e.g., *Overcoming Shyness and Social Phobia* by Rapee; *Overcoming Social Anxiety and Shyness* by Butler; or *The Shyness and Social Anxiety Workbook* by Antony and Swinson).

6. Verbalize an understanding of the rationale for treatment of panic. (10)

10. Discuss with the veteran/service member how cognitive restructuring and exposure serve as an arena to desensitize learned fear, build social skills and confidence, and reality-test biased thoughts.

7. Learn and implement calming and coping strategies to manage anxiety symptoms during moments of social anxiety. (11)

11. Teach the veteran/service member relaxation and attentional focusing skills (e.g., staying focused externally and on behavioral goals, muscular relaxation, evenly paced diaphragmatic breathing, ride the wave of anxiety) to manage social anxiety symptoms.

8. Identify, challenge, and replace biased, fearful self-talk with reality-based, positive self-talk. (12, 13)

12. Explore the veteran's/service member's schema and self-talk that mediate his/her social fear response and challenge the biases (or assign "Journal and Replace Self-Defeating Thoughts" in the *Adult Psychotherapy Homework Planner*, 2nd ed. by Jongsma); assist him/her in generating appraisals that correct for the biases and build confidence.

13. Assign the veteran/service member a homework exercise in which he/she identifies fearful self-talk and creates reality-based alternatives; review and reinforce success, providing corrective feedback for failure (see "Restoring Socialization Comfort" in the *Adult Psychotherapy Homework Planner*, 2nd ed. by Jongsma; *The Shyness and Social Anxiety Workbook* by Antony and Swinson; *Overcoming Shyness and Social Phobia* by Rapee).

9. Undergo gradual repeated exposure to feared social situations within therapy. (14, 15)

14. Direct and assist the veteran/service member in construction of a hierarchy of anxiety-producing situations associated with the phobic response (e.g., standing in front of a promotion board).

15. Select initial *in vivo* or role-played exposures that have a high likelihood of being a successful experience for the veteran/service member; do cognitive restructuring within and after the exposure, use behavioral strategies (e.g., modeling, rehearsal, social reinforcement) to facilitate the exposure (see "Social Anxiety Disorder" by Turk, Heimberg, and Hope in *Clinical Handbook of Psychological Disorders* by Barlow [Ed.]).

10. Undergo gradual repeated exposure to feared social situations in daily life. (16)

16. Assign the veteran/service member a homework exercise in which he/she does an *in vivo* exposure exercise and records responses (or assign "Gradually Reducing Your Phobic Fear" in the *Adult Psychotherapy Homework Planner*, 2nd ed. by Jongsma; also see *The Shyness and Social Anxiety Workbook* by Antony and Swinson; *Overcoming Shyness and Social Phobia* by Rapee); review and reinforce success, providing corrective feedback toward improvement.

11. Learn and implement social skills to reduce anxiety and build confidence in social interactions. (17, 18)

17. Use instruction, modeling, and role-playing to build the veteran's/service member's general social and/or communication skills (see *Social Effectiveness Therapy* by Turner, Beidel, and Cooley).

18. Assign the veteran/service member to read about general social and/or communication skills in books or treatment manuals on building social skills (e.g., *Your Perfect Right* by Alberti and Emmons; *Conversationally Speaking* by Garner). EBT

EBT 12. Implement relapse prevention strategies for managing possible future anxiety symptoms. (19, 20, 21, 22)

19. Discuss with the veteran/service member the distinction between a lapse and relapse, associating a lapse with an initial and reversible return of symptoms, fear, or urges to avoid and relapse with the decision to return to fearful and avoidant patterns. EBT

20. Identify and rehearse with the veteran/service member the management of future situations or circumstances in which lapses could occur. EBT

21. Instruct the veteran/service member to routinely use strategies learned in therapy (e.g., using cognitive restructuring, social skills, and exposure) while building social interactions and relationships. EBT

22. Develop a "coping card" on which coping strategies and other important information (e.g., "pace your breathing," "focus on the task at hand," "you can manage it," and "it will go away") are written for the veteran's/service member's later use. EBT

13. Explore past experiences that may be the source of low self-esteem and social anxiety currently. (23, 24)

23. Probe the veteran's/service member's childhood experiences of criticism, abandonment, or abuse that would foster low self-esteem and shame, process these.

24. Assign the veteran/service member to read the books *Healing the Shame That Binds You* by Bradshaw and *Facing Shame* by Fossum and Mason; process key ideas.

14. Verbally describe the defense mechanisms used to avoid close relationships. (25)

25. Assist the veteran/service member in identifying defense mechanisms that keep others at a distance and prevent him/her from developing trusting relationships; identify ways to minimize defensiveness.

15. Return for a follow-up session to track progress, reinforce gains, and problem-solve barriers. (26)

26. Schedule a follow-up or "booster session" for the veteran/service member for one to three months after therapy ends.

__. ____________________

__. ____________________

__. ____________________

__. ____________________

__. ____________________

__. ____________________

DIAGNOSTIC SUGGESTIONS

ICD-9-CM	*ICD-10-CM*	*DSM-5* Disorder, Condition, or Problem
300.23	F40.10	Social Anxiety Disorder (Social Phobia)
300.4	F34.1	Persistent Depressive Disorder
296.xx	F32.x	Major Depressive Disorder, Single Episode
296.xx	F33.x	Major Depressive Disorder, Recurrent Episode
300.7	F45.22	Body Dysmorphic Disorder
301.82	F60.6	Avoidant Personality Disorder
301.0	F60.0	Paranoid Personality Disorder
310.22	F21	Schizotypal Personality Disorder
______	______	____________________
______	______	____________________

SPIRITUAL AND RELIGIOUS ISSUES

BEHAVIORAL DEFINITIONS

1. Reports conflicts between religious beliefs and military service.
2. Verbalizes feelings of spiritual emptiness.
3. Reports a longing and desire to be closer to a higher power.
4. Reports an inability to connect with a particular religion due to lack of education and understanding about different religions.
5. Expresses a belief that there is no God due to past hurt, rejection, and/or childhood traumas.
6. Reports being discriminated against by the military due to spiritual/religious beliefs.

—. ____

____

—. ____

____

—. ____

____

LONG-TERM GOALS

1. Resolve conflicts between military service and spiritual/religious beliefs.
2. Develop a connection with a higher power that provides satisfaction and fulfillment.
3. Become versed in a chosen religion and implement practices as desired.
4. Develop connections and supports with others that share same spiritual/religious beliefs.

—. ____

____

—. ____

____

—. ____

____

SHORT-TERM OBJECTIVES

1. Describe in detail the nature of the spiritual/religious issues. (1, 2)

2. Describe current spiritual belief system. (3, 4, 5)

3. Talk with a military chaplain about spiritual and religious beliefs and conflicts between belief system and the military. (6, 7, 8)

THERAPEUTIC INTERVENTIONS

1. Establish a therapeutic relationship with the veteran/service member that conveys an accepting and non-judgmental stance.

2. Assess the veteran's/service member's type, intensity, and frequency of spiritual/religious concerns and the impact on social, occupational, and interpersonal functioning.

3. Ask the veteran/service member to describe his/her spiritual belief system and how it fits in with traditional religion.

4. Assist the veteran/service member in identifying what influenced his/her current beliefs (e.g., family, friends, television, school).

5. Assist the veteran/service member in processing any significant emotional material that arises from this discussion.

6. Encourage the service member to talk with a military chaplain to help identify the rationale behind the conflict between his/her belief system and serving in the military.

7. Encourage the service member to discuss his/her beliefs with a second military chaplain if he/she feels his/her questions were not answered or concerns were not appreciated.
8. Discuss with the service member the importance religion has played in the military during times of war.

4. Describe in detail the religious atmosphere and practices of the family of origin. (9, 10)

9. Assist the veteran/service member in understanding how early life experiences in his/her family helped shape his/her current beliefs (or assign the "My History of Spirituality" exercise in the *Adult Psychotherapy Homework Planner*, 2nd ed. by Jongsma).
10. Instruct the veteran/service member to construct a list of those beliefs that are no longer consistent with his/her current beliefs.

5. Verbalize an understanding of the need to separate past negative childhood experiences regarding religion from the present. (11, 12)

11. Assist the veteran/service member in challenging the validity and/or usefulness of his/her current views about religion that were fueled by past negative experiences in the family, school, or from friends.
12. Encourage the veteran/service member to forgive those that instilled fear in him/her regarding religion and that conditioned him/her to view religion as critical, judgmental, and punitive.

6. Identify the differences between religion, spirituality, and a higher power. (13)

13. Educate the veteran/service member on the differences between religion, spirituality, and a higher power; refer to a minister/chaplain if necessary.

7. Verbalize an understanding of the tenets of the chosen belief system. (14, 15)

14. Assist the veteran/service member in identifying the main principles of his/her chosen belief system and how they apply to his/her everyday life.

15. Encourage the veteran/service member to create a list of those aspects of his/her belief system that conflict with his/her view of life and/or service in the military; encourage the veteran/service member to discuss conflicts with a spiritual/religious leader or someone he/she respects for their spiritual/religious values.

8. Verbalize how spirituality and/or religion will fill a perceived emptiness or void. (16, 17)

16. Assign the veteran/service member to write a narrative statement regarding how he/she feels his/her life has a void and lacks meaning and purpose.

17. Assign the veteran/service member to write a narrative statement in response to the previous narrative statement addressing how including spirituality and religion in his/her life will fill this void; encourage the veteran/service member to be specific.

9. Describe the concept of faith and how it applies to religion. (18, 19)

18. Explore with the veteran/service member about what faith means and how it is a primary tenet of any religion.

19. Assist the veteran/service member in identifying other areas of his/her life when he/she has used faith; process relevant content.

10. Engage in daily prayer, reflection, or meditation. (20, 21)

20. Recommend that the veteran/service member pray and/or meditate daily; process his/her feelings about the experience.

21. Recommend that the protestant

veteran/service member read *The Purpose-Driven Life* by Warren.

11. Attend religious services on a regular basis. (22, 23, 24)

22. Encourage the veteran/service member to attend a church/synagogue/mosque weekly that he/she feels is a good fit with his/her beliefs; reinforce attendance.

23. Encourage the veteran/service member to maintain a "church diary" so that he/she can write reflections and make notes about lessons learned during the sermons; encourage the veteran/service member to review it throughout the week.

24. Encourage the veteran/service member to attend worship/prayer services more frequently as he/she feels comfortable.

12. Attend religious-based community support groups/activities. (25)

25. Assist the veteran/service member in identifying religious-based community groups and activities (e.g., Bible study classes, church socials, religious training classes) and encourage attendance.

13. Talk with another service member with strong spiritual/religious beliefs about conflicts he/she encountered. (26)

26. Assist the service member in identifying a fellow comrade that he/she respects for their spiritual/religious beliefs and encourage him/her to talk with the fellow service member about their own struggles with religion, particularly with experiences related to ridicule and discrimination; process this experience.

___. ______________________ ___. ______________________

______________________ ______________________

___. ______________________ ___. ______________________

______________________ ______________________

___. ______________________ ___. ______________________

______________________ ______________________

DIAGNOSTIC SUGGESTIONS

ICD-9-CM	*ICD-10-CM*	*DSM-5* Disorder, Condition, or Problem
V62.89	Z65.8	Religious or Spiritual Problem
309.0	F43.21	Adjustment Disorder, With Depressed Mood
311	F32.9	Unspecified Depressive Disorder
311	F32.8	Other Specified Depressive Disorder
300.00	F41.9	Unspecified Anxiety Disorder
296.xx	F32.x	Major Depressive Disorder, Single Episode
296.xx	F33.x	Major Depressive Disorder, Recurrent Episode
______	______	______________________
______	______	______________________

SUBSTANCE ABUSE / DEPENDENCE

BEHAVIORAL DEFINITIONS

1. Demonstrates a maladaptive pattern of substance use, manifested by increased tolerance and withdrawal.
2. Fails to stop or cut down use of mood-altering drug once started, despite the verbalized desire to do so and the negative consequences continued use brings.
3. Presents with blood work (e.g., elevated liver enzymes, electrolyte imbalance) and physical indicators (e.g., stomach pain, high blood pressure, malnutrition) that reflect the results of a pattern of heavy substance use.
4. Denies that chemical dependence is a problem, despite feedback from family, friends, unit leaders, or subordinates that the use of the substance is negatively affecting him/her and others.
5. Experiences frequent blackouts when using.
6. Continues substance use despite knowledge of experiencing persistent physical, legal, financial, vocational, social, and/or relationship problems that are directly caused by the use of the substance.
7. Demonstrates increased tolerance for the drug, as there is the need to use more to become intoxicated or to recall the desired effect.
8. Exhibits physical withdrawal symptoms (e.g., shaking, seizures, nausea, headaches, sweating, anxiety, insomnia, depression) when going without the substance for any length of time.
9. Has a history of altercations with military or civilian police for substance abuse-related offenses (e.g., driving under the influence [DUI], minor in possession [MIP], domestic disturbance, assault, possession/delivery of a controlled substance, shoplifting, breaking and entering [B&E]).

---

10. Reports repeated lateness to morning accountability or physical training formations as a result of substance use.

—. ______________________________

—. ______________________________

—. ______________________________

LONG-TERM GOALS

1. Accept the unmanageability over mood-altering substances, and participate in a recovery-based program.
2. Establish a sustained recovery, free from the use of all mood-altering substances.
3. Establish and maintain total abstinence, while increasing knowledge of the disease and the process of recovery.
4. Acquire the necessary 12-step skills to maintain long-term sobriety from all mood-altering substances, and live a life free of substance abuse.
5. Improve quality of life by maintaining an ongoing abstinence from all mood-altering chemicals.

—. ______________________________

—. ______________________________

—. ______________________________

SHORT-TERM OBJECTIVES

1. Cooperate with medical assessment and an evaluation of the necessity for pharmacological intervention. (1, 2)

THERAPEUTIC INTERVENTIONS

1. Refer the veteran/service member to a military healthcare provider to perform a physical examination, assess the need for psychotropic medication for any mental/emotional comorbidities, and discuss the use of acamprosate

(Campral), naltrexone (Vivitrol), or disulfiram (Antabuse) where applicable.

2. Refer the veteran/service member to a pharmacology-based treatment/recovery program (e.g., acamprosate, naltrexone), where applicable.

2. Take prescribed medications as directed by the military healthcare provider. (3, 4)

3. Healthcare provider will monitor the effectiveness and side effects of medication, titrating as necessary.

4. Staff will administer prescribed medications and monitor for effectiveness and side effects.

3. Report acute withdrawal symptoms to the staff. (5)

5. Assess and monitor the veteran's/service member's condition during withdrawal, using a standardized procedure (e.g., Narcotic Withdrawal Scale) as needed.

4. Complete psychological testing or objective questionnaires for assessing substance dependence. (6)

6. Administer to the veteran/service member psychological instruments designed to objectively assess substance dependence (e.g., Substance Use Disorders Diagnostic Schedule-IV [SUDDS-IV], Substance Abuse Subtle Screen Inventory-3 [SASS-3]); give the veteran/service member feedback regarding the results of the assessment; re-administer as needed to assess outcome.

5. Provide honest and complete information for a chemical dependence biopsychosocial history. (7)

7. Complete a thorough family and personal biopsychosocial history that has a focus on addiction (e.g., family history of addiction and treatment, other substances used, progression of substance abuse, consequences of abuse).

6. Attend didactic sessions and read assigned material in order to increase knowledge of

8. Assign the veteran/service member to attend a chemical dependence didactic series to increase

addiction and the process of recovery. (8, 9, 10, 11)

his/her knowledge of the patterns and effects of chemical dependence; ask him/her to identify several key points attained from each didactic and process these points with the therapist.

9. Assign the veteran/service member to read a workbook describing evidence-based treatment approaches to addiction recovery (e.g., *Overcoming Your Alcohol or Drug Problem*, 2nd ed. by Daley and Marlatt); use the readings to reinforce key concepts and practices throughout therapy.

10. Assign the veteran/service member to read material on addiction (e.g., *Willpower's Not Enough* by Washton; *The Addiction Workbook* by Fanning, or *Alcoholics Anonymous*); process key points gained from the reading.

11. Require the veteran/service member to read the book *Narcotics Anonymous* and gather five key points from it to process with the therapist.

7. Attend group therapy sessions to share thoughts and feelings associated with, reasons for, consequences of, feelings about, and alternatives to addiction. (12, 13)

12. Assign the veteran/service member to attend group therapy.

13. Direct group therapy that facilitates the veteran/service member sharing causes for, consequences of, feelings about, and alternatives to addiction.

8. List and discuss negative consequences resulting from or exacerbated by substance dependence. (14, 15, 16)

14. Ask the veteran/service member to make a list of the ways chemical use has negatively impacted his/her life (or assign "Substance Abuse Negative Impact Versus Sobriety's Positive Impact" in the *Adult Psychotherapy Homework Planner*, 2nd ed. by Jongsma);

process the list in individual or group sessions.

15. Confront the veteran's/service member's use of denial to minimize the severity of and negative consequences of substance abuse.

16. Using the biopsychosocial history and the veteran's/service member's list of negative consequences of substance abuse, assist him/her in understanding the need to stay in treatment.

9. Verbalize recognition that mood-altering chemicals were used as the primary coping mechanism to escape from stress or pain, and resulted in negative consequences. (17)

17. Explore how addiction was used to escape from stress, physical and emotional pain, and boredom; confront the negative consequences of this pattern.

10. List and discuss the negative emotions that were caused or exacerbated by substance dependence. (18)

18. Probe the veteran's/service member's sense of shame, guilt, and low self-worth that has resulted from addiction and its consequences.

11. List and discuss reasons to work on a plan for recovery from addiction. (19)

19. Assign the veteran/service member to write a list of reasons to be abstinent from addiction (or assign "Making Change Happen" or "A Working Recovery Plan" in the *Addiction Treatment Homework Planner*, 4th ed. by Finley and Lenz).

12. List lies used to hide substance dependence. (20, 21)

20. Help the veteran/service member see the dishonesty that goes along with addiction; ask him/her to list lies told to hide substance use.

21. Teach the veteran/service member why honesty is essential to recovery.

13. Verbalize ways a higher power can assist in recovery. (22)

22. Teach the veteran/service member about the AA concept of a higher power and how this can assist in recovery (e.g., God

can help with chronic pain or craving, regular prayer and meditation can reduce stress).

14. Identify and accept the need for substance abuse treatment. (23)

23. Conduct Motivational Interviewing to assess the veteran's/service member's stage of preparation for change; intervene accordingly, moving from building motivation, through strengthening commitment to change, to participation in treatment (see *Motivational Interviewing: Preparing People for Change* by Miller and Rollnick).

15. Identify realistic goals for substance abuse recovery. (24, 25, 26)

24. Assign the veteran/service member to meet with an AA/NA member who has been working the 12-step program for several years and find out specifically how the program has helped him/her to stay sober; afterward process the meeting.

25. Request that the veteran/service member write out basic treatment expectations (e.g., physical changes, social changes, emotional needs) regarding sobriety, and process these with the clinician.

26. Emphasize the goal of substance abuse recovery and the need for sobriety, despite lapses or relapses.

16. Verbalize a commitment to abstain from the use of mood-altering drugs. (27)

27. Develop an abstinence contract with the veteran/service member regarding the termination of the use of his/her drug; process the veteran's/service member's feelings related to the commitment.

17. Identify and make changes in social relationships that will support recovery. (28)

28. Review the negative influence of the veteran/service member continuing his/her alcohol-related friendships ("drug buddies") and assist him/her in making a plan

to develop new sober relationships including "sobriety buddies;" revisit routinely and facilitate toward development of a new social support system.

18. Identify the positive impact that sobriety will have on intimate and family relationships. (29)

29. Assist the veteran/service member in identifying positive changes that will be made in family relationships during recovery.

19. Agree to make amends to significant others who have been hurt by the life dominated by substance abuse. (30, 31)

30. Discuss the negative effects the veteran's/service member's substance abuse has had on family, friends, and work relationships and encourage a plan to make amends for such hurt.

31. Elicit from the veteran/service member a verbal commitment to make initial amends now to key individuals and further amends later or if working Steps Eight and Nine of an AA program (see *The Alcoholism and Drug Abuse Patient Workbook* by Perkinson).

20. Participate in behavioral marital or family therapy. (32)

32. Refer to or provide behavioral couples or family therapy to learn and implement ways to improve relations, resolve conflicts, solve problems, and communicate effectively.

21. Learn and implement personal coping strategies to manage urges to lapse back into chemical use. (33)

33. Teach the veteran/service member tailored coping strategies involving calming strategies (e.g., relaxation, breathing), thought-stopping, positive self-talk, and attentional focusing skills (e.g., distraction from urges, staying focused on behavioral goals of abstinence) to manage triggered urges to use chemical substances.

22. Identify, challenge, and replace destructive self-talk with positive, strength building self-talk. (34, 35)

34. Use cognitive therapy approaches to explore the veteran's/service member's schema and self-talk that weaken his/her resolve to

remain abstinent; challenge the biases; assist him/her in generating realistic self-talk that correct for the biases and build resilience. ▽

35. Rehearse situations in which the veteran/service member identifies his/her negative self-talk and generates empowering alternatives (or assign "Journal and Replace Self-Defeating Thoughts" in the *Adult Psychotherapy Homework Planner*, 2nd ed. by Jongsma); review and reinforce success. ▽

▽ 23. Participate in gradual repeated exposure to triggers of urges to lapse back into chemical substance use. (36, 37)

36. Direct and assist the veteran/service member in construction of a hierarchy of urge-producing cues to use substances (or assign "Identifying Relapse Triggers and Cues" or "Relapse Prevention Planning" in the *Addiction Treatment Homework Planner*, 4th ed. by Finley and Lenz). ▽

37. Select initial *in vivo* or role-played cue exposures that have a high likelihood of being a successful experience for the veteran/service member; facilitate coping and cognitive restructuring within and after the exposure, use behavioral strategies (e.g., modeling, rehearsal, social reinforcement) to facilitate the exposure, review with the veteran/service member. ▽

▽ 24. Learn and implement personal skills to manage common day-to-day challenges without the use of substances. (38, 39)

38. Assess current skill in managing common everyday stressors (e.g., work, social, family role demands); use behavioral techniques (e.g., instruction, modeling, role-playing) to build social and/or communication skills to manage these challenges without the use of substances. ▽

39. Assign the veteran/service member to read about general social and/or communication skills in books or treatment manuals on building social skills (e.g., *Your Perfect Right* by Alberti and Emmons; *Conversationally Speaking* by Garner).

25. Learn and implement pain management techniques as an alternative to coping through substance use. (40)

40. Teach or refer the veteran/service member to a pain management program to learn alternatives to substance use for managing pain (see the chapter on Chronic Pain After Injury in this *Planner*).

26. Implement relapse prevention strategies for managing possible future situations with high-risk for relapse. (41, 42, 43, 44, 45)

41. Discuss with the veteran/service member the distinction between a lapse and relapse, associating a lapse with an initial, temporary, and reversible use of a substance and relapse with the decision to return to a repeated pattern of abuse.

42. Using a 12-step recovery program's relapse prevention exercise, help the veteran/service member uncover his/her triggers for relapse (see *The Alcoholism and Drug Abuse Patient Workbook* by Perkinson).

43. Identify and rehearse with the veteran/service member the management of future situations or circumstances in which lapses could occur.

44. Request that the veteran/service member identify feelings, behaviors, and situations that place him/her at a higher risk for substance abuse (or assign "Relapse Triggers" in the *Adult Psychotherapy Homework Planner*, 2nd ed. by Jongsma).

45. Instruct the veteran/service member to routinely use strategies learned in therapy (e.g., using cognitive restructuring, social skills, and exposure) while building social interactions and relationships (or assign "Aftercare Plan Components" in the *Adult Psychotherapy Homework Planner*, 2nd ed. by Jongsma).▽

▽ 27. Verbalize that there are options to substance use in dealing with stress and in finding pleasure or excitement in life. (46, 47, 48, 49)

46. Teach the veteran/service member the importance of getting pleasure out of life without using mood-altering substances.▽

47. Assist the veteran/service member in developing a list of pleasurable activities (see *Inventory of Rewarding Activities* by Birchler and Weiss); assign engagement in selected activities daily.▽

48. Encourage the veteran/service member to establish a daily routine of physical exercise to build body stamina, self-esteem, and reduce depression (see *Exercising Your Way to Better Mental Health* by Leith), or revisit effectiveness of the physical training plan already in place.▽

49. Instruct veteran/service member to discuss his/her current level of fitness with his/her Platoon Sergeant or First Sergeant and develop a specialized exercise program if needed.▽

28. Verbalize the results of turning problems over to God each day. (50)

50. Using a Step Three exercise, teach the veteran/service member about the recovery concept of "turning it over;" then assign turning over problems to a higher power each day; ask the veteran/service member to record the event and discuss the results.

__. ______________________ __. ______________________

______________________ ______________________

__. ______________________ __. ______________________

______________________ ______________________

__. ______________________ __. ______________________

______________________ ______________________

DIAGNOSTIC SUGGESTIONS

ICD-9-CM	*ICD-10-CM*	*DSM-5* Disorder, Condition, or Problem
305.60	F14.10	Cocaine Use Disorder, Mild
305.90	F19.10	Other (or Unknown) Substance Use Disorder, Mild
305.90	F19.20	Other (or Unknown) Substance Use Disorder, Moderate or Severe
305.40	F13.10	Sedative, Hypnotic, or Anxiolytic Use Disorder, Mild
303.90	F10.20	Alcohol Use Disorder, Moderate or Severe
305.20	F12.10	Cannabis Use Disorder, Mild
305.70	F15.10	Amphetamine-Type Substance Use Disorder, Mild
305.00	F10.10	Alcohol Use Disorder, Mild
304.40	F15.20	Amphetamine-Type Substance Use Disorder, Moderate or Severe
304.30	F12.20	Cannabis Use Disorder, Moderate or Severe
304.20	F14.20	Cocaine Use Disorder, Moderate or Severe
304.50	F16.20	Other Hallucinogen Use Disorder, Moderate or Severe
304.30	F16.10	Other Hallucinogen Use Disorder, Mild
304.00	F11.20	Opioid Use Disorder, Moderate or Severe
304.90	F16.20	Phencyclidine Use Disorder, Moderate or Severe
304.10	F13.20	Sedative, Hypnotic, or Anxiolytic Use Disorder, Moderate or Severe
________	________	______________________
________	________	______________________

SUICIDAL IDEATION

BEHAVIORAL DEFINITIONS

1. Reports recurrent thought of suicide or preoccupation with death and dying.
2. Possesses suicidal intent.
3. Acknowledges a detailed plan of suicide.
4. Reports feelings of hopelessness and/or chronic feelings of emptiness.
5. Reports past suicide attempts or suicidal gestures.
6. Engages in risky and dangerous behavior during combat missions (e.g., enters a house without back-up).
7. Reports past completed suicide by a family member or close friend.
8. Acknowledges a positive history for major depression.
9. Displays akathisia resulting from prescription medication (e.g., antidepressants) or illicit drug use (cocaine).
10. Displays a lack of future orientation.
11. Recently given away personal and meaningful possessions to friends, families, or strangers (e.g., stereo, clothes, video games).
12. Displays a recent onset of uncharacteristic disrespectful and hostile behavior towards superiors.

__. ____

____

__. ____

____

__. ____

____

LONG-TERM GOALS

1. Eliminate suicidal ideation and intent.
2. Decrease feelings of hopelessness and increase self-esteem.

3. Increase healthy coping skills.
4. Reestablish a sense of purpose and future orientation.
5. Return to previous highest level of occupational functioning.

__. ____

____

__. ____

____

__. ____

____

SHORT-TERM OBJECTIVES

1. Verbalize the level of suicidal feelings, including frequency of thoughts and details of plan. (1, 2, 3, 4, 5)

THERAPEUTIC INTERVENTIONS

1. Assess the veteran's/service member's suicidal ideation including plan, intent, and overall level of risk.
2. Administer the veteran/service member the Beck Depression Inventory Second Edition (BDI-II), Beck Hopelessness Scale (BHS), and the Suicide Probability Scale (SPS) to assess for risk of suicide; provide feedback to the veteran/service member.
3. Inform veteran's/service member's family members and/or chain of command if level of risk is high.
4. Provide the veteran/service member with a clear plan for seeking help if he/she feels suicidal prior to the next appointment (e.g., call veteran's/service member's First Sergeant, relative, or friend).
5. Schedule a follow-up appointment for the veteran/service member at the end of the session.

2. Agree to a verbal or written no-harm contract with the therapist. (6, 7)

6. Create a written no-harm contract for the veteran/service member to sign or have the veteran/service member verbally agree to a no-harm contract.

7. Review the no-harm contract each session or as needed.

3. Agree to a commitment to treatment contract. (8)

8. Create a written commitment to treatment contract for the veteran/service member to sign, or have the veteran/service member verbally agree to a treatment contract.

4. Cooperate with recommendations regarding making the environment safe (e.g., removal of firearms from the home). (9, 10)

9. Inform the veteran's/service member's family members or significant others about his/her suicidal ideation; assist them with making the home safer by removing all weapons and handling all prescription medications.

10. Inform the service member's chain of command about his/her suicidal ideation; assist them with making the work environment safer by restricting access to weapons and limit the service member to low risk training.

5. Cooperate with hospitalization if suicidal intent develops. (11, 12)

11. Facilitate hospitalization if the veteran/service member is considered to be at imminent risk.

12. Inform family members and/or chain of command if hospitalization is required.

6. Develop a safety plan with chain of command that includes a "battle buddy." (13)

13. Develop a safety plan with the service member's chain of command that requires the service member to be in sight of a peer 24 hours a day.

7. Discuss suicidal feelings with family and friends in order to increase social support. (14, 15)

14. Meet with the veteran's/service member's significant others to answer any questions they may have about the veteran's/service member's suicidal ideation, how they can help, and what behaviors may be counterproductive.

15. Arrange a family therapy session to process the emotions of all parties involved.

8. Identify psychosocial factors that contribute to the suicidal ideation. (16)

16. Discuss interpersonal, social, and occupational stressors that contribute to the suicidal ideation; develop coping strategies to manage the stressors.

9. Identify past periods of suicidal ideation and how those feelings were overcome. (17, 18)

17. Discuss the veteran's/service member's past episodes of suicidal ideation, specifically focusing on triggers.

18. Highlight the veteran's/service member's past successes in overcoming suicidal ideation.

10. Complete a psychiatric evaluation to assess the need for antidepressant medication. (19, 20)

19. Arrange for a psychiatric evaluation to determine if antidepressant medication is needed.

20. Inform a family member and/or chain of command if the veteran/service member does not attend the scheduled appointment.

11. Take medications as prescribed. (21)

21. Monitor medication compliance, side effects, efficacy, and progress.

12. Describe positive aspects of his/her current and future life. (22)

22. Identify areas of the veteran's/service member's life, both current and future, that are positive; reinforce any positive comments and thoughts the veteran/service member may have.

13. Identify and change dysfunctional and maladaptive beliefs about self, others, and the world. (23, 24, 25)

23. Assist the veteran/service member in identifying maladaptive thought patterns that perpetuate suicidal ideation (e.g., I am worthless, I am not worthy of love); or assign "Negative Thoughts Trigger Negative Feelings" in the *Adult Psychotherapy Homework Planner*, 2nd ed. by Jongsma.

24. Teach the veteran/service member how to become more aware of automatic thoughts by maintaining a daily automatic thoughts journal/log (or assign "Journal of Distorted, Negative Thoughts" in the *Adult Psychotherapy Homework Planner*, 2nd ed. by Jongsma).

25. Utilize cognitive restructuring to teach the veteran/service member to replace his/her maladaptive distortions (e.g., all-or-nothing thinking, overgeneralization, magnification) with positive, reality-based thoughts.

14. Report an absence of suicidal ideation. (26)

26. Continually query about the presence of suicidal ideation in the veteran/service member; acknowledge and reinforce the absence of suicidal ideation.

15. Verbalize spiritual beliefs about life, death, and suicide. (27)

27. Assist the veteran/service member in gaining a clearer understanding of his/her beliefs about taking his/her life; process the emotions and thoughts related to veteran's/service member's beliefs about the social, family, and spiritual consequences of suicide (or assign "The Aftermath of Suicide" in the *Adult Psychotherapy Homework Planner*, 2nd ed. by Jongsma).

16. Meet with the unit Chaplain. (28)

28. Encourage the veteran/service member to meet with his/her unit Chaplain or his/her Chaplain at the local Veterans Affairs hospital.

17. Develop a plan of care if the service member is scheduled to deploy. (29, 30)

29. Assist the service member in identifying mental health resources at the location where he/she will be deployed.

30. Ensure that the service member has enough medication to get him/her through the deployment transition.

—. ______________________

—. ______________________

—. ______________________

—. ______________________

—. ______________________

—. ______________________

DIAGNOSTIC SUGGESTIONS

ICD-9-CM	*ICD-10-CM*	*DSM-5* Disorder, Condition, or Problem
296.xx	F32.x	Major Depressive Disorder, Single Episode
296.xx	F33.x	Major Depressive Disorder, Recurrent Episode
300.4	F34.1	Persistent Depressive Disorder
296.xx	F31.xx	Bipolar I Disorder
296.89	F31.81	Bipolar II Disorder
301.83	F60.3	Borderline Personality Disorder
301.81	F60.81	Narcissistic Personality Disorder
________	________	______________________
________	________	______________________

SURVIVOR'S GUILT

BEHAVIORAL DEFINITIONS

1. Reports feeling guilty for surviving or being injured when fellow comrade(s) was killed or seriously injured.
2. Blames self for the loss of life of a comrade.
3. Reports constant thoughts about doing nothing or too little to prevent or minimize the loss of life or injury to a comrade.
4. Complains of feelings of worthlessness and self-loathing.
5. Expresses a desire to die or suffer the same fate as his/her comrade.
6. Engages in an increased amount of fighting, drug and alcohol use, and other self-destructive behaviors.

—. ____

____

—. ____

____

—. ____

____

LONG-TERM GOALS

1. Eliminate feelings of guilt associated with the loss.
2. Regain self-confidence and self-esteem.
3. Accept that loss is a part of life.
4. View self as a fortunate survivor.

__. ____

____

__. ____

____

__. ____

____

SHORT-TERM OBJECTIVES

1. Describe in detail the nature and impact of the guilt. (1, 2, 3)

2. Cooperate with a psychiatric evaluation to determine if psychotropic medication is needed. (4, 5)

3. Share openly and honestly about the reaction to the loss. (6, 7, 8)

THERAPEUTIC INTERVENTIONS

1. Establish a therapeutic relationship with the veteran/service member that conveys an attitude of acceptance and understanding.
2. Explore the incident that led to the veteran/service member feeling guilt; allow him/her to talk about it in as much detail as possible.
3. Assess the intensity, frequency, and severity of the veteran's/service member's guilt and the impact on social, occupational, and interpersonal functioning.
4. Arrange for a psychiatric evaluation for the veteran/service member to determine if antidepressant, anxiolytic, or hypnotic medication is needed to relieve more significant mood or anxiety symptoms and/or sleep disturbances.
5. Monitor the veteran's/service member's medication compliance, side effects, and efficacy; keep in communication with prescribing professional.
6. Encourage the veteran/service member to share the history of his/her feelings and experiences

after the loss; process the most relevant material.

7. Utilize basic counseling techniques (e.g., reflection, empathic responding) as a means to convey caring, empathy, and respect.

8. Educate the veteran/service member on the importance of acknowledging and connecting with strong emotions; encourage an emotional catharsis related to the loss.

4. Verbalize an understanding that brief feelings of grief, guilt, and self-blame are normal after this type of event. (9, 10)

9. Normalize the veteran's/service member's feelings by educating him/her about how experiencing shame, self-blame, and self-loathing is common after this type of event.

10. Educate the veteran/service member on symptoms that are not considered typical and expected (e.g., suicidal ideation, increased substance use, domestic violence).

5. Verbalize the importance of developing a "survivor" identity. (11, 12)

11. Explore with the veteran/service member any impediments (e.g., gets sympathy from others) to adapting a view of self as a "survivor."

12. Educate the veteran/service member on how those who see themselves as "survivors" are able to regain a sense of control and self-determination; use examples from the veteran's/service member's military training and career to illustrate the point.

6. Focus on the event as being a result of misfortune and not the survivor's responsibility. (13, 14, 15)

13. Assign the veteran/service member to create a list of reasons supporting the idea that the event was related to

misfortune and events outside of his/her control; process the list.

14. Identify, challenge, and replace the veteran's/service member's maladaptive thoughts that promote misplaced self-blame.

15. If the event was related to the veteran's/service member's actions or lack of actions, explain to him/her that accidents happen during the stress and chaos of combat and that extreme circumstances can negatively impact decision making.

7. Restore a sense of safety and stability by adhering to a routine. (16, 17)

16. Educate the veteran/service member about how following a routine promotes familiarity, contentment, and predictability.

17. Instruct the veteran/service member to exercise and attend work daily while only missing either due to sickness or other extreme circumstances.

8. Grieve for the loss of the comrade(s). (18, 19, 20)

18. Facilitate closure by encouraging the veteran/service member to acknowledge the loss, discuss the impact of the loss on his/her life, and say goodbye by participating in a ritual (e.g., funeral/memorial service, visiting the burial site, writing a farewell letter or talking to a picture).

19. Instruct the veteran/service member to visit with someone who knew the fellow comrade(s) and share pleasant memories of the deceased.

20. Encourage the veteran/service member to plan an annual memorial service honoring the fellow comrade(s).

9. Acknowledge joy about being alive. (21)

21. Instruct the veteran/service member to make a list of why it is good to be alive; process the list in session.

10. Complete an assets and strengths inventory. (22, 23)

22. Instruct the veteran/service member to compile a list of his/her personal emotional and social strengths and assets that have helped him/her through difficult times in the past.

23. Explain to the veteran/service member that his/her situation may be worse if it were not for his/her inner resolve and fortitude.

11. Reflect on the meaning of life. (24, 25)

24. Explore with the veteran/service member his/her meaning of life and purpose on earth.

25. Encourage the veteran/service member to talk with someone with more wisdom and experience that is able to share his/her philosophy of life and death.

12. Talk with someone else who has been through a similar experience. (26)

26. Encourage the veteran/service member to talk with a veteran or fellow service member that has experienced the same type of loss and feelings.

13. Develop spiritual contacts/ resources. (27)

27. Encourage the veteran/service member to meet with a military chaplain and discuss his/her emotional and spiritual conflicts about the loss.

14. Develop and attend support groups. (28)

28. Instruct the veteran/service member to locate a local support group for other members who have lost someone close.

15. Assist with recovery and clean-up efforts. (29)

29. If applicable, encourage the veteran/service member to participate in clean-up and recovery activities; ensure that the veteran/service member is psychologically and physically ready to participate.

__. ____________________ __. ____________________

__. ____________________ __. ____________________

__. ____________________ __. ____________________

DIAGNOSTIC SUGGESTIONS

ICD-9-CM	*ICD-10-CM*	*DSM-5* Disorder, Condition, or Problem
V62.82	Z63.4	Uncomplicated Bereavement
309.0	F43.21	Adjustment Disorder, With Depressed Mood
296.xx	F32.x	Major Depressive Disorder, Single Episode
296.xx	F33.x	Major Depressive Disorder, Recurrent Episode
305.00	F10.10	Alcohol Use Disorder, Mild
303.90	F10.20	Alcohol Use Disorder, Moderate or Severe
______	______	________________
______	______	________________

TOBACCO USE

BEHAVIORAL DEFINITIONS

1. Regularly uses cigarettes, cigars, or pipes and/or smokeless tobacco that causes physical health problems.
2. Exhibits decreased physical fitness as a result of using tobacco.
3. Frequency of use of tobacco is increasing.
4. Has failed in past attempts at tobacco cessation.
5. Displays withdrawal symptoms (e.g., insomnia, irritability, restlessness) after brief periods of being abstinent from tobacco.
6. Complains of discolored teeth, bad breath, and/or foul smelling clothes that are due to tobacco use and cause significant social dissatisfaction.
7. Reports intense nicotine cravings after awakening in the morning or when unable to use tobacco for several hours at a time.
8. Lies to family and/or friends to try to hide tobacco use.
9. Continues using tobacco despite having someone close die from tobacco related cancer or pulmonary disease.
10. Fails required physical training tests due to decreased lung capacity.

__. ____

____

__. ____

____

__. ____

____

LONG-TERM GOALS

1. Develop adequate coping resources to refrain from all tobacco use.
2. Develop coping strategies to manage nicotine cravings.
3. Improve physical health and physical fitness.
4. Eliminate social alienation due to negative effects of smoking (e.g., bad breath, stained teeth).

__. ____
____

__. ____
____

__. ____
____

SHORT-TERM OBJECTIVES

1. Discuss in detail the history and current pattern of tobacco use. (1, 2)

2. Verbalize a desire and commitment to stop using tobacco. (3, 4)

3. Cooperate with a physical examination to assess for any negative physical effects caused by past tobacco use. (5)

THERAPEUTIC INTERVENTIONS

1. Gather data regarding the history of the veteran's/service member's tobacco use including duration, frequency, and type.

2. Assess the impact that the veteran's/service member's tobacco use has had on his/her physical, occupational, social, and interpersonal functioning.

3. Explain the five stages of change (Precontemplation, Contemplation, Preparation, Action, and Maintenance) to the veteran/service member (see *The Transtheoretical Approach: Crossing Traditional Boundaries of Therapy* by Prochaska and DiClemente).

4. Assess the veteran/service member as to whether he/she verbalizes a desire to stop using tobacco that is consistent with Prochaska's and DiClemente's stage two of change (Contemplation).

5. Refer the veteran/service member for a physical evaluation to assess for any complications of long-term tobacco use (e.g., respiratory problems, oral decay).

4. Acknowledge the health risks associated with continued tobacco use. (6, 7)

6. Educate the veteran/service member on the health risks of using tobacco in smoke or smokeless form.

7. Instruct the veteran/service member to read material on the health hazards of smoking; provide the veteran/service member with the following web links: www.cancer.gov/cancer topics/factsheet/tobacco/ cancer and www.cancer.org.

5. Acknowledge the physical and social benefits of not using tobacco. (8, 9)

8. Instruct the veteran/service member to create a list of how using tobacco has limited his/her physical and social functioning (e.g., failed a physical training test, girlfriend/boyfriend left due to tobacco use); process the list in session.

9. Instruct the veteran/service member to create a list of how his/her life will be better if he/she quits using tobacco (e.g., more dates, save more money, clothes won't smell, run faster on physical training test).

6. Decide on and commit to a specified date to quit using tobacco. (3, 10)

3. Explain the five stages of change (Precontemplation, Contemplation, Preparation, Action, and Maintenance) to the veteran/service member (see *The Transtheoretical Approach: Crossing Traditional Boundaries of Therapy* by Prochaska and DiClemente).

10. Consistent with Prochaska's and DiClemente's stage three of change (Preparation), instruct the veteran/service member to set a specific date to stop using tobacco.

7. Remove all tobacco paraphernalia from home, car, and office. (11)

11. Instruct the veteran/service member to remove all tobacco paraphernalia (e.g., cigarette

lighters, unused packs of cigarettes and cans of smokeless tobacco, ashtrays) from his/her home, office, and car as a way to prevent temptation and limit impulsive tobacco use.

8. Verbalize an understanding that a combined approach (i.e., pharmacotherapy and cognitive-behavioral therapy) provides the greatest opportunity for success. (12, 13)

12. Educate the veteran/service member on the medical and psychological literature indicating that a combined approach of pharmacotherapy and cognitive-behavioral therapy provides the greatest chance of success in cessation of tobacco use.

13. Discuss with the veteran/service member the benefits, limitations, and risks of pharmacotherapy and cognitive-behavioral therapy; address any concerns the veteran/service member may have.

9. Comply with pharmacological treatment (nicotine replacement, medication) for tobacco cessation. (14, 15, 16)

14. Refer the veteran/service member to a prescribing practitioner for an evaluation for nicotine replacement therapy (e.g., nicotine patch and/or gum) or medication (Wellbutrin, Zyban, Chantix).

15. Provide the veteran/service member with educational material on the various pharmacological treatments available to include information on common and rare side effects, length of time needed to see benefit, and how long the treatment will need to be used.

16. Monitor the veteran/service member for compliance with, as well as side effects and effectiveness of, pharmacological treatments.

10. Attend a cognitive-behavioral treatment program for tobacco cessation. (17)

17. Refer the veteran/service member to a structured smoking cessation group that utilizes a cognitive-behavioral approach to tobacco cessation.

11. Utilize cognitive-behavioral techniques to assist with tobacco cessation. (18, 19, 20)

18. Instruct the veteran/service member to consistently practice cognitive techniques learned in group (e.g., cognitive rehearsal to deal with high-risk situations, review top five reasons why it's important to quit throughout the day).

19. Instruct the veteran/service member to consistently practice behavioral techniques learned in group (e.g., delaying or fading techniques, aversion).

20. Reinforce the veteran's/service member's use of cognitive-behavioral techniques.

12. Verbalize an understanding that triggers increase cravings and create risk for tobacco use. (21)

21. Educate the veteran/service member on triggers typically identified by individuals attempting to quit using tobacco.

13. Recognize internal triggers that lead to tobacco use. (22)

22. Instruct the veteran/service member to identify internal triggers that increase likelihood of tobacco use (e.g., feeling angry or sad, lack of sleep, anxiety); have the veteran/service member create a list and process that list in session.

14. Recognize external triggers that lead to tobacco use. (23)

23. Instruct the veteran/service member to identify external triggers that increase likelihood of tobacco use (e.g., alcohol use, being around others that smoke, going to a bar); have the veteran/service member create a list and process that list in session.

15. Practice stress management and relaxation skills to reduce overall stress levels and attain a feeling of comfort. (24, 25, 26)

24. Using progressive relaxation or biofeedback, teach the veteran/service member how to relax; assign him/her to relax twice a day for 10 to 20 minutes.

25. Using current physical fitness levels, urge the veteran/service member to exercise three times a week to promote stress

reduction; increase the exercise by 10 percent a week, until he/she is exercising at a training heart rate for at least 20 minutes at least three times a week.

26. Assist the veteran/service member in clarifying how he/she was using nicotine to cope with stress, and help him/her to identify adaptive ways to obtain the sought-after result such as using relaxation techniques (or assign "Learning to Self-Soothe" in the *Addiction Treatment Homework Planner*, 4th ed. by Finley and Lenz).

16. Make a written plan to cope with each high-risk trigger situation that may precipitate relapse. (27)

27. After identifying the veteran's/service member's about high-risk situations (e.g., negative emotions, social pressure, interpersonal conflict, positive emotions, alcohol use, testing personal control); assist the veteran/service member in making a written plan to cope with each high-risk situation using behavioral and cognitive techniques learned (or assign "Avoiding Nicotine Relapse Triggers" in the *Addiction Treatment Homework Planner*, 4th ed. by Finley and Lenz).

17. Develop healthy strategies to neutralize cravings for tobacco use. (28)

28. Encourage the veteran/service member to replace the "habit" of smoking with healthier strategies (e.g., eating carrot sticks or sugar-free candy, relaxation exercises, increase water intake, chew on a toothpick) that promote abstinence.

18. Increase aerobic exercise as a means to improve physical stamina and improve emotional well-being. (29)

29. Encourage the veteran/service member to increase his/her level of physical activity; explain to the veteran/service member the benefits of exercise when

attempting to stop using tobacco (e.g., control weight, improve mood, relieve restlessness and anxiety).

19. Reward self for remaining abstinent from tobacco at predetermined times (e.g., one week, two weeks, one month). (30, 31, 32)

30. Design with the veteran/service member a behavior modification program that targets nicotine abuse and reinforces periods of abstinence.

31. Instruct the veteran/service member to reward himself/herself after meeting predetermined abstinence goals (e.g., buy a music CD after one week of being tobacco-free); review, process, and redirect the behavior modification program to maximize success.

32. Encourage the veteran/service member to calculate the amount of money spent on tobacco products each year; encourage the veteran/service member to save the money and buy a substantial purchase (e.g., pay for a trip, down payment on a car/boat) at the end of the year.

__. ____________________

__. ____________________

__. ____________________

__. ____________________

__. ____________________

__. ____________________

DIAGNOSTIC SUGGESTIONS

ICD-9-CM	*ICD-10-CM*	*DSM-5* Disorder, Condition, or Problem
305.10	F17.200	Tobacco Use Disorder, Moderate or Severe
292.0	F17.203	Tobacco Withdrawal
292.9	F17.209	Unspecified Tobacco-Related Disorder
______	______	____________
______	______	____________

Appendix A

BIBLIOTHERAPY SUGGESTIONS

GENERAL

Many references are made throughout the chapters to a therapeutic homework resource that was developed by the authors as a corollary to *The Complete Adult Psychotherapy Treatment Planner, Fourth Edition* (Jongsma, A. E. and Peterson, L. M.). The assignments referenced are judged to be easily applicable to the adult clients focused on in this *Veteran's and Active Duty Military Treatment Planner*. This frequently cited homework resource book is:

Jongsma, A. E. (2006). *Adult Psychotherapy Homework Planner* (2nd ed.). Hoboken, NJ: John Wiley & Sons.

Adjustment To Killing

Artwohl, A., & Christensen, L. W. (1997). *Deadly Force Encounters: What Cops Need to Know to Mentally and Physically Prepare for and Survive a Gunfight.* Boulder, CO: Paladin Press.

Dinter, E. (1985). *Hero or Coward: Pressures Facing the Soldier in Battle*. London: Frank Cass and Company.

Grossman, D. (1995). *On Killing: The Psychological Cost of Learning to Kill in War and Society*. New York: Back Bay.

Grossman, D. & Christensen, L. W. (2007). *On Combat: The Psychology and Physiology of Deadly Conflict in War and in Peace* (2nd ed.). Millstadt, IL: PPCT Research Publications.

Holmes, R. (1985). *Acts of War: The Behavior of Men in Battle.* New York: Free Press.

Klinger, D. (2004). *Into the Kill Zone: A Cop's Eye View of Deadly Force.* San Francisco: Josey-Bass.

Shalit, B. (1998). *The Psychology of Conflict and Combat*. New York: Praeger Publishers.

ADJUSTMENT TO THE MILITARY CULTURE

Department of the Army. (2007). *The Soldier's Guide: The Complete Guide to U.S. Army Traditions, Training, Duties, and Responsibilities*. New York: Skyhorse Publishing.

Leahy, J. F. (2002). *Honor, Courage, Commitment: Navy Boot Camp*. Annapolis, MD: U.S. Naval Institute Press.

Leyva, M. (2003). *Married to the Military: A Survival Guide for Military Wives, Girlfriends, and Women in Uniform*. New York: Fireside.

Nicolls, B. (2007). *Airman's Guide* (7th ed.). Mechanicsburg, PA: Stackpole Books.

AMPUTATION, LOSS OF MOBILITY, AND/OR DISFIGUREMENT

Cristian, A. (2005). *Lower Limb Amputation: A Guide to Living a Quality Life*. NewYork: Demos Medical Publishing.

Flacco, A. (2005). *Tiny Dancer: The Incredible True Story of a Young Burn Victim's Journey from Afghanistan*. New York: Thomas Dunne Books.

Garrison, K. S. (2005). *It's Just a Matter of Balance*. New York: Print Vantage.

Riley, R. L. (2005). *Living with a Below-Knee Amputation: A Unique Insight from a Prosthetist/Amputee*. Thorofare, NJ: Slack Incorporated.

Ritter, R. (2005). *Coping with Physical Loss and Disability: A Workbook*. Ann Arbor, MI: Loving Healing Press.

Wilder, E. I. (2006). *Wheeling and Dealing: Living with Spinal Cord Injury*. Nashville, TN: Vanderbilt University Press.

ANGER MANAGEMENT AND DOMESTIC VIOLENCE

Alberti, R., & Emmons, M. (2008). *Your Perfect Right*. San Luis Obispo, CA: Impact.

Bilodeau, L. (1992). *The Anger Workbook*. Minneapolis, MN: Compare Publications.

Deffenbacher, J. L., & McKay, M. (2000). *Overcoming Situational and General Anger: Client Manual (Best Practices for Therapy)*. Oakland, CA: New Harbinger Publications.

Gottlieb, M. (1999). *The Angry Self: A Comprehensive Approach to Anger Management*. Redding, CT: Zeig, Tucker & Theisen.

Harbin, T. J. (2000). *Beyond Anger: A Guide for Men: How to Free Yourself from the Grip of Anger and Get More Out of Life*. New York: Marlowe & Co.

Kubany, E. S., McCaig, M. A., & Laconsay, J. R. (2004). *Healing the Trauma of Domestic Violence: A Workbook for Women*. Oakland, CA: New Harbinger Publications.

Lee, J., & Stott, B. (1995). *Facing the Fire: Experiencing and Expressing Anger Appropriately*. New York: Bantam Doubleday Dell.

Lerner, H. (1997). *The Dance of Anger: A Woman's Guide to Changing the Patterns of Intimate Relationships.* New York: HarperCollins.

McKay, M., & Rogers, P. (2000). *The Anger Control Workbook.* Oakland, CA: New Harbinger Publications.

McKay, M., Rogers, P. D., & McKay, J. (2003). *When Anger Hurts: Quieting the Storm Within.* Oakland, CA: New Harbinger Publications.

Rosellini, G., & Worden, M. (1997). *Of Course You're Angry.* San Francisco: Harper Hazelden.

Rubin, T. I. (1998). *The Angry Book.* New York: Touchstone.

Smedes, L. (2007). *Forgive and Forget: Healing the Hurts We Don't Deserve.* San Francisco: HarperOne.

Weisinger, H. (1985). *Dr. Weisinger's Anger Work-out Book.* New York: Quill.

Weiss, E. (2004). *Surviving Domestic Violence: Voices of Women Who Broke Free.* Volcano, CA: Volcano Press.

Williams, R., & Williams, V. (1998). *Anger Kills: Seventeen Strategies for Controlling the Hostility That Can Harm Your Health.* New York: Harper Mass Market Paperbacks.

ANTISOCIAL BEHAVIOR IN THE MILITARY

Bilodeau, L. (1992). *The Anger Workbook.* Minneapolis, MN: Compare Publications.

Carnes, P. (1983). *Out of the Shadows: Understanding Sexual Addictions.* Minneapolis, MN: CompCare.

Gottlieb, M. (1999). *The Angry Self: A Comprehensive Approach to Anger Management.* Redding, CT: Zeig, Tucker & Theisen.

Katherine, A. (1998). *Boundaries: Where You End and I Begin.* New York: MJF Books.

Pittman, F. (1998). *Grow Up!* New York: Golden Books.

Sharp, B. (2000). *Changing Criminal Thinking: A Treatment Program.* Lanham, MD: American Correctional Association.

Williams, R., & Williams, V. (1993). *Anger Kills.* New York: Times Books.

Wolman, B. (1999). *Antisocial Behavior: Personality Disorders from Hostility to Homicide.* Amherst, NY: Prometheus Books.

ANXIETY

Antony, M., Craske, M., & Barlow, D. (2006). *Mastering Your Fears and Phobias, Workbook* (2nd ed.). New York: Oxford University Press.

Antony, M., & Swinson, R. (2008). *The Shyness & Social Anxiety Workbook: Proven Techniques for Overcoming Your Fears.* Oakland, CA: New Harbinger Publications.

Barlow, D., & Craske, M. (2007). *Mastery of Your Anxiety and Panic, Workbook* (4th ed.). New York: Oxford University Press.

Bradshaw, J. (2005). *Healing the Shame That Binds You.* Deerfield Beach, FL: Health Communications.

Burns, D. (1985). *Intimate Connections: The New Clinically Tested Program for Overcoming Loneliness.* New York: William Morrow.

Craske, M. & Barlow, D. (2006). *Mastery of your Anxiety and Worry—Workbook.* New York: Oxford University Press.

Dayhoff, S. (2000). *Diagonally Parked in a Parallel Universe: Working Through Social Anxiety.* Placitas, NM: Effectiveness-Plus Publications.

Goldman, C., & Babior, S. (1996). *Overcoming Panic, Anxiety, & Phobias: New Strategies to Free Yourself from Worry and Fear.* Duluth, MN: Whole Person Associates.

Hayes, S. C. (2005). *Get Out of Your Mind and Into Your Life: The New Acceptance and Commitment Therapy*. Oakland, CA: New Harbinger Publications.

Helmstetter, S. (1990). *What to Say When You Talk to Yourself.* New York: Pocket.

Hofmann, S., & Dibartolo, P. (Eds.). (2000). *From Social Anxiety to Social Phobia: Multiple Perspectives.* Needham Heights, MA: Allyn & Bacon.

Leahy, R. L. (2006). *The Worry Cure: Seven Steps to Stop Worry from Stopping You.* New York: Three Rivers Press.

Perkinson, R. (2003). *The Alcohol and Drug Abuse Patient Workbook.* Thousand Oaks, CA: Sage Publications.

Peurifoy, R. (1995). *Anxiety, Phobias, and Panic: A Step-by-Step Program for Regaining Control of Your Life.* New York: Warner Books.

Rapee, R. (1999). *Overcoming Shyness and Social Phobia: A Step-by-Step Guide.* Northvale, NJ: Jason Aronson.

Zimbardo, P. (1990). *Shyness: What It Is and What to Do About It.* Reading, MA: Addison-Wesley.

ATTENTION AND CONCENTRATION DEFICITS

Hollowell, E. M., & Ratey, J. J. (1995). *Driven to Distraction: Recognizing and Coping with Attention Deficit Disorder from Childhood through Adulthood.* New York: Simon & Schuster.

Ingersoll, B. (1995). *Distant Drums, Different Drummers: A Guide for Young People with ADHD.* Buffalo, NY: Cape Publishing.

Kelly, K., & Ramundo, P. (2006). *You Mean I'm Not Lazy, Stupid or Crazy?!: A Self-Help Book for Adults with Attention Deficit Disorder.* New York: Fireside.

Murphy, K. R., & Levert, S. (1995). *Out of the Fog: Treatment Options and Coping Strategies for Adult Attention Deficit Disorder.* New York: Hyperion.

Nadeau, K. (1996). *Adventures in Fast Forward.* Levittown, PA: Brunner/Mazel.

Quinn, P. O., & Stern, J. M. (2001). *Putting on the Brakes: Young People's Guide to Understanding Attention Deficit Hyperactive Disorder.* Washington, D.C.: Magination.

Safren, S. A. (2005). *Mastering Your Adult ADHD: A Cognitive-Behavioral Treatment Program—Client Workbook.* New York: Oxford University Press.

Weis, Lynn. (1994). *The Attention Deficit Disorder in Adults Workbook.* Dallas, TX: Taylor Publishing.

Wender, P. (1987). *The Hyperactive Child, Adolescent, and Adult.* New York: Oxford University Press.

BEREAVEMENT DUE TO THE LOSS OF A COMRADE

Grossman, D. (1995). *On Killing: The Psychological Cost of Learning to Kill in War and Society.* New York: Back Bay.

Grossman, D. & Christensen, L.W. (2007). *On Combat: The Psychology and Physiology of Deadly Conflict in War and in Peace* (2nd ed.). Millstadt, IL: PPCT Research Publications.

Harris-Lord, J. (2006). *No Time for Goodbyes: Coping with Sorrow, Anger, and Injustice After a Tragic Death.* Burnsville, NC: Compassion Books.

James, J., & Friedman, R. (1998). *The Grief Recovery Handbook: The Action Program for Moving Beyond Death, Divorce, and Other Losses.* New York: HarperCollins.

Smith, H. I. (2002). *When Your Friend Dies.* Minneapolis, MN: Augsburg Fortress Publishing.

Westberg, G. (2004). *Good Grief: A Constructive Approach to the Problem of Loss.* Minneapolis, MN: Fortress Press.

Zonnebelt-Smeenge, S., & DeVries, R. (2006). *Traveling through Grief: Learning to Live Again after the Death of a Loved One.* Grand Rapids, MI: Baker.

BORDERLINE PERSONALITY

Cudney, M., & Handy, R. (1993). Self-Defeating Behaviors. San Francisco: HarperCollins.

Finley, J., & Lenz, B. (2009). *Addiction Treatment Homework Planner* (4th ed.). Hoboken, NJ: John Wiley & Sons.

Fruzetti, A. E., & Linehan, M. M. (2003). *The High Conflict Couple: A Dialectical Behavior Therapy Guide to Finding Peace, Intimacy, & Validation.* Oakland, CA: New Harbinger Publications.

Herman, J. (1997). *Trauma and Recovery*. New York: Basic Books.

Katherine, A. (1998). *Boundaries: Where You End and I Begin.* New York: MJF Books.

Kreisman, J. J., & Straus, H. (1991). *I Hate You—Don't Leave Me: Understanding Borderline Personality Disorder.* New York: Avon.

Kreisman, J. J., & Straus, H. (2006). *Sometimes I Act Crazy: Living with Borderline Personality Disorder.* Hoboken, NJ: John Wiley & Sons.

Marra, T. (2004). *Depressed and Anxious: The Dialectical Behavior Therapy Workbook for Overcoming Depression & Anxiety*. Oakland, CA: New Harbinger Publications.

Mason, P. T., Kreger, R., & Siever, L. J. (1998). *Stop Walking on Eggshells: Coping When Someone You Care About Has Borderline Personality Disorder.* Oakland, CA: New Harbinger Publications.

McKay, M., Wood, J., & Brantley, J. (2007). *Dialectical Behavior Therapy Workbook: Practical DBT Exercises for Learning Mindfulness, Interpersonal Effectiveness, Emotion Regulation, & Distress Tolerance.* Oakland, CA: New Harbinger Publications.

Miller, D. (1994). *Women Who Hurt Themselves: A Book of Hope and Understanding.* New York: HarperCollins.

Moskovitz, R. A. (2001). *Lost in the Mirror: An Inside Look at Borderline Personality Disorder.* Dallas, TX: Taylor Publishers.

Reiland, R. (2004). *Get Me Out of Here: My Recovery from Borderline Personality Disorder*. Center City, MN: Hazeldon Foundation.

Santoro, J., & Cohen, R. (2001). *The Angry Heart: Overcoming Borderline and Addictive Disorders: An Interactive Self-Help Guide.* New York: MJF Books.

Spradlin, S. E. (2003). *Don't Let Your Emotions Run Your Life: How Dialectical Behavior Therapy Can Put You in Control.* Oakland, CA: New Harbinger Publications.

Thornton, M. F., Peterson, E. W., & Barley, W. D. (1997). *Eclipses: Behind the Borderline Personality Disorder.* Madison, AL: Monte Sano Publishers.

BRIEF REACTIVE PSYCHOTIC EPISODE

Adamec, C., & Jaffe, D. (1996). *How to Live with a Mentally Ill Person: A Handbook of Day-to-Day Strategies.* New York: John Wiley & Sons.

Mondimore, F. (2006). *Bipolar Disorder: A Guide for Patients and Families.* Baltimore: Johns Hopkins University Press.

Mueser, K., & Gingerich, S. (2006). *The Complete Family Guide to Schizophrenia: Helping Your Loved One Get the Most Out of Life.* New York: Guilford Press.

Olson, B., & Olson, M. (1999). *Win the Battle: The 3-Step Lifesaving Formula to Conquer Depression and Bipolar Disorder.* Worchester, MA: Chandler House Press.

Torrey, F. (2001). *Surviving Schizophrenia: A Manual for Families, Consumers and Providers.* New York: Harper Perennial Library.

CHRONIC PAIN AFTER INJURY

Bernstein, D. A., and Borkovec, T. D. (1973). *Progressive Relaxation Training.* Champaign, IL: Research Press.

Burns, D. (1999). *The Feeling Good Handbook.* New York: Plume.

Burns, D. (1999). *Ten Days to Self Esteem!* New York: Collins Living.

Catalano, E. M., and Hardin, K. N. (1996). *The Chronic Pain Control Workbook: A Step-by-Step Guide for Coping with and Overcoming Pain.* Oakland, CA: New Harbinger Publications.

Caudill, M. (2001). *Managing Pain before It Manages You.* New York: Guilford Press.

Duckro, P., Richardson, W., & Marshall, J. (1999). *Taking Control of Your Headaches.* New York: Guilford Press.

Hunter, M. (1996). *Making Peace with Chronic Pain.* New York: Brunner/Mazel.

Lewandowski, M. (2006). *The Chronic Pain Care Workbook: A Self-treatment Approach to Pain Relief Using the Behavioral Assessment of Pain Questionnaire.* Oakland, CA: New Harbinger Publications.

Otis, John. (2007). *Managing Chronic Pain: A Cognitive-Behavioral Treatment Program.* New York: Oxford University Press.

Willhoff, J. (2004). *Living Well with Chronic Pain.* New York: Thornton Publishing.

COMBAT AND OPERATIONAL STRESS REACTION

Department of the Army. (2003). *U.S. Army Combat Stress Control Handbook.* Guilford, CT: The Lyons Press.

Grossman, D., & Christensen, L. W. (2007). *On Combat: The Psychology and Physiology of Deadly Conflict in War and in Peace* (2nd ed.). Millstadt, IL: PPCT Research Publications.

Solomon, Z. (1993). *Combat Stress Reaction: The Enduring Toll of War.* New York: Springer Publishing.

United States Marine Corps. (2004). *Combat Stress.* Honolulu, HI: University Press of the Pacific.

CONFLICT WITH COMRADES

Cava, R. (2006). *Dealing with Difficult People: How to Deal with Nasty Customers, Demanding Bosses and Annoying Co-workers.* Tonawanda, NY: Firefly Books.

Godwin, A. (2008). *How to Solve Your People Problems: Dealing with Your Difficult Relationships.* Eugene, OR: Harvest House Publisher.

Littauer, F. (2006). *How to Get Along with Difficult People.* Eugene, OR: Harvest House Publisher.

DEPRESSION

Addis, M. E., & Martell, C. R. (2004). *Overcoming Depression One Step at a Time: The New Behavioral Activation Approach to Getting Your Life Back.* Oakland, CA: New Harbinger Publications.

Burns, D. (1999). *The Feeling Good Handbook.* New York: Plume.

Burns, D. (1999). *Ten Days to Self Esteem!* New York: Collins Living.

Copeland, M., & McKay, M. (2004). *The Depression Workbook: A Guide for Living with Depression and Manic Depression.* Oakland, CA: New Harbinger Publications.

Cronkite, K. (1995). *On the Edge of Darkness: Conversations About Conquering Depression.* New York: Delta.

Gilson, M., & Freeman, A. (2004). *Overcoming Depression: A Cognitive Therapy Approach for Taming the Depression BEAST Client Workbook.* New York: Oxford University Press.

Golant, M., & Golant, S. K. (2007). *What to Do When Someone You Love Is Depressed: A Practical, Compassionate and Helpful Guide.* New York: Holt.

Hayes, S. C. (2005). *Get Out of Your Mind and Into Your Life: The New Acceptance and Commitment Therapy.* Oakland, CA: New Harbinger Publications.

Lewinsohn, P. (1992). *Control Your Depression.* New York: Fireside.

Miklowitz, D. J. (2002). *Bipolar Disorder Survival Guide: What You and Your Family Need to Know.* New York: Guilford Press.

O'Connor, R. (1999). *Undoing Depression: What Therapy Doesn't Teach You and Medication Can't Give You.* New York: Berkley Publishing Group.

Pettit, J. W., Joiner, T. E., & Rehm, L. P. (2005). *The Interpersonal Solution to Depression: A Workbook for Changing How You Feel by Changing How You Relate.* Oakland, CA: New Harbinger Publications.

Rosen, L. E., & Amador, X. F. (1997). *When Someone You Love Is Depressed: How to Help Your Loved One Without Losing Yourself.* New York: Fireside.

Segal, Z. V., Williams, J. M. G., & Teasdale, J. D. (2001). *Mindfulness-Based Cognitive Therapy for Depression: A New Approach to Preventing Relapse.* New York: Guilford Press.

Thorn, J., & Rothstein, L. (1993). *You Are Not Alone: Words of Experience and Hope for the Journey Through Depression.* New York: Harper Perennial.

Weissman, M. M. (2005). *Mastering Depression through Interpersonal Psychotherapy: Patient Workbook.* New York: Oxford University Press.

Yapko, M. (1998). *Breaking the Patterns of Depression.* New York: Main Street Books.

DIVERSITY ACCEPTANCE

Kottak, C., & Kozaitis, K. (2007). *On Being Different: Diversity and Multiculturalism in the North American Mainstream.* Columbus, OH: Mc-Graw Hill.

Toropov, B., & Buckles, L. (2004). *The Complete Idiot's Guide to World Religions* (3rd ed.). New York: Alpha Books.

FINANCIAL DIFFICULTIES

Abentrod, S. (1996). *10-Minute Guide to Beating Debt.* New York: Macmillan.

Burkett, L. (2001). *Debt-Free Living.* Chicago: Moody Press.

Hunt, M. (2005). *Debt-Proof Living: The Complete Guide to Living Financially Free.* Long Beach, CA: DPL Press.

Loungo, T. (1997). *10-Minute Guide to Household Budgeting.* New York: Macmillan.

Ramsey, D. (2007). *The Total Money Makeover: A Proven Plan for Financial Fitness.* Nashville, TN: Thomas Nelson.

HOMESICKNESS/LONELINESS

Andre, R. (2000). *Positive Solitude: A Practical Program for Mastering Loneliness and Achieving Self-Fulfillment*. Bloomington, IN: AuthorHouse.

Anthony, M. M., & Swinson, R. P. (2008). *Shyness & Social Anxiety Workbook*. Oakland, CA: New Harbinger Publications.

Boothman, N. (2008). *How to Make People Like You in 90 Seconds or Less*. New York: Workman Publishing Company.

Burgess, P. H. (2008). *Defeating Loneliness*. Bloomington, IN: AuthorHouse.

Deavours, D. (2007). *Letters from Home—Thoughts to Carry with You Upon Leaving the Nest*. Eureka, MT: EnDeavours Publishing.

Watts, J. (2007). *Leaving the Nest for College: Some Helpful Hints to Help Smooth the Transition*. Frederick, MD: Publish America.

INSOMNIA

Breus, M. (2006). *Good Night: The Sleep Doctor's 4-Week Program to Better Sleep and Better Health*. New York: Dutton.

Foldvary, N. (2006). *Getting a Good Night's Sleep (A Cleveland Clinic Guide)*. Cleveland, OH: Cleveland Clinic Press.

Hewish, J. (1985). *Relaxation*. Chicago: NTC Publishing Group.

Krakow, B. (2007). *Sound Sleep, Sound Mind: 7 Keys to Sleeping through the Night*. Hoboken, NJ: John Wiley & Sons.

Leith, L. (1998). *Exercising Your Way to Better Mental Health*. Morgantown, WV: Fitness Information Technology.

MILD TRAUMATIC BRAIN INJURY

Denton, G. (2008). *Brainlash: Maximize Your Recovery from Mild Brain Injury*. New York: Demos Medical Publishing.

Mason, D. (2004). *The Mild Traumatic Brain Injury Workbook: Your Program for Regaining Cognitive Function and Overcoming Emotional Pain*. Oakland, CA: New Harbinger Publications.

Osborn, C. (2000). *Over My Head: A Doctor's Own Story of Head Injury from the Inside Looking Out*. Kansas City: Andrews McMeels Publishing, LLC.

Sullivan, C. (2008). *Brain Injury Survival Kit: 365 Tips, Tools and Tricks to Deal with Cognitive Function Loss*. New York: Demos Medical Publishing.

NIGHTMARES

Carranza, C. R., & Dill, J. R. (2004). *Banishing Night Terrors and Nightmares: A Breakthrough Program to Heal the Traumas That Shatter Peaceful Sleep*. New York: Kensington Books.

Hewish, J. (1985). *Relaxation.* Chicago: NTC Publishing Group.

Krakow, B. (2007). *Sound Sleep, Sound Mind: 7 Keys to Sleeping Through the Night.* Hoboken, NJ: John Wiley & Sons.

OPIOID DEPENDENCE

Catalono, E. M., & Hardin, K. N. (1996). *The Chronic Pain Control Workbook: A Step-by-Step Guide for Coping with and Overcoming Pain.* Oakland, CA: New Harbinger Publications.

Denning, P., Little, J., & Glickman, A. (2003). *Over the Influence: The Harm Reduction Guide for Managing Drugs and Alcohol.* New York: Guilford Press.

Faber, W. (2007). *Pain, Pain Go Away: Free Yourself from Chronic Pain.* Charleston, SC: BookSurge.

Hiesiger, E. (2003). *Your Pain Is Real: Free Yourself from Chronic Pain with Breakthrough Medical Treatments.* New York: Collins Living.

Inaba, D. S., & Cohen, W. E. (2007). *Uppers, Downers, All-Arounders.* Ashland, OR: CNS Publications.

Jamison, R. N. (1996). *Learning to Master Your Chronic Pain.* Sarasota, FL: Professional Resource Press.

Leith, L. (1998). *Exercising Your Way to Better Mental Health.* Morgantown, WV: Fitness Information Technology.

Marlatt, G. A. (2002). *Harm Reduction: Pragmatic Strategies for Managing High-Risk Behaviors.* New York: Guilford Press.

Narcotics Anonymous World Service. (1988). *Narcotics Anonymous.* Los Angeles: Narcotics Anonymous World Service.

PANIC/AGORAPHOBIA

Antony, M., & McCabe, R. (2004). *10 Simple Solutions to Panic: How to Overcome Panic Attacks, Calm Physical Symptoms, and Reclaim Your Life.* Oakland, CA: New Harbinger Publications.

Barlow, D., & Craske, M. (2007). *Mastery of Your Anxiety and Panic, Workbook* (4th ed.). New York: Oxford University Press.

Bourne, E. (2005). *The Anxiety and Phobia Workbook* (4th ed.). Oakland, CA: New Harbinger Publications.

Goldman, C., & Babior, S. (1996). *Overcoming Panic, Anxiety, & Phobias: New Strategies to Free Yourself from Worry and Fear.* Duluth, MN: Whole Person Associates.

McKay, M., Davis, M., & Farming, P. (2007). *Thoughts and Feelings: Taking Control of Your Moods and Your Life* (3rd ed.). Oakland, CA: New Harbinger Publications.

Peurifoy, R. (1995). *Anxiety, Phobias, and Panic: A Step-by-Step Program for Regaining Control of Your Life.* New York: Warner Books.

Swede, S., & Jaffe, S. (2000). *The Panic Attack Recovery Book. Step-by-Step Techniques to Reduce Anxiety and Change Your Life—Natural, Drug-Free, Fast Results.* New York: New American Library.

Wilson, R. (2009). *Don't Panic: Taking Control of Anxiety Attacks* (3rd ed.). New York: Harper & Row.

PARENTING PROBLEMS RELATED TO DEPLOYMENT

Andrews, B., & Wright, H. (2007). *I Miss You: A Military Kid's Book About Deployment.* Amherst, NY: Prometheus Books.

Cline, F., & Fay, J. (2006). *Parenting with Love and Logic: Updated and Expanded Edition.* Colorado Springs, CO: Navpress.

Dinkmeyer, D., McKay, G. D., & Dinkmeyer, D. (2007). *The Parent's Handbook: Systematic Training for Effective Parenting.* Bowling Green, KY: STEP Publishers.

Dreikurs, R. (1964). *Children: The Challenge.* New York: Hawthorn Books.

Edwards, C. (1999). *How to Handle a Hard-to-Handle Kid.* Minneapolis, MN: Free Spirit Publishing.

Faber, A., & Mazlish, E. (1982). *How to Talk So Kids Will Listen and Listen So Kids Will Talk.* New York: Avon.

Gordon, T. (2000). *Parent Effectiveness Training.* New York: Three Rivers Press.

Greene, R. (2005). *The Explosive Child: A New Approach for Understanding and Parenting Easily Frustrated, Chronically Inflexible Children.* New York: HarperCollins.

McBride, S. G. (2008). *My Mommy Wears Combat Boots.* Bloomington, IN: AuthorHouse.

Phelan, T. (2004). *1-2-3 Magic: Effective Discipline for Children 2–12.* Glen Ellyn, IL: Parentmagic, Inc.

PERFORMANCE-ENHANCING SUPPLEMENT USE

Etingoff, K. (2007). *Abusing Over-the-Counter Drugs: Illicit Uses for Everyday Drugs.* Broomall, PA: Mason Crest Publishers.

Inaba, D. S., & Cohen, W. E. (2001). *Uppers, Downers, All-Arounders.* Ashland, OR: CNS Productions.

Marlatt, G. A. (2002). *Harm Reduction: Pragmatic Strategies for Managing High-Risk Behaviors.* New York: Guilford Press.

PHOBIA

Bourne, E. (2005). *The Anxiety and Phobia Workbook* (4th ed.). Oakland, CA: New Harbinger.

Gold, M. (1988). *The Good News about Panic, Anxiety, and Phobias.* New York: Villard/Random House.

Marks, I. (2002). *Living with Fear: Understanding and Coping with Anxiety* (2nd ed.). New York: McGraw-Hill.

McKay, M., Davis, M., & Farming, P. (2007). *Thoughts and Feelings: Taking Control of Your Moods and Your Life* (3rd ed.). Oakland, CA: New Harbinger.

PHYSIOLOGICAL STRESS REACTIONS

Department of the Army. (2003). *U.S. Army Combat Stress Control Handbook*. Guilford, CT: The Lyons Press.

Grossman, D., & Christensen, L.W. (2007). *On Combat: The Psychology and Physiology of Deadly Conflict in War and in Peace* (2nd ed.). Millstadt, IL: PPCT Research Publications.

Solomon, Z. (1993). *Combat Stress Reaction: The Enduring Toll of War*. New York: Springer Publishing.

United States Marine Corps. (2004). *Combat Stress*. Honolulu, HI: University Press of the Pacific.

POST-DEPLOYMENT REINTEGRATION PROBLEMS

Armstrong, K., Best, S., & Domenici, P. (2005). *Courage After Fire: Coping Strategies for Troops Returning from Iraq and Afghanistan and Their Families*. Berkeley, CA: Ulysses Press.

Cantrell, B. C., & Dean, C. (2005). *Down Range: To Iraq and Back*. Los Angeles, CA: Wordsmith Books.

Friedman, M. J., & Slone, L. B. (2008). *After the War Zone: A Practical Guide for Returning Troops and Their Families*. New York: De Capo Press.

Matsakis, A. (2007). *Back from the Front: Combat Trauma, Love, and the Family*. Baltimore, MD: Sidran Press.

POSTTRAUMATIC STRESS DISORDER (PTSD)

Cantrell, B. C., & Dean, C. (2005). *Down Range: To Iraq and Back*. Los Angeles, CA: Wordsmith Books.

Friedman, M. J., & Slone, L. B. (2008). *After the War Zone: A Practical Guide for Returning Troops and Their Families*. New York: De Capo Press.

Grossman, D., & Christensen, L. W. (2007). *On Combat: The Psychology and Physiology of Deadly Conflict in War and in Peace* (2nd ed.). Millstadt, IL: PPCT Research Publications.

Hart, A. (2000). *An Operator's Manual for Combat PTSD: Essays for Coping*. Lincoln, NB: Writer's Showcase Press.

Matsakis, A. (2007). *Back from the Front: Combat Trauma, Love, and the Family*. Baltimore, MD: Sidran Press.

Rothbaum, B. (2007). *Reclaiming Your Life from a Traumatic Experience: A Prolonged Exposure Treatment Program, Workbook.* New York: Oxford University Press.

Schiraldi, G. (2000). *The Post-Traumatic Stress Disorder Sourcebook: A Guide to Healing, Recovery, and Growth.* Lincolnwood, IL: Lowell House.

Shay, J. (1995). *Achilles in Vietnam: Combat Trauma and the Undoing of Character.* New York: Simon & Schuster.

Smyth, L. (2004). *Overcoming Post-Traumatic Stress Disorder—Client Manual.* Oakland, CA: New Harbinger Publications.

Solomon, Z. (1993). *Combat Stress Reaction: The Enduring Toll of War*. New York: Springer Publishing.

Tick, E. (2005). *War and the Soul: Healing Our Nation's Veterans from Post-Traumatic Stress Disorder.* New York: Quest Books.

Williams, M. B., & Poijula, S. (2002). *The PTSD Workbook: Simple, Effective Techniques for Overcoming Traumatic Stress Symptoms.* Oakland, CA: New Harbinger Publications.

PRE-DEPLOYMENT STRESS

Mengesha, T. A. (2008). *The Service Member's Guide to Deployment: What Every Soldier, Sailor, Airmen and Marine Should Know Prior to Being Deployed.* Southfield, MI: Mengesha Publishing.

SEPARATION AND DIVORCE

Abrams-Spring, J. (1996). *After the Affair.* New York: HarperCollins.

Asker, S. (1999). *Plan B: How to Get Unstuck from Work, Family, and Relationship Problems.* New York: Perigee.

Bach, G., & Wyden, P. (1976). *The Intimate Enemy: How to Fight Fair in Love and Marriage.* New York: Avon Books.

Beck, A. (1989). *Love Is Never Enough: How Couples Can Overcome Misunderstanding, Resolve Conflicts, and Solve Relationship Problems Through Cognitive Therapy.* New York: HarperCollins.

Bernstein, J., & Magee, S. (2007). *Why Can't You Read My Mind? Overcoming the 9 Toxic Thought Patterns that Get in the Way of a Loving Relationship.* Cambridge, MA: DaCapo Press.

Christensen, A., & Jacobson, N. S. (2000). *Reconcilable Differences.* New York: Guilford Press.

Colgrove, M., Bloomfield, H., & McWillilams, P. (1991). *How to Survive the Loss of a Love.* Los Angeles: Prelude Press.

Crenshaw, R. (1981). *Expressing Your Feelings: The Key to an Intimate Relationship.* New York: Irvington Publications.

Finley, J., & Lenz, B. (2009). *Addiction Treatment Homework Planner* (4th ed.). Hoboken, NJ: John Wiley & Sons.

Fisher, B. (1981). *Rebuilding: When Your Relationship Ends.* San Luis Obispo, CA: Impact.

Fromm, E. (1956). *The Art of Loving.* New York: Harper & Row.

Gorski, T. (1993). *Getting Love Right: Learning the Choices of Healthy Intimacy.* New York: Simon & Schuster.

Gottman, J., & Silver, N. (2000). *The Seven Principles for Making Marriage Work.* New York: Three Rivers Press.

Gray, J. (1992). *Men Are from Mars, Women Are from Venus.* New York: HarperCollins.

Gray, J. (1993). *Men and Women and Relationships: Making Peace with the Opposite Sex.* Hillsboro, OR: Beyond Words.

Harley, W. (1994). *His Needs, Her Needs: Building an Affair-Proof Marriage.* Grand Rapids, MI: Revell.

Hendrix, H. (2007). *Getting the Love You Want: A Guide for Couples.* New York: Holt.

Lerner, H. (1989). *The Dance of Intimacy: A Woman's Guide to Courageous Acts of Change in Key Relationships.* New York: Harper Perennial.

Lindbergh, A. (1955). *A Gift from the Sea.* New York: Pantheon.

Markman, H., Stanley S., & Blumberg, S. (1994). *Fighting for Your Marriage.* San Francisco: Jossey-Bass.

Oberlin, L. (2005). *Surviving Separation and Divorce: A Woman's Guide.* Avon, MA: Adams Media.

Page, S. (1998). *How One of You Can Bring the Two of You Together: Breakthrough Strategies to Resolve Your Conflicts and Re-ignite Your Love.* New York: Broadway.

Robinson, J. (1997). *Communication Miracles for Couples: Easy and Effective Tools to Create More Love and Less Conflict.* Berkeley, CA: Conari Press.

Stern, S. (1999). *He Just Doesn't Get It: Simple Solutions to the Most Common Relationship Problems.* New York: Pocket Books.

Synder, D., Baucom, D., & Gordon, K. (2007). *Getting Past the Affair: A Program to Help You Cope, Heal, and Move On—Together or Apart.* New York: Guilford Press.

Weiner-Davis, M. (1993). *Divorce Busting: A Step-by-Step Approach to Making Your Marriage Loving Again.* New York: Simon & Schuster.

SEXUAL ASSAULT BY ANOTHER SERVICE MEMBER

Bradshaw, J. (2005). *Healing the Shame That Binds You.* Deerfield Beach, FL: Health Communications, Inc.

Burns, D. (1999). *Ten Days to Self-Esteem!* Deerfield Beach, FL: Health Communications, Inc.

Copeland, M. E., & Harris, M. (2000). *Healing the Trauma of Abuse: A Women's Workbook.* Oakland, CA: New Harbinger Publications.

Davis, L. (1990). *The Courage to Heal Workbook: For Men and Women Survivors of Child Sexual Abuse.* San Francisco: HarperCollins.

Forward, S., & Buck, C. (1988). *Betrayal of Innocence: Incest and Its Devastation, Revised Edition.* New York: Penguin Books.

Koh, M. R. (2001). *Beauty Restored: Finding Life and Hope after Date Rape.* Ventura, CA: Regal Books.

Scott, K. (1993). *Sexaul Assault: Will I Ever Feel O.K. Again?* Ada, MI: Bethany House.

Zehr, H. (2001). *Transcending: Reflections of Crime Victims.* Intercourse, PA: Good Books.

SHIFT WORK SLEEP DISORDER

Foldvary, N. (2006). *Getting a Good Night's Sleep (A Cleveland Clinic Guide).* Cleveland, OH: Cleveland Clinic Press.

Hewish, J. (1985). *Relaxation.* Chicago: NTC Publishing Group.

Hirshkowitz, M., & Smith, P. B. (2004). *Sleep Disorders for Dummies.* Hoboken, NJ: John Wiley & Sons.

Krakow, B. (2007). *Sound Sleep, Sound Mind: 7 Keys to Sleeping Through the Night.* Hoboken, NJ: John Wiley & Sons.

SOCIAL DISCOMFORT

Antony, M., & Swinson, R. (2008). *The Shyness & Social Anxiety Workbook: Proven Step-by-Step Techniques for Overcoming Your Fears.* Oakland, CA: New Harbinger Publications.

Bradshaw, J. (2005). *Healing the Shame That Binds You.* Deerfield Beach, FL: Health Communications.

Burns, D. (1985). *Intimate Connections: The New Clinically Tested Program for Overcoming Loneliness.* New York: William Morrow.

Burns, D. (1999). *The Feeling Good Handbook.* New York: Plume.

Burns, D. (1999). *Ten Days to Self Esteem!* New York: Collins Living.

Dayhoff, S. (2000). *Diagonally Parked in a Parallel Universe: Working through Social Anxiety.* Placitas, NM: Effectiveness-Plus Publications.

Dyer, W. (1978). *Pulling Your Own Strings.* New York: Thomas Crowell.

Fossum, M. A., & Mason, M. J. (1986). *Facing Shame: Families in Recovery.* New York: W. W. Norton.

Harris, A., & Harris, T. (1969). *I'm OK, You're OK.* New York: Harper & Row.

Helmstetter, S. (1990). *What to Say When You Talk to Yourself.* New York: Pocket.

Hilliard, E. (2005). *Living Fully with Shyness and Social Anxiety: A Comprehensive Guide to Gaining Social Confidence.* Cambridge, MA: Da Capo Press.

Rapee, R. (1999). *Overcoming Shyness and Social Phobia: A Step-by-Step Guide.* Northvale, NJ: Jason Aronson.

SPIRITUAL AND RELIGIOUS ISSUES

Carter, L. (1997). *The Choosing to Forgive Workbook.* Nashville, TN: Thomas Nelson.

Foster, R. (1988). *Celebration of Discipline: The Path to Spiritual Growth.* San Francisco: Harper & Row.

Graham, B. (2000). *Peace with God: The Secret of Happiness.* Nashville, TN: Thomas Nelson.

Parachin, J. (1999). *Engaged Spirituality: Ten Lives of Contemplation and Action.* St. Louis, MO: Chalice Press.

Perkinson, R. (2000). *God Talks to You.* Bloomington, IN: 1stBooks.

Smedes, L. (2007). *Forgive and Forget: Healing the Hurts We Don't Deserve.* San Francisco: HarperOne.

Toropov, B., & Buckles, L. (2004). *The Complete Idiot's Guide to World Religions* (3rd ed.). New York: Alpha Books.

Willard, D. (1990). *The Spirit of the Disciplines.* New York: Harper & Row.

SUBSTANCE ABUSE/DEPENDENCE

Alcoholics Anonymous World Services. (2001). *Alcoholics Anonymous.* New York: Alcoholics Anonymous World Services.

Daley, D. C., & Marlatt, G. A. (2006). *Overcoming Your Alcohol or Drug Problem: Effective Recovery Strategies Workbook.* New York: Oxford University Press.

Denning, P., Little, J., & Glickman, A. (2003). *Over the Influence: The Harm Reduction Guide for Managing Drugs and Alcohol.* New York: Guilford Press.

Inaba, D. S., & Cohen, W. E. (2001). *Uppers, Downers, All-Arounders.* Ashland, OR: CNS Productions.

Marlatt, G. A. (2002). *Harm Reduction: Pragmatic Strategies for Managing High-Risk Behaviors.* New York: Guilford Press.

Miller, W. R., & Munoz, R. F. (2004). *Controlling Your Drinking: Tools to Make Moderation Work for You.* New York: Guilford Press.

Sales, P. (1999). *Alcohol Abuse: Straight Talk Straight Answers.* Honolulu, HI: Ixia Publications.

Solowji, N. (2006). *Cannabis and Cognitive Functioning.* New York: Cambridge University Press.

Washton, A., & Boundy, D. (1990). *Willpower's Not Enough: Understanding and Recovering from Addictions of Every Kind.* New York: HarperCollins.

Washton, A., & Zweben, J. (2009). *Cocaine and Methamphetamine Addiction: Treatment, Recovery, and Relapse Prevention.* New York: Norton.

SUICIDAL IDEATION

Arena, J. (1996). *Step Back from the Exit: 45 Reasons to Say No to Suicide.* Milwaukee, WI: Zebulon Press.

Burns, D. (1999). *The Feeling Good Handbook.* New York: Plume.
Burns, D. (1999). *Ten Days to Self Esteem!* New York: Collins Living.
Copeland, M., & McKay, M. (2004). *The Depression Workbook: A Guide for Living with Depression and Manic Depression.* Oakland, CA: New Harbinger Publications.
Cronkite, K. (1995). *On the Edge of Darkness: Conversations about Conquering Depression.* New York: Delta.
Ellis, T. E., & Newman, C. F. (1996). *Choosing to Live: How to Defeat Suicide Though Cognitive Therapy.* Oakland, CA: New Harbinger Publications.
Jamison, K. R. (2000). *Night Falls Fast: Understanding Suicide.* New York: Vintage Books.
O'Connor, R. (1999). *Undoing Depression: What Therapy Doesn't Teach You and Medication Can't Give You.* New York: Berkley Publishing Group.
Thorn, J., & Rothstein, L. (1993). *You Are Not Alone: Words of Experience and Hope for the Journey Through Depression.* New York: Harper Perennial.
Yapko, M. (1998). *Breaking the Patterns of Depression.* New York: Main Street Books.

SURVIVIOR'S GUILT

Kushner, H. (2004). *When Bad Things Happen to Good People.* New York: Anchor.
Luttrell, M. (2007). *Lone Survivor: The Eyewitness Account of Operation Redwing and the Lost Heroes of SEAL Team 10.* Boston, MA: Little, Brown and Company.
Matsakis, A. (1999). *Survivor Guilt.* Oakland, CA: New Harbinger Publications.
Obershaw, R. (2004). *Cry Until You Laugh: Comforting Guidance for Coping with Grief.* Edina, MN: Beavers Pond Press.
Smedes, L. (2007). *Forgive and Forget: Healing the Hurts We Don't Deserve.* San Francisco: HarperOne.
Westberg, G. (2004). *Good Grief: A Constructive Approach to the Problem of Loss.* Minneapolis, MN: Fortress Press.

TOBACCO USE

Ashelman, M. W. (2000). *Stop Smoking Naturally.* New York: NTC/Contemporary Publishing.
Baer, A. (1998). *Quit Smoking for Good: A Supportive Program for Permanent Smoking Cessation.* Freedom, CA: Crossing Press.
Brizer, D. (2003). *Quitting Smoking for Dummies.* Hoboken NJ: John Wiley & Sons.
Fisher, E. B., & Koop, C. E. (1998). *American Lung Association 7 Steps to a Smoke Free Life.* New York: John Wiley & Sons.
Johnson, D. L., & Johnson, C. A. (2000). *Stop Smoking and Chewing Tobacco for Life Changes.* West Conshohocken, PA: Infinity Publishing.
Rogers, J. (1995). *You Can Stop Smoking.* New York: Pocket Books.
Wetherall, R. (2007). *Quit: Read This Book and Stop Smoking.* Philadelphia, PA: Running Press Miniature Editions.

Appendix B

PROFESSIONAL REFERENCES FOR EVIDENCE-BASED CHAPTERS

EVIDENCE-BASED PSYCHOLOGICAL AND PSYCHOPHARMACOLOGICAL TREATMENTS IN GENERAL

APA Presidential Task Force on Evidence-Based Practice. (2006). Evidence-based practice in psychology. *American Psychologist, 61,* 271–285.

Bruce, T. J., & Sanderson, W. C. (2005). Evidence-based psychosocial practices: Past, present, and future. In C. Stout & R. Hayes (Eds.), *Handbook of Evidence-Based Practice in Behavioral Healthcare: Applications and New Directions.* Hoboken, NJ: John Wiley & Sons.

Castonguay, L. G., & Beutler, L. E. (2006). *Principles of Therapeutic Change that Work.* New York: Oxford University Press.

Chambless, D. L., Baker, M. J., Baucom, D., Beutler, L. E., Calhoun, K. S., Crits-Christoph, P., … Woody, S. R. (1998). Update on empirically validated therapies: II. *The Clinical Psychologist, 51*(1), 3–16.

Chambless, D. L., & Ollendick, T. H. (2001). Empirically supported psychological interventions: Controversies and evidence. *Annual Review of Psychology, 52,* 685–716.

Chambless, D. L., Sanderson, W. C., Shoham, V., Johnson, S. B., Pope, K. S., Crits-Christoph, P., … McCurry, S. (1996). An update on empirically validated therapies. *The Clinical Psychologist, 49*(2), 5–18.

Drake, R. E., & Goldman, H. (2003). *Evidence-based Practices in Mental Health Care.* Washington, D.C.: American Psychiatric Association.

Drake, R. E., Merrens, M. R., & Lynde, D. W. (2005). *Evidence-Based Mental Health Practice: A Textbook.* New York: W.W. Norton & Company.

Hofmann, S. G., & Tompson, M. G. (2002). *Treating Chronic and Severe Mental Disorders: A Handbook of Empirically Supported Interventions.* New York: Guilford Press.

Institute of Medicine. (2007). *Treatment of PTSD: An Assessment of the Evidence.* Available online at http://www.iom.edu/?id=47389.

Nathan, P. E., & Gorman, J. M. (Eds.). (2007). *A Guide to Treatments that Work* (3rd ed.). New York: Oxford University Press.

National Center for PTSD. (2004). *The Iraq War Clinician Guide* (2nd ed.). Available online at http://www.ncptsd.va.gov/ncmain/ncdocs/manuals/iraq_clinician_guide_v2.pdf.

Personal Improvement Computer Systems. *Therapyadvisor.* Available online at http://www.therapyadvisor.com.

Society of Clinical Psychology, American Psychological Association Division 12. *Website on Research-supported Psychological Treatments.* Available online at http://www.psychology.sunysb.edu/eklonsky-/division12/index.html.

Stout, C., & Hayes, R. (1995). *The Handbook of Evidence-Based Practice in Behavioral Healthcare: Applications and New Directions.* New York: John Wiley & Sons.

Substance Abuse and Mental Health Administration (SAMHSA). *National Registry of Evidence-based Programs and Practices (NREPP).* Available online at http://nrepp.samhsa.gov/index.asp.

ANGER MANAGEMENT AND DOMESTIC VIOLENCE

Babcock, J., & LaTaillade, J. (2000). Evaluating interventions for men who batter. In J. Vincent & E. Jouriles (Eds.), *Domestic Violence: Guidelines for Research-informed Practice* (pp. 37–77). Philadelphia: Jessica Kingsley.

Deffenbacher, J., Story, D., Brandon, A., Hogg, J., & Hazaleus, S. (1988). Cognitive and cognitive relaxation treatment of anger. *Cognitive Therapy and Research, 12,* 167–184.

Deffenbacher, J. L., Dahlen, E. R., Lynch, R. S., Morris, C. D., & Gowensmith, W. N. (2000). An application of Beck's cognitive therapy to general anger reduction. *Cognitive Therapy and Research, 24,* 689–687.

Deffenbacher, J. L., Oetting, E. R., Huff, M. E., Cornell, G. R., & Dallagher, C. J., et al. (1996). Evaluation of two cognitive-behavioral approaches to general anger reduction. *Cognitive Therapy and Research, 20,* 551–573.

DiGiuseppe, R., & Tafrate, R. C. (2003). Anger treatment for adults: A meta-analytic review. *Clinical Psychology: Science & Practice, 10,* 70–84.

Easton, C., Mandel, D., Hunkele, K., Nich, C., Rounsaville, B., & Carroll, K. (2007). A Cognitive Behavioral Therapy for Alcohol-dependent Domestic Violence Offenders: An Integrated Substance Abuse-Domestic Violence Treatment Approach (SADV). *American Journal on Addictions, 16*(1), 24–31.

Feindler, E., & Ecton, R. (1986). *Adolescent Anger Control: Cognitive-Behavioral Techniques.* New York: Pergamon Press.

Gilchrist, E. (2007). The cognition of domestic abusers: Explanations, evidence and treatment. *Aggressive offenders' cognition: Theory, research and practice* (pp. 247–266). Hoboken, NJ: John Wiley & Sons.

Meichenbaum, D. (1985). *Stress Inoculation Training.* New York: Pergamon Press.

Meichenbaum, D. (1993). Stress inoculation training: A twenty-year update. In R. L. Woolfolk & P. M. Lehrer (Eds.), *Principles and Practices of Stress Management*. New York: Guilford Press.

Meichenbaum, D. (2001). *Treatment of Individuals with Anger Control Problems and Aggressive Behaviors: A Clinical Handbook*. Clearwater, FL: Institute Press.

Novaco, R. (1975). *Anger Control: The Development and Evaluation of an Experimental Treatment*. Lexington, MA: Lexington Books.

Novaco, R. (1976). The functions and regulation of the arousal of anger. *American Journal of Psychiatry, 133*, 1124–1128.

Novaco, R. (1977). A stress inoculation approach to anger management in the training of law enforcement officers. *American Journal of Community Psychology, 5*, 327–346.

ANXIETY

Barlow, D. H., Allen, L. B., & Basden, S. L. (2007). Psychological treatments for panic disorders, phobias, and generalized anxiety disorder. In P. E. Nathan & J. M. Gorman (Eds.), *A Guide to Treatments that Work* (3rd ed.; pp. 351–394). New York: Oxford University Press.

Beck, A. T., & Emory, G. (1990). *Anxiety Disorders and Phobias: A Cognitive Perspective*. New York: Basic Books.

Bernstein, D. A., & Borkovec, T. D. (1973). *Progressive Relaxation Training*. Champaign, IL: Research Press.

Brown, T. A., DiNardo, P. A., & Barlow, D. H. (2006). *Anxiety Disorders Interview Schedule Adult Version (ADIS-IV): Client Interview Schedule.* New York: Oxford University Press.

Brown, T. A., O'Leary, T., & Barlow, D. H. (2001). Generalized anxiety disorder. In D. H. Barlow (Ed.), *Clinical Handbook of Psychological Disorders: A Step-by-Step Treatment Manual* (3rd ed.; pp. 154–208). New York: Guilford Press.

Chambless, D. L, Baker, M. J., Baucom, D., Beutler, L. E., Calhoun, K. S., Crits-Christoph, P., … Woody, S. R. (1998). Update on empirically validated therapies: II. *The Clinical Psychologist, 51*(1), 3–16.

Chambless, D. L., & Ollendick, T. H. (2001). Empirically supported psychological interventions: Controversies and evidence. *Annual Review of Psychology, 52*, 685–716.

Meyer, T. J., Miller, M. L., Metzger, R. L., & Borkovec, T. D. (1990). Development and validation of the Penn State Worry Questionnaire. *Behaviour Research and Therapy, 28*, 487–495.

Roy-Byrne, P. P., & Cowley, D. S. (2007). Pharmacological treatments for panic disorder, generalized anxiety disorder, specific phobia, and social anxiety disorder. In P. E. Nathan & J. M. Gorman (Eds.), *A Guide to Treatments that Work* (3rd ed.; pp. 395–430). New York: Oxford University Press.

Rygh, J. L. & Sanderson, W. C. (2004). *Treating GAD: Evidence-Based Strategies, Tools, and Techniques*. New York: Guilford Press.

Zinbarg, R. E., Craske, M. G., & Barlow, D. H. (2006). *Mastery of Your Anxiety and Worry—Therapist Guide*. New York: Oxford University Press.

ATTENTION AND CONCENTRATION DEFICITS

Safren, S. A. (2006). Cognitive-behavioral approaches to ADHD treatment in adulthood. *Journal of Clinical Psychiatry, 67*(8), 46–50.

Safren, S. A., Otto, M. W., Sprich, S, Winett, C. L., Wilens, T. E., & Biederman, J. (2005). Cognitive-behavioral therapy for ADHD in medication-treated adults with continued symptoms. *Behaviour Research and Therapy*, *43*(7), 831–842.

Safren, S. A., Sprich, S., Perlman, C. A., & Otto, M. W. (2005) *Mastery of Your Adult ADHD—Therapist Manual.* New York: Oxford University Press.

Weiss, M., Safren, S. A., Solanto, M., Hechtman, L., Rostain, A. L., Ramsay, R., & Murray, C. (2008). Research forum on psychological treatment of adults with ADHD. *Journal of Attention Disorders, 11*, 642–651.

BORDERLINE PERSONALITY

Beck, A. T., Rush, A. J., Shaw, B. F., & Emery, G. (1979). *Cognitive Therapy of Depression*. New York: Guilford Press.

Crits-Christoph, P. & Barber, J. P. (2007). Psychological treatments for personality disorders. In P. E. Nathan & J. M. Gorman (Eds.), *A Guide to Treatments that Work* (3rd ed.; pp. 641–658). New York: Oxford University Press.

Freeman, A. (2002). Cognitive behavioral therapy for severe personality disorders. In S. G. Hofmann & M. C. Tompson (Eds.). *Treating Chronic and Severe Mental Disorders: A Handbook of Empirically Supported Interventions* (pp. 382–402). New York: Guilford Press.

Koenigsberg, H. W., Woo-Ming, A. M., & Siever, L. J. (2007). Psychopharmacological treatment of personality disorders. In P. E. Nathan & J. M. Gorman (Eds.), *A Guide to Treatments that Work* (3rd ed.; pp. 659–680). New York: Oxford University Press.

Linehan, M. M. (1993). *Cognitive Behavioral Treatment for Borderline Personality Disorder*. New York: Guilford Press.

Linehan, M. M. (1993). *Skills Training Manual for Treating Borderline Personality Disorder*. New York: Guilford Press.

Linehan, M. M., Armstrong, H., Suarez, A. Allmon, D., & Heard, H. (1991). Cognitive-behavioral treatment of chronically parasuicidal borderline patients. *Archives of General Psychiatry, 48,* 1060–1064.

Linehan, M., Cochran, & Kehrer, K. (2001). Dialectical Behavior Therapy for Borderline Personality Disorder. In D. H. Barlow (Ed.), *Clinical Handbook of Psychological Disorders: A Step-by-Step Treatment Manual* (3rd ed.). New York: Guilford Press.

Linehan, M., Dimeff, L. A., & Koerner, K. (2007). *Dialectical Behavior Therapy in Clinical Practice: Applications across Disorders and Settings*. New York: Guilford Press.

Linehan, M. M., Heard, H. L., & Armstrong, H. E. (1993). Naturalistic follow-up of a behavioral treatment for chronically parasuicidal borderline patients. *Archives of General Psychiatry, 50,* 971–974.

Linehan, M. M., Schmidt, H., Dimeff, L. A., Craft, J. C., Kanter, J., & Comtois, K. A. (1999). Dialectical behavior therapy for patients with borderline personality disorder and drug-dependence. *American Journal on Addiction, 8*(4), 279–292.

Linehan, M. M., Tutek, D., Heard, H., & Armstrong, H. (1992). Interpersonal outcome of cognitive behavioral treatment for chronically suicidal borderline patients. *American Journal of Psychiatry, 151*(12), 1771–1775.

Resick, P. A., & Calhoun, K. S. (2001). Posttraumatic stress disorder. In D. H. Barlow (Ed.), *Clinical Handbook of Psychological Disorders: A Step-By-Step Treatment Manual* (3rd ed.). New York: Guilford Press.

Safer, D. L., Telch, C. F., & Agras, W. S. (2001). Dialectical behavior therapy for bulima nervosa. *American Journal of Psychiatry, 158*(4), 632–634.

Whitehurst, T., Ridolfi, M. E., & Gunderson, J. (2002). Multiple family group treatment for borderline personality disorder. In S. G. Hofmann & M. C. Tompson (Eds.), *Treating Chronic and Severe Mental Disorders: A Handbook of Empirically Supported Interventions* (pp. 343–363). New York: Guilford Press.

CHRONIC PAIN AFTER INJURY

Bradley, L. A., Young, L. D., Anderson, J. O., Turner, R. A., Agudelo, C. A., McDaniel, L. K., Pisko, E. J., Semble, E. J., & Morgan, T. M. (1987). Effects of psychological therapy on pain behavior of rheumatoid arthritis patients: Treatment outcome and six-month follow-up. *Arthritis & Rheumatism, 30,* 1105–1114.

Guzman, J., Esmail, R., Karjalainen, K., Malmivaara, A., Irvin, E., & Bombardier, C. (2001). Multidisciplinary bio-psycho-social rehabilitation for chronic low back pain. *The Cochrane Database of Systematic Reviews, 1,* Art No.: CD000963.

Hoffman, B. M., Chatkoff, D. K., Papas, R. K., & Kerns, R. D. (2007). Meta-analysis of psychological interventions for chronic low back pain. *Health Psychology, 26,* 1–9.

Keefe, F. J., Beaupre, P. M., Gil, K. M., Rumble, M. E., & Aspnes, A. K. (2002). Group therapy for patients with chronic pain. In D. C. Turk & R. J. Gatchel (Eds.), *Psychological Approaches to Pain Management: A Practitioner's Handbook* (2nd ed.). New York: Guilford Press.

Keefe, F. J., Caldwell, D. S., Williams, D. A., Gil, K.M., Mitchell, D., Robertson, D., … Helms, M. (1990). Pain coping skills training in the management of osteoarthritic knee pain: A comparative study. *Behavior Therapy, 21,* 49–62.

Keefe, F. J., & Gil, K. M. (1986). Behavioral concepts in the analysis of chronic pain syndromes. *Journal of Consulting and Clinical Psychology, 54,* 776–783.

Ostelo, R. W., Van Tulder, M. W., Vlaeyan, J. W., Linton, S. J., Morley, S. J., & Assendelft, W. J. (2005). Behavioral treatment for chronic low back pain (Review). *The Chochrane Library*, 4, 1–25.

Syrjala, K. L., Donaldson, G. W., Davies, M. W., Kippes, M. E., & Carr, J. E. (1995). Relaxation and imagery and cognitive-behavioral training reduce pain during cancer treatment: A controlled clinical trial. *Pain, 63,* 189–198.

Turk, D. C., Meichenbaum, D., & Genest, M. (1983). *Pain and Behavioral Medicine: A Cognitive-behavioral Perspective.* New York: Guilford Press.

Turner, J. A., & Clancy, S. (1988). Comparison of operant-behavioral and cognitive-behavioral group treatment for chronic low back pain. *Journal of Consulting and Clinical Psychology, 58,* 573–579.

DEPRESSION

Beck, A. T., Rush, A. J., Shaw, B. F., & Emery, G. (1979). *Cognitive Therapy of Depression.* New York: Guilford Press.

Beck, A. T., & Steer, R. A. (1988). *Beck Hopelessness Scale.* San Antonio, TX: The Psychological Corporation.

Beck, A. T., Steer, R. A., & Brown, G. K. (1996). *Beck Depression Inventory Manual* (2nd ed.). San Antonio, TX: The Psychological Corporation.

Beck, J. S. (1995). *Cognitive Therapy: Basics and Beyond.* New York: Guilford Press.

Bowman, D., Scogin, F., & Lyrene, B. (1995). The efficacy of self-examination and cognitive bibliotherapy in the treatment of mild to moderate depression. *Psychotherapy Research, 5,* 131–140.

Brown, S., Glasner-Edwards, S., Tate, S., McQuaid, J., Chalekian, J., & Granholm, E. (2006). Integrated cognitive behavioral therapy versus twelve-step facilitation therapy for substance-dependent adults with depressive disorders. *Journal of Psychoactive Drugs, 38*(4), 449–460.

Craighead, W. E., Sheets, E. S., Brosse, A. L. & Ilardi, S. S. (2007). Psychosocial treatments for major depressive disorder. In P. E. Nathan & J. M. Gorman (Eds.), *A Guide to Treatments that Work* (3rd ed.; pp. 289–307). New York: Oxford University Press.

Klerman, G. L., Weissman, M. M., Rounasacille, B. J., & Chevron, E. S. (1984). *Interpersonal Psychotherapy of Depression.* New York: Basic Books.

Lewinsohn, P. M., Antonuccio, D. O., Steinmetz, J. L., & Teri, L. (1984). *The Coping with Depression Course: A Psychoeducational Intervention for Unipolar Depression.* Eugene, OR: Castalia.

Lewinson, P. M. (1974) A behavioural approach to depression. In R. J. Friedman & Katz (Eds.), *The Psychology of Depression.* Washington, D.C.: Winston & Sons.

Nemeroff, C. B., & Schatzberg, A. F. (2007). Pharmacological treatments for unipolar depression. In P. E. Nathan & J. M. Gorman (Eds.), *A Guide to Treatments that Work* (3rd ed.; pp. 271–287). New York: Oxford University Press.

Nezu, A. M., Nezu, C. M., & Perri, M. G. (1989). *Problem-Solving Therapy for Depression: Theory, Research, and Clinical Guidelines.* New York: John Wiley & Sons.

Scogin, F., Jamison, C., & Gochneaur, K. (1989). Comparative efficacy of cognitive and behavioral bibliotherapy for mildly and moderately depressed adults. *Journal of Consulting and Clinical Psychology, 57,* 403–407.

Weissman, M. M., Markowitz, J. C., & Klerman, G. L. (2000). *Comprehensive Guide to Interpersonal Psychotherapy.* New York: Basic Books.

Zimmerman, M., Coryell, W., Corenthal, C., & Wilson, S. (1986). A self-report scale to diagnose major depressive disorder. *Archives of General Psychiatry, 43*, 1076–1081.

INSOMNIA

Currie, S., Wilson, K., Pontefract, A., & deLaplante, L. (2000). Cognitive-behavioral treatment of insomnia secondary to chronic pain. *Journal of Consulting and Clinical Psychology, 68*(3), 407–416.

Edinger, J., Wohlgemuth, W., Radtke, R., Marsh, G., & Quillian, R. (2001). Cognitive behavioral therapy for treatment of chronic primary insomnia: A randomized controlled trial. *JAMA: Journal of the American Medical Association, 285*(14), 1856–1864.

Morin, C. M., Hauri, P. J., Espie, C. A., Spielman, A. J., Buysse, D. J., & Bootzin, R. R. (1999) Non-pharmacological treatment of chronic insomnia. An American Academy of Sleep Medicine review. *Sleep 22,* 1134–1156.

Wang, M., Wang, S., & Tsai, P. (2005). Cognitive behavioural therapy for primary insomnia: A systematic review. *Journal of Advanced Nursing, 50*(5), 553–564.

NIGHTMARES

Krakow, B., Hollifield, M., Johnston, L., Koss, M., Schrader, R., Warner, T., et al. (2001). Imagery rehearsal therapy for chronic nightmares in sexual assault survivors with posttraumatic stress disorder: A randomized controlled trial. *JAMA: Journal of the American Medical Association, 286*(5), 537–545.

Krakow, B., & Zadra, A. (2006). Clinical management of chronic nightmares: Imagery rehearsal therapy. *Behavioral Sleep Medicine, 4,* 45–70.

Lamarche, L., & De Koninck, J. (2007). Sleep disturbance in adults with posttraumatic stress disorder: A review. *Journal of Clinical Psychiatry, 68*(8), 1257–1270.

Raskind, M., Peskind, E., Hoff, D., Hart, K., Holmes, H., Warren, D., et al. (2007). A Parallel Group Placebo Controlled Study of Prazosin for Trauma Nightmares and Sleep Disturbance in Combat Veterans with Post-Traumatic Stress Disorder. *Biological Psychiatry, 61*(8), 928–934.

OPIOID DEPENDENCE

Abbot, P. J., Weller, S. B., Delaney, H. D., & Moore, B. A. (1998). Community reinforcement approach in the treatment of opiate addicts. *American Journal of Drug and Alcohol Abuse, 24*(1), 17–30.

Finney, J. W., Wilbourne, P. L., & Moos, R. H. (2007). Psychosocial treatments for substance use disorders. In P. E. Nathan & J. M. Gorman (Eds.), *A Guide to Treatments that Work* (3rd ed.; pp. 179–202). New York: Oxford University Press.

Marlatt, G. A., & Donovan, D. M. (Eds.) (2005). *Relapse Prevention: Maintenance Strategies in the Treatment of Addictive Behaviors* (2nd ed.). New York: Guilford Press.

Marlatt, G. A., & Gordon, J. R. (1985). *Relapse Prevention: Maintenance Strategies in the Treatment of Addictive Behaviors*. New York: Guilford Press.

McCrady, B. S., & Nathan, P. E. (2006). Treatment factors in treating substance use disorders. In L. G. Castonguay & L. E. Beutler (Eds.), *Principles of Therapeutic Change That Work* (pp. 319–340). New York: Oxford University Press.

Miller, W. R., & Rollnick, S. (2002). *Motivational Interviewing: Preparing People for Change* (2nd ed.). New York: Guilford Press.

O'Brien, C. P., & McKay J. (2007). Psychopharmacological treatments for substance use disorders. In P. E. Nathan & J. M. Gorman (Eds.), *A Guide to Treatments That Work* (3rd ed.; pp. 145–177). New York: Oxford University Press.

Ouimette, P. C., Finney, J. W., & Moos, R. H. (1997). Twelve step and cognitive-behavioral treatment for substance abuse: A comparison of treatment effectiveness. *Journal of Consulting and Clinical Psychology, 65*, 230–240.

PANIC/AGORAPHOBIA

Craske, M. G., & Barlow, D. H. (2006). *Mastery of Your Anxiety and Panic: Therapist Guide.* New York: Oxford University Press.

Barlow, D. H., Craske, M. G., Cerny, J. A., et al. (1986). Behavioral treatment of panic disorder. *Behavior Therapy, 20*, 261–282.

Chambless, D. L, Baker, M. J., Baucom, D., Beutler, L. E., Calhoun, K. S., Crits-Christoph, P., … Woody, S. R. (1998). Update on Empirically Validated Therapies: II. *The Clinical Psychologist, 51*(1), 3–16.

Chambless, D. L., Caputo, G. C., Jasin, S. E., Gracel, E. J., & Williams, C. (1985). The mobility inventory for agoraphobia. *Behaviour Research and Therapy, 23*, 35–44.

Chambless, D. L., & Ollendick, T. H. (2001). Empirically supported psychological interventions: Controversies and evidence. *Annual Review of Psychology, 52*, 685–716.

Clark, D. M., Salkovskis, P. M., Hackman, A., et al. (1994). A comparison of cognitive therapy, applied relaxation, and imipramine in the treatment of panic disorder. *British Journal of Psychiatry, 164*, 759–769.

DiNardo, P. A., Brown, T. A., & Barlow, D. H. (1994). *Anxiety Disorders Interview Schedule for* DSM-IV: *Lifetime Version.* San Antonio, TX: The Psychological Corporation.

Nathan, P. E., & Gorman, J. M. (Eds.). (2007). *A Guide to Treatments That Work* (3rd ed.). New York: Oxford University Press.

Reiss, S., Peterson, R. A., Gursky, D. M., & McNally, R. J. (1986). Anxiety sensitivity, anxiety frequency, and the prediction of fearfulness. *Behaviour Research and Therapy, 24*, 1–8.

Roy-Byrne, P. P., & Cowley, D. S. (2007). Pharmacological treatments for panic disorder, generalized anxiety disorder, specific phobia, and social anxiety disorder. In P. E. Nathan & J. M. Gorman (Eds.), *A Guide to Treatments that Work* (3rd ed.; pp. 395–430). New York: Oxford University Press.

Teng, E., Bailey, S., Chaison, A., Petersen, N., Hamilton, J., & Dunn, N. (2008). Treating comorbid panic disorder in veterans with posttraumatic stress disorder. *Journal of Consulting and Clinical Psychology, 76*(4), 704–710.

PARENTING PROBLEMS RELATED TO DEPLOYMENT

Brestan, E., & Eyberg, S. (1998). Effective psychosocial treatments of conduct-disordered children and adolescents: 29 years, 82 studies, and 5,272 kids. *Journal of Clinical Child Psychology, 27*, 180–189.

Forgatch, M., & DeGarmo, D. (1999). Parenting through change: An effective prevention program for single mothers. *Journal of Consulting and Clinical Psychology, 67*, 711–724.

Graziano, A., & Diament, D. (1992). Parent behavioral training: An examination of the paradigm. *Behavior Modification, 16*, 3–38.

Kazdin, A. (1997). Parent management training: Evidence, outcomes, and issues. *Journal of the American Academy of Child & Adolescent Psychiatry, 36*, 1349–1356.

Long, P., Forehand, R., Wierson, M., & Morgan, A. (1994). Does parent training with young noncompliant children have long-term effects? *Behaviour Research and Therapy, 32*, 101–107.

Serketich, W., & Dumas, J. (1996). The effectiveness of behavioral parent training to modify antisocial behavior in children: A meta-analysis. *Behavior Therapy, 27*, 171–186.

van den Hoofdakker, B., van der Veen-Mulders, L., Sytema, S., Emmelkamp, P., Minderaa, R., & Nauta, M. (2007). Effectiveness of behavioral parent training for children with ADHD in routine clinical practice: A randomized controlled study. *Journal of the American Academy of Child & Adolescent Psychiatry, 46*(10), 1263–1271.

Webster-Stratton, C. (1994). Advancing videotape parent training: A comparison study. *Journal of Consulting and Clinical Psychology, 62*, 583–593.

PHOBIA

Antony, M.M. (2001). Measures for specific phobia. In M. M. Antony, S. M. Orsillo, & I. Roemer (Eds.), *Practitioner's Guide to Empirically-Based Measures of Anxiety*. New York: Kluwer Academic/Plenum.

Antony, M. M., Craske, M. C., & Barlow, D. H. (2004). *Mastery of Your Specific Phobia—Client Workbook*. New York: Oxford University Press.

Bruce, T. J. & Sanderson, W. C. (1998). *Specific Phobias: Clinical Applications of Evidence-Based Psychotherapy*. Northvale, NJ: Jason Aronson.

Craske, M. G., Antony, M. M., & Barlow, D. H. (2006). *Mastering Your Fears and Phobias: Therapist Guide.* New York: Oxford University Press.

DiNardo, P. A., Brown, T. A., & Barlow, D. H. (1994). *Anxiety Disorders Interview Schedule for* DSM-IV*: Lifetime Version.* San Antonio, TX: The Psychological Corporation.

Marks, I. (1978). *Living with Fear*. New York: McGraw Hill.

Ost, L. G., Fellenius, J., & Sterner, U. (1991). Applied tension, exposure in vivo, and tension-only in the treatment of blood phobia. *Behaviour Research and Therapy, 29*(6), 561–574.

POSTTRAUMATIC STRESS DISORDER (PTSD)

Bryant, R. A., & Harvey, A. G. (2000). *Acute Stress Disorder: A Handbook of Theory, Assessment, and Treatment*. Washington, D.C.: American Psychological Association.

Dunmore, E., Clark, D. M., & Ehlers, A. (2001). A prospective investigation of the role of cognitive factors in persistent Posttraumatic Stress Disorder (PTSD) after physical or sexual assault. *Behaviour Research and Therapy, 39*, 1063–1084.

Ehlers, A., & Clark, D. M. (2000). A cognitive model of posttraumatic stress disorder. *Behaviour Research and Therapy, 38*, 319–345.

Foa, E. B., Dancu, C. V., Hembree, E. A., Jaycox, L. H., Meadows, E. A., & Street, G. (1999). A comparison of exposure therapy, stress inoculation training and their combination for reducing posttraumatic stress disorder in female assault victims. *Journal of Consulting and Clinical Psychology, 67*, 194–200.

Foa, E. B., Hembree, E. A , & Rothbaum, B. O. (2007). *Prolonged Exposure Therapy for PTSD: Emotional Processing of Traumatic Experiences, Therapist's Guide*. Oxford University Press: New York.

Foa, E. B., Keane, T. M., & Friedman, M. J., & Cohen, J. A. (2008). *Effective Treatments for PTSD, Second Edition: Practice Guidelines from the International Society for Traumatic Stress Studies*. New York: Guilford Press.

Friedman, M. J. (2006). *Post-traumatic and Acute Stress Disorders: The Latest Assessment and Treatment Strategies.* Sudbury, MA: Jones and Bartlett Publishers.

Friedman, M. J., Keane, T. M., & Resick, P. A. (2007). *Handbook of PTSD: Science and Practice.* New York: Guilford Press.

Golier, J. A., Legge, J., & Yehuda, R. (2007). Pharmacological treatment of posttraumatic stress disorder. In P. E. Nathan & J. M. Gorman (Eds.), *A Guide to Treatments That Work* (3rd ed.; pp. 475–512). New York: Oxford University Press.

Kanas, N. (2005). Group Therapy for Patients with Chronic Trauma-Related Stress Disorders. *International Journal of Group Psychotherapy, 55*(1), 161–165.

Marks, I., Lovell, K., Noshirvani, H., et al., (1998). Treatment of post-traumatic stress disorder by exposure and/or cognitive restructuring: A controlled study. *Archives of General Psychiatry, 55*, 317–325.

McNally, R. J. (2003). *Remembering Trauma*. Cambridge, MA: Harvard University Press.

Najavits, L. M. (2002). *Seeking Safety: A Treatment Manual for PTSD and Substance Abuse*. New York: Guilford Press.

Najavits, L. M. (2007). Psychosocial treatments for posttraumatic stress disorder. In P. E. Nathan & J. M. Gorman (Eds.), *A Guide to Treatments That Work* (3rd ed.; pp. 513–530). New York: Oxford University Press.

Padesky, C. A., Candido, D., Cohen, A., Gluhoski, V., McGinn, L. K., Sisti, M., & Westover, S. (2002). *Academy of Cognitive Therapy's Trauma Task Force Report*. Available online at: http://academyofct.org

Schnurr, P., Friedman, M., Engel, C., Foa, E., Shea, M., Chow, B., et al. (2007). Cognitive behavioral therapy for posttraumatic stress disorder in women: A randomized controlled trial. *JAMA: Journal of the American Medical Association, 297*(8), 820–830.

Teng, E., Bailey, S., Chaison, A., Petersen, N., Hamilton, J., & Dunn, N. (2008). Treating comorbid panic disorder in veterans with posttraumatic stress disorder. *Journal of Consulting and Clinical Psychology, 76*(4), 704–710.

Wilson, J. P., & Keane, T. M. (2004). *Assessing Psychological Trauma and PTSD* (2nd ed.). New York: Guilford Press.

SHIFT WORK SLEEP DISORDER

Barion, A., & Zee, P. (2007). A clinical approach to circadian rhythm sleep disorders. *Sleep Medicine, 8*(6), 566–577.

Bootzin, R. (1972). A stimulus control treatment for insomnia. *American Psychological Association Proceedings*, 395–396.

Edinger, J., Wohlgemuth, W., Radtke, R., Marsh, G., & Quillian, R. (2001). Cognitive behavioral therapy for treatment of chronic primary insomnia: A randomized controlled trial. *JAMA: Journal of the American Medical Association, 285*(14), 1856–1864.

Lu, B., Manthena, P., & Zee, P. (2006). Circadian rhythm sleep disorders. In *Handbook of Sleep Medicine* (pp. 137–164). Philadelphia: Lippincott Williams & Wilkins Publishers.

Morin, C. M., Hauri, P. J., Espie, C. A., Spielman, A. J., Buysse, D. J., & Bootzin, R. R. (1999) Non-pharmacological treatment of chronic insomnia. An American Academy of Sleep Medicine review. *Sleep 22*, 1134–1156.

Wang, M., Wang, S., & Tsai, P. (2005). Cognitive behavioural therapy for primary insomnia: A systematic review. *Journal of Advanced Nursing, 50*(5), 553–564.

SOCIAL DISCOMFORT

Antony, M. M., & Swinson, R. P. (2000). *Phobic Disorders and Panic in Adults: A Guide to Assessment and Treatment*. Washington, D.C.: American Psychological Association.

Beidel, D. C., & Turner, S. M. (1998). *Shy Children, Phobic Adults: Nature and Treatment of Social Phobia.* Washington, D.C.: American Psychological Association.

Bruce, T. J., & Saeed, S. A. (1999). Social anxiety disorder: A common, underrecognized mental disorder. *American Family Physician, 60*(8), 2311–2320.

Chambless, D. L, Baker, M. J., Baucom, D., Beutler, L. E., Calhoun, K. S., Crits-Christoph, … Woody, S. R. (1998). Update on Empirically Validated Therapies: II. *The Clinical Psychologist, 51*(1), 3–16.

Chambless, D. L., & Ollendick, T. H. (2001). Empirically supported psychological interventions: Controversies and evidence. *Annual Review of Psychology, 52*, 685–716.

Crozier, W. R., & Alden, L. E. (2001). *International Handbook of Social Anxiety: Concepts, Research and Interventions Relating to the Self and Shyness.* New York: John Wiley & Sons.

DiNardo, P. A., Brown, T. A., & Barlow, D. H. (1994). *Anxiety Disorders Interview Schedule for* DSM-IV*: Lifetime Version.* San Antonio, TX: The Psychological Corporation.

Heimberg, R. G., & Becker, R. E. (2002). *Cognitive-Behavioral Group Therapy for Social Phobia: Basic Mechanisms and Clinical Strategies.* New York: Guilford Press.

Hofmann, S. G., & DiBartolo, P. M. (2001). *From Social Anxiety to Social Phobia: Multiple Perspectives.* Needham Heights, MA: Allyn & Bacon.

Hope, D. A., Heimberg, R. G., Juster, H. R., & Turk, C. L. (2006). *Managing Social Anxiety: A Cogntive Behavioral Therapy Approach—Therapist Guide.* New York: Oxford University Press.

Koszycki, D., Benger, M., Shlik, J., & Bradwejn, J. (2007). Randomized trial of a meditation-based stress reduction program and cognitive behavior therapy in generalized social anxiety disorder. *Behaviour Research and Therapy, 45*(10), 2518–2526.

Mattick, R. P., & Clarke, J. C. (1998). Development and validation of measures of social phobia scrutiny fear and social interaction anxiety. *Behaviour Research and Therapy, 36*, 455–470.

Paleg, K., & Jongsma, A. E. (2005). *The Group Therapy Treatment Planner* (2nd ed.). Hoboken, NJ: John Wiley & Sons.

Westra, H., & Dozois, D. (2006). Preparing Clients for Cognitive Behavioral Therapy: A Randomized Pilot Study of Motivational Interviewing for Anxiety. *Cognitive Therapy and Research, 30*(4), 481–498.

SUBSTANCE ABUSE/DEPENDENCE

Abbot, P. J., Weller, S. B., Delaney, H. D., & Moore, B. A. (1998). Community reinforcement approach in the treatment of opiate addicts. *American Journal of Drug and Alcohol Abuse, 24*(1), 17–30.

Drake, R. E., McHugo, G., & Noordsy, D. L. 1993). Treatment of alcoholism among schizophrenic outpatients: Four-year outcomes. *American Journal of Psychiatry, 150,* 328–329.

Epstein, E. E., & McGrady, B. S. (1998). Behavioral couples treatment of alcohol and drug use disorders: Current status and innovations. *Clinical Psychology Review, 18*, 689–711.

Finney, J. W., Wilbourne, P. L., & Moos, R. H. (2007). Psychosocial treatments for substance use disorders. In P. E. Nathan & J. M. Gorman (Eds.), *A Guide to Treatments that Work* (3rd ed.; pp. 179–202). New York: Oxford University Press.

Marlatt, G. A., & Donovan, D. M. (Eds.). (2005). *Relapse prevention: Maintenance Strategies in the Treatment of Addictive Behaviors* (2nd ed.). New York: Guilford Press.

McCrady, B. S. (2001). Alcohol use disorders. In D. H. Barlow (Ed.), *Clinical Handbook of Psychological Disorders* (3rd ed.). New York: Guilford Press.

McGovern, M. P., & Carroll, K. M. (2003). Evidence-based practice for substance use disorders. *Psychiatric Clinics of North America, 26*, 991–1010.

Miller, W. R., & Rollnick, S. (2002). *Motivational Interviewing: Preparing People for Change* (2nd ed.). New York: Guilford Press.

Miller, W. R., Wilbourne, P. L., & Hettema, J. E. (2003). What works? A summary of alcohol treatment outcome research. In R. K. Hester & W. R. Miller (Eds.), *Handbook of Alcoholism Treatment Approaches: Effective Alternatives* (3rd ed.; pp. 13–63). Boston: Allyn & Bacon.

Mueser, K. T., Noordsy, D. L., Drake, R. E., & Fox, L. (2003). *Integrated Treatment for Dual Disorders: A Guide to Effective Practice.* New York: Guilford Press.

O'Brien, C. P., & McKay J. (2007). Psychopharmacological treatments for substance use disorders. In P. E. Nathan & J. M. Gorman (Eds.), *A Guide to Treatments That Work* (3rd ed.; pp. 145–177). New York: Oxford University Press.

O'Farrell, T. J., Choquette, K. A., & Cutter, H. S. G. (1998). Couples relapse prevention sessions after Behavioral Marital Therapy for male alcoholics: Outcomes during the three years after starting treatment. *Journal of Studies on Alcohol, 59*, 357–370.

O'Farrell, T. J., Choquette, K. A., Cutter H. S. G., Brown, E. D., & McCourt, W. F. (1993). Behavioral Marital Therapy with and without additional couples relapse prevention sessions for alcoholics and their wives. *Journal of Studies on Alcohol, 54*, 652–666.

Ouimette, P. C., Finney, J. W., & Moos, R. H. (1997). Twelve step and cognitive-behavioral treatment for substance abuse: A comparison of treatment effectiveness. *Journal of Consulting and Clinical Psychology, 65*, 230–240.

Prochaska, J. O., DiClemente, C. C., & Norcross, J. C. (1992). In search of how people change: Applications to addictive behavior. *American Psychologist, 47*(9), 1102–1114.

Project MATCH Research Group. (1997). Matching alcoholism treatments to client heterogeneity: Project MATCH posttreatment drinking outcomes. *Journal of Studies on Alcohol, 58*, 7–29.

Smith, J. E., Meyers, R. J., & Delaney, H. D. (1998). The community reinforcement approach with homeless alcohol-dependent individuals. *Journal of Consulting and Clinical Psychology, 66*, 541–548.

TOBACCO USE

Agency for Healthcare Research and Quality. (2008). *AHCPR-supported Clinical Practice Guidelines: Treating Tobacco Use and Dependence* (2008 update). Available online at: http://www.ncbi.nlm.nih.gov/books/bv.fcgi?rid=hstat2.chapter.28163.

Appendix C

RECOVERY MODEL OBJECTIVES AND INTERVENTIONS

The Objectives and Interventions that follow are created around the 10 core principles developed by a multidisciplinary panel at the 2004 National Consensus Conference on Mental Health Recovery and Mental Health Systems Transformation, convened by the Substance Abuse and Mental Health Services Administration (SAMHSA, 2004):

1. **Self-direction:** Consumers lead, control, exercise choice over, and determine their own path of recovery by optimizing autonomy, independence, and control of resources to achieve a self-determined life. By definition, the recovery process must be self-directed by the individual, who defines his or her own life goals and designs a unique path toward those goals.

2. **Individualized and person-centered:** There are multiple pathways to recovery based on an individual's unique strengths and resiliencies as well as his or her needs, preferences, experiences (including past trauma), and cultural background in all of its diverse representations. Individuals also identify recovery as being an ongoing journey and an end result as well as an overall paradigm for achieving wellness and optimal mental health.

3. **Empowerment:** Consumers have the authority to choose from a range of options and to participate in all decisions—including the allocation of resources—that will affect their lives, and are educated and supported in so doing. They have the ability to join with other consumers to collectively and effectively speak for themselves about their needs, wants, desires, and aspirations. Through empowerment, an individual gains control of his or her own destiny and influences the organizational and societal structures in his or her life.

4. **Holistic:** Recovery encompasses an individual's whole life, including mind, body, spirit, and community. Recovery embraces all aspects of life, including housing, employment, education, mental health and healthcare treatment and services, complementary and naturalistic services, addictions treatment, spirituality, creativity, social networks, community participation, and family supports as determined by the person. Families, providers, organizations, systems, communities, and society play crucial roles in creating and maintaining meaningful opportunities for consumer access to these supports.

5. **Nonlinear:** Recovery is not a step-by-step process but one based on continual growth, occasional setbacks, and learning from experience. Recovery begins with an initial stage of awareness in which a person recognizes that positive change is possible. This awareness enables the consumer to move on to fully engage in the work of recovery.

6. **Strengths-based:** Recovery focuses on valuing and building on the multiple capacities, resiliencies, talents, coping abilities, and inherent worth of individuals. By building on these strengths, consumers leave stymied life roles behind and engage in new life roles (e.g., partner, caregiver, friend, student, employee). The process of recovery moves forward through interaction with others in supportive, trust-based relationships.

7. **Peer support:** Mutual support—including the sharing of experiential knowledge and skills and social learning—plays an invaluable role in recovery. Consumers encourage and engage other consumers in recovery and provide each other with a sense of belonging, supportive relationships, valued roles, and community.

8. **Respect:** Community, systems, and societal acceptance and appreciation of consumers—including protecting their rights and eliminating discrimination and stigma—are crucial in achieving recovery. Self-acceptance and regaining belief in one's self are particularly vital. Respect ensures the inclusion and full participation of consumers in all aspects of their lives.

9. **Responsibility:** Consumers have a personal responsibility for their own self-care and journeys of recovery. Taking steps toward their goals may require great courage. Consumers must strive to understand and give meaning to their experiences and identify coping strategies and healing processes to promote their own wellness.

10. **Hope:** Recovery provides the essential and motivating message of a better future—that people can overcome the barriers and obstacles that confront them. Hope is internalized, but can be fostered by peers, families, friends, providers, and others. Hope is the catalyst of the recovery process. Mental health recovery not only benefits individuals with mental health

> disabilities by focusing on their abilities to live, work, learn, and fully participate in our society, but also enriches the texture of American community life. America reaps the benefits of the contributions individuals with mental disabilities can make, ultimately becoming a stronger and healthier Nation.[1]

The numbers used for Objectives in the treatment plan that follows correspond to the numbers for the 10 core principles. Each of the 10 Objectives was written to capture the essential theme of the like-numbered core principle. The numbers in parentheses after the Objectives denote the Interventions designed to assist the client in attaining each respective Objective. The clinician may select any or all of the Objectives and Intervention statements to include in the client's treatment plan.

One generic Long-Term Goal statement is offered should the clinician desire to emphasize a recovery model orientation in the client's treatment plan.

LONG-TERM GOAL

1. To live a meaningful life in a self-selected community while striving to achieve full potential during the journey of healing and transformation.

SHORT-TERM OBJECTIVES

1. Make it clear to therapist, family, and friends what path to recovery is preferred. (1, 2, 3, 4)

THERAPEUTIC INTERVENTIONS

1. Explore the client's thoughts, needs, and preferences regarding his/her desired pathway to recovery (from depression, bipolar disorder, posttraumatic stress disorder [PTSD], etc.).
2. Discuss with the client the alternative treatment interventions and community support resources that might facilitate his/her recovery.
3. Solicit from the client his/her preferences regarding the direction treatment will take; allow for these preferences to be

[1] From: Substance Abuse and Mental Health Services Administration's (SAMHSA) National Mental Health Information Center: Center for Mental Health Services (2004). *National consensus statement on mental health recovery.* Washington, DC: Author. Available from http://mentalhealth.samhsa.gov/publications/allpubs/sma05-4129/

communicated to family and significant others.

4. Discuss and process with the client the possible outcomes that may result from his/her decisions.

2. Specify any unique needs and cultural preferences that must be taken under consideration during the treatment process. (5, 6)

5. Explore with the client any cultural considerations, experiences, or other needs that must be considered in formulating a mutually agreed-upon treatment plan.

6. Modify treatment planning to accommodate the client's cultural and experiential background and preferences.

3. Verbalize an understanding that decision making throughout the treatment process is self-controlled. (7, 8)

7. Clarify with the client that he/she has the right to choose and select among options and participate in all decisions that affect him/her during treatment.

8. Continuously offer and explain options to the client as treatment progresses in support of his/her sense of empowerment, encouraging and reinforcing the client's participation in treatment decision making.

4. Express mental, physical, spiritual, and community needs and desires that should be integrated into the treatment process. (9, 10)

9. Assess the client's personal, interpersonal, medical, spiritual, and community strengths and weaknesses.

10. Maintain a holistic approach to treatment planning by integrating the client's unique mental, physical, spiritual, and community needs and assets into the plan; arrive at an agreement with the client as to how these integrations will be made.

5. Verbalize an understanding that during the treatment process there will be successes and failures, progress and setbacks. (11, 12)

11. Facilitate realistic expectations and hope in the client that positive change is possible, but does not occur in a linear process of straight-line successes; emphasize a recovery process involving

growth, learning from advances as well as setbacks, and staying this course toward recovery.

12. Convey to the client that you will stay the course with him/her through the difficult times of lapses and setbacks.

6. Cooperate with an assessment of personal strengths and assets brought to the treatment process. (13, 14, 15)

13. Administer to the client the *Behavioral and Emotional Rating Scale (BERS): A Strength-Based Approach to Assessment* (Epstein).
14. Identify the client's strengths through a thorough assessment involving social, cognitive, relational, and spiritual aspects of the client's life; assist the client in identifying what coping skills have worked well in the past to overcome problems and what talents and abilities characterize his/her daily life.
15. Provide feedback to the client of his/her identified strengths and how these strengths can be integrated into short-term and long-term recovery planning.

7. Verbalize an understanding of the benefits of peer support during the recovery process. (16, 17, 18)

16. Discuss with the client the benefits of peer support (e.g., sharing common problems, receiving advice regarding successful coping skills, getting encouragement, learning of helpful community resources, etc.) toward the client's agreement to engage in peer activity.
17. Refer the client to peer support groups of his/her choice in the community and process his/her experience with follow-through.
18. Build and reinforce the client's sense of belonging, supportive relationship building, social value, and community integration by processing the

gains and problem-solving the obstacles encountered through the client's social activities.

8. Agree to reveal when any occasion arises that respect is not felt from the treatment staff, family, self, or the community. (19, 20, 21)

19. Discuss with the client the crucial role that respect plays in recovery, reviewing subtle and obvious ways in which disrespect may be shown to or experienced by the client.

20. Review ways in which the client has felt disrespected in the past, identifying sources of that disrespect.

21. Encourage and reinforce the client's self-concept as a person deserving of respect; advocate for the client to increase incidents of respectful treatment within the community and/or family system.

9. Verbalize acceptance of responsibility for self-care and participation in decisions during the treatment process. (22)

22. Develop, encourage, support, and reinforce the client's role as the person in control of his/her treatment and responsible for its application to his/her daily life; adopt a supportive role as a resource person to assist in the recovery process.

10. Express hope that better functioning in the future can be attained. (23, 24)

23. Discuss with the client potential role models who have achieved a more satisfying life by using their personal strengths, skills, and social support to live, work, learn, and fully participate in society toward building hope and incentive motivation.

24. Discuss and enhance internalization of the client's self-concept as a person capable of overcoming obstacles and achieving satisfaction in living; continuously build and reinforce this self-concept using past and present examples supporting it.